FEMINIST HUMOR & SATIRE

Edited by

**GLORIA KAUFMAN AND
MARY KAY BLAKELY**

INDIANA UNIVERSITY PRESS
BLOOMINGTON

This book is dedicated to the poets and scholars, mothers and teachers, movers and shakers of the women's movement who have raised the consciousness, pressed the boundaries, and entertained their sisters with their laughter and wit.

First Midland Book Edition 1980
Copyright © 1980 Indiana University Press
All rights reserved
No part of this book may be reproduced or utilized in any form or by any means, electronic or mechanical, including photocopying and recording, or by any information storage and retrieval system, without permission in writing from the publisher. The Association of American University Presses' Resolution on Permissions constitutes the only exception to this prohibition.

Manufactured in the United States of America

Library of Congress Cataloging in Publication Data
Main entry under title:
Pulling our own strings.

1. Women—Anecdotes, facetiae, satire, etc.
2. American wit and humor—Women authors. I. Kaufman, Gloria J., 1929–   II. Blakely, Mary Kay, 1948–
PN6231.W6P78   817'.008'09287   79-3382
ISBN 0-253-13034-4   4 5 6 7 86 85 84 83
ISBN 0-253-20251-5 (pbk.)

CONTENTS

CONTENTS

CONTENTS

CONTENTS

Dear Gloria,

I have been suffering an interminable cognitive hangover ever since I mailed off the manuscript for the introduction to the book. Every time I move my head too abruptly, another phrase of that tedious, didactic essay comes crashing into consciousness. I want to run to South Bend and collect the copy I sent off and bury it with the other Something's Wrong Here manuscripts under my socks in the bottom drawer.

I should have noticed the warning signs and listened to my friend Cathryn, who is always telling me to "trust my instincts." She manages to give me the impression that *she* trusts my instincts, and *I'm* crazy not to. When I had to write and rewrite and over-write it, I should have paid more attention to my rebellion. The worst indicator of trouble was that when I finished it (or, more accurately, when it finished me), it wasn't a piece that I wanted to share with my friends, my peers, my pushers-to-excellence. Like Joan, who knits her eyebrows at me whenever she thinks I'm "holding back" on what I think. I didn't want to read it to Joan.

It wasn't a total exercise in futility, however. I think it was necessary for me to go through the ritual of writing a "regular" introduction. It was a "learning experience"— that terrible euphemism for failures, misfires, perilous attempts, and ruinous outcomes. I tried my best to convince myself that the introduction should satisfy all of the questions raised about feminist humor inside and outside the Press: "What, exactly, *is* feminist humor?" (Whenever I hear that question, I have to stifle a strong urge to head for the nearest available exit. You either understand $E = mc^2$ or you don't. I have no desire to be the one beating her brains out for a month trying to explain it.) "Who, exactly, would en*joy* feminist humor—women or feminists?" (Who, exactly, benefits from technology—companies or computer programmers? Who asks stupid questions— people or interviewers?) "How in the world are feminists able to laugh through clenched teeth?" (We are ventriloquists.)

I dunno. I tried to convince myself that addressing the issues of style and form and genre and technique was the mission of the introduction writer, and I unhappily made it my mission as well. You are by now familiar with the less than spectacular results. My anxiety about the appropriateness, the correctness, of the introduction was relieved only when I made the decision to abandon it altogether. I am, in other words, jumping ship.

It's ironic actually. I've made some discoveries about feminist humor while undertaking the chore of writing a summary of it. I have some conclusions about this three-year sojourn we have had into the exciting territory of feminist art and culture—teeming with funny feminists/clever women/witty visionaries. But now I find myself singularly unable to write (even with the late arrival of Hard Evidence and Real Conclusions for ballast) the kind of introduction that will produce relief in our long-suffering editor. (Long-suffering, I'm sure Suzy would agree, is built into the job description of editors.) So while this letter is not exactly an apology, I do hope to explain why I am the Wrong Woman For The Job.

Immediately before I began this reckless assignment, I read the advice of a friend, a word technician who has some experience in the matter of introduction-writing, who counseled me not to write a "rah-rah feminist statement." It's the kind of advice, I have come to discover, that well-wishers offer when they fear you are walking too close to the edge of respectability, on the verge of Going Too Far, about to depart irretrievably from reality, to return only as a tourist. The advice came, I think, as a last-ditch effort to save my objectivity, which is connected like a Siamese twin to my credibility.

But the point is, it was too late. Like my journalist friend who announced at lunch the other day, "It's finally happened! I've lost my objectivity!" I, too, find that once it's gone, it's gone.

In spite of a dogged effort, I could not acquire the cool detachment I imagined to be the necessary equipment of a born introduction writer. The subject here was feminist humor—a subject from which I have about as much distance and objectivity as a five-year-old at a Ringling Brothers circus. I tried to suppress myself, put my enthusiasm on hold, let the scholarly attitude take over. I ended up writing a long, belabored overbearing account of the best and the brightest feminist comedy. There's nothing like good, pedantic send-off on your way into a book of humor.

What we have here instead, I'm afraid, is a giddy introduction writer, one who has the family album in her hands, who wants to tell the story of the family tree—its painful prunings and its delicious growth—who keeps pointing proudly at the ubiquitous progeny; who is irrepressibly excited over the family achievements; who borders on obnoxious in her display of family affection. I'm not an introduction-writer, Gloria, I'm a *cheer*leader. (I accept the rightness, the naturalness, of this seemingly unprofessional stance—this demonstration of almost adolescent superabundance—through the teachings of my five-year-old sage. He watched the runners in the Lincoln 10,000-meter race stoicly and solemnly until the youngest entry, #345, who needed three strides to keep up with each one of his mother's, came into view. At the sight of #345, my son broke into wild ecstasy, grinning and clapping with abandon from the street curb. "Why did you cheer for #345?" I asked him. "Well, mom," he said, drawing on the vast patience needed to explain obvious truths to adults, "you *have* to cheer for your *group*!" Of course you do.)

It's a relief, in a way, to admit my defeat—my defection, actually, from the introduction—to be through with the shoe that never fit, to be back to trusting my own instincts, biased and pressingly personal though they may be.

The problem was, I couldn't hush the voices I kept hearing, the chorus of voices gathered here in the family album—the writers and thinkers, the scholars and comics, the speakers and street fighters, the movers and shakers. I couldn't quiet them down. They are a rowdy bunch: slicing through the myths with their saucy satire; burlesquing rude sex-role assumptions; talking back to the patriarchs with their one-liners; rattling their "invisible" chains—giving a clever name to each embarrassing link; overhauling motherhood with their warm wit; indulging, now and again, in a fantasy reversal; and just generally living it up at the bottom of the pedestal. How can you write with all that racket going on?

I couldn't write because I kept hearing the voices, the fascinating intonations, the fluctuating moods, and yes, yes, yes, I listened to the tremors of revolution that our humor inspires. I lost interest in diagramming the sentences, explicating the themes . . . I wanted to listen.

I heard the faint voice of self-consciousness in our humor, the nervous laugh of the messenger who doesn't want her head cut off for reporting the damaging news: The natives are restless. We use our humor to deliver our complaints about the status quo. We tend to be a bit edgy at times because we know from experience just how many potential toes we are stepping on.

We are expected, somehow, not to offend anyone on our way to liberation. There's an absurd expectation that the women's movement must be the first revolution in history to accomplish its goals without hurting anyone's feelings. We are to be the Boston Tea Party that serves crumpets with its resolutions. We are to curtsey throughout our crusades. We ought to smile politely as we outline our injustices. By all means, we are to be kind. (Pardon me, sir, but could you kindly move over? You're stepping on my body, my paycheck, my choices. It's hurting me, sir. Would it be too much trouble to please move over?)

And then I would hear the voice of Robin Tyler, ending her comic routine, "If you were offended by anything, you needed it."

We're sensitive at times because we've had more than our share of advice on how to be an acceptable feminist. (Acceptable feminist? Does that suggest a contradiction, like "military intelligence"?) The advice usually comes from an armchair supporter, an almost-ally: "It certainly makes *sense*, this equality business, *BUT* (emphasis mine) couldn't you feminists just be a little . . . softer . . . nicer . . . more sensitive?"

I'm keeping a list of all the phrases that follow: You could get your point across much better if you would only . . . Speak Up. Slow Down. Move Over. Come Around.

It's no wonder, actually, that our self-confidence has a quicksand quality about it. We seem to be miles away from having the Right Personality as humorists and satirists because we are miles away from having the Right Personality as women. We are too emotional, too hysterical, too moody, too illogical, too (fill in the blank). We always seem to be carrying the wrong baggage with us: We bring our feelings into the conference rooms and we bring our logic into the emergency rooms. The messages have been confounding: we are cute when we are angry, and angry when we are funny; we are threatening when we are glib, and amusing when we are upset. It has taken us decades to discover, singly and collectively, who we are.

I listened uncomfortably to the voices of those who found some of the early movement humor "too obvious" for our now raised awareness. The Equal Pay Act was passed in 1964, and most employers still haven't gotten the message. Textbooks published in 1979 are still offering pictures of mommies in aprons. Television commercials still cling to the belief that women have orgasms over laundry that is whiter than white. *What raised awareness?* I look for it regularly.

I heard the impatience in our voices; we are eager for relief. It's worth noting, I think, that subtlety, distance, a laid-back and mellow delivery are the luxuries reserved for the more powerful classes in a culture. They have the *time* to linger on stage and mull it over. We sometimes rush our punchlines because getting the word out through our humor is a risky business. (Joan and I were invited to a small town in Indiana to do a routine called "Women's Liberation Is Gonna Get Your Mama and Your Sister and Your Girlfriend"—a lighthearted number, we thought. Before we went on stage, Joan looked out at the sea of polyester Hoosier suits and said, worried, "What if they don't *get* it?" "Worse, Joan," I said, looking at what appeared to be an entire row of football coaches, "What if they *do?* We could get hurt!")

I heard the voices of the war buddies at the barricades of change. This particular album contains many snapshots of the women who have seen action. There are the mad, impossible confrontations we marched bravely into, trying to make sense of the resistance we faced. Susan B. Anthony was startled to be asked to speak on the suffrage issue to the inmates of an insane asylum. "Bless me!" she said. "It's as much as I can do to speak to the sane! What could I say to an audience of lunatics!" But her companion, Virginia Minor, recovered quickly to add, "This is a golden moment for you, the first opportunity you have ever had, according to the Constitution, to talk to your *peers,* for is not the right of suffrage denied to 'idiots, criminals, lunatics, and women'?"

There are the little portraits of the incredible odds we faced and the courage we mustered to make our unpopular points: Joan, scheduled to perform a program on women's history, arrived at the home of a wealthy woman. Observing the display of affluence and luxury, she whispered to her colleagues, "Listen, I think we better skip the part about 'throwing off your shackles and following us into freedom.' "

I heard the poignant struggle in our humor: To remove the limiting biases, to isolate the prejudices, to avoid blaming the victim. It isn't easy to plow our way through "150 Years of the Experts' Advice to Women" and still arrive at our own ponderous truths. We use extreme caution, for example, when we begin the delicate operation of separating the "institution of motherhood" from the "experience of motherhood." "It's not splitting hairs," said one mother. "It's splitting arteries."

It's the silliness of our circumstances, however, and not our commitments, that feminist humor satirizes. In fact, I have grown overly fond of looking ahead through our humor. The "distortions" it presents seem so logical and sane to me now, and the reality I see is ridiculous. (Isn't it incredible, for example, that 99 percent of the 2,800 equal-employment officers in the state of Indiana are white male? And *they* are calling *us* the protected classes. How, I'd be grateful to know, did this happen?)

It isn't hard for me to name the most troublesome voice I had to listen to while I tried to write that introduction: I kept tiptoeing around the edge of the hostility in the humor. I was protective of it. I had a severe case of what Cathryn calls "aggressive nuturance"—taking care of people who aren't in need of help. I was gentle with the anger that leaps from the pages. I was dangerously close to dishonest in my need to soften it, to make it understandable. That's why I couldn't read it to Kathy or Joan, why I couldn't send it to Cathryn or Carolen, why I never dropped it off for Alice to edit and comment on. I hated to mail it to you and to Suzy. I knew you would see my reluctance, my reticence, with the truth. The truth is, we are angry. Getting over my need to protect people from my anger, from our anger, has been the hardest piece of conditioning for me to cough up.

I keep believing I'm making progress in this area. Insights about women's anger are delivered to me daily. I was giving a lecture once in a Women's Studies class on the period of the "wasteland"—the eras of the fifties and the sixties, with their cracker-barrel psychology and patronizing women's magazines—and keeping an eye on a woman in the front row, a guest that evening, the mother of one of my students. Her facial expression never changed as she listened intently in her Butte knit suit and prim bun, her ankles crossed and seams perfectly straight. I worried that she would disapprove of my obvious feminism, my clear outrage at the lousy, limited lives of women. I worried that she would see me as bitter.

In the discussion that followed, one of the students wondered aloud, "Well, what was *wrong* with women then? Why didn't they just put their food down?" Then, with the conviction available only to youth, she added, "I wouldn't have stood for it."

Before I could say anything, the carefully maintained expressionless face in front of me changed, and, dropping all poses, the woman addressed the young student. "I'll tell you why we stood for it. Because for fifty years women like myself have been man*ip*ulated! We didn't *make* very many choices then, because we didn't *have* very many choices then." The woman I was protecting from my anger whipped fifty years of rage out of her handbag.

I discussed it later with Joan, and she nodded, "You can't lie to women, Mary Kay. I don't care where they come from to get to the threshold of this movement, but once they get here, we can't tell them any more lies." However much I may want to, I can't soften the blunt reality women face when they start to ask the questions and listen for the answers. Our humor is honest. I wish it weren't true, but the Argus poster is right: "The truth will make you free, but first it will make you miserable." Our humor turns our anger into a fine art.

I heard the exhaustion in some of the voices, and I identified with the urgency of it: Sexism is hurting us, it's taking a serious toll. There is a weariness in our humor over the excuse that "change takes time."

Change takes time, it appears, because nobody out there is paying attention. Change takes time because we have to say everything four hundred times. Isn't anybody out there taking notes? Change takes time because we are so busy with the nets to catch the casualties as they topple from the pedestal—with the shelters and the crisis centers and the hot lines—that we barely have time for the roots of the problems. Nobody knows better than the feminists who are trying it that "change takes time." Change doesn't take time. Resistance takes time.

I heard the chorus of feminist voices I have spoken to and written to during our three years of collecting their wit. "Humor?" they asked. "What could be funny?" they snorted. "It's a jungle out here!" they reported. "Get the book out quick," they pleaded. "We could use some comic relief!" they laughed. With our humor we learn how to live in a society, despite its sexism, without compromising too many of our principles or sacrificing too much of our happiness. We use our humor as a cure for burnout.

I know that I, for one, am burned out. I see the symptoms. I have been making menacing comments to my TV—yelling at the guy with ring around the collar to wash his dirty neck. When Bert Parks comes on, I'm rude.

I know that I'm burned out because lately I have excluded from my company all but small children. Their questions, for one thing, are infinitely more cheerful. Instead of "How do you explain the 43 percent earnings gap?" they ask questions you can answer: "Mom, where do pancakes come from?"

I see the signs, I see the signs. And it is my firm belief that burnouts should have as little as possible to do with introduction writing.

So much went wrong with that introduction—I experienced so much struggle and strain to describe a feminist philosophy with which I am intimately familiar. I felt so much distance from a movement in which I consider myself a lifer, it's a pretty clear indication to me, anyway, that the whole thing ought to be canned.

Maybe it's important to discuss the sources of our humor, the conflicts of it, the balance of it, the blues of it, the revelous pleasure of it. Maybe it is.

But I feel strongly that My Time Is Up. I hear the voices, and it's time to get up from my typewriter and out where the emergencies arrive as frequently as ever. I'm not an introduction writer, Gloria. I'm a correspondent from the front lines.

Fondly, MK

INTRODUCTION

By Gloria Kaufman

It is easy to identify overtly political humor as feminist ("Rock the boat, not the cradle" or "A woman's place is in the White House"). We need, however, a definition that encompasses indirect and subtle feminist humor as well as the obvious kinds.

Feminist humor is based on the perception that societies have generally been organized as systems of oppression and exploitation, and that the largest (but not the only) oppressed group has been the female. It is also based on conviction that such oppression is undesirable and unnecessary. It is a humor based on visions of change.

The persistent attitude that underlies feminist humor is the attitude of social revolution—that is, we are ridiculing a social system that can be, that must be changed. *Female* humor may ridicule a person or a system from an accepting point of view ("that's life"), while the *nonacceptance* of oppression characterizes feminist humor and satire. The following anecdote exemplifes feminist humor:

It was New Year's Eve of 1961. At a lively party in Watertown, Massachusetts, a psychiatrist was conversing with an attractive divorced woman.

"So you have only one child?"

"Yes," she said, "a four-year-old."

"That means," he said, magnanimously sharing his expertise, "that you don't yet know what it means to be a mother."

"Well, then," she returned, "when you have a child, I'm sure you'll tell me."

The professional man is playing an authority role, but the woman does not accept the authority he assumes for himself. Her remark, which exhibits an amused awareness of his intellectual limitation, clearly demonstrates the feminist stance of nonacceptance. In contrast, the Lithuanian joke that follows is an example of female (nonfeminist) humor:

A farmer loudly asserted to his wife that she did not enjoy the same rights in the house as he. She was a mere woman, not a member of mankind. The next day, when he was putting on his boots, she heard him curse.

"What's the matter, dear?"

"There's shit in my boot, God damn it!"

"Was it the cat, dear?"

"No—it's not cat stuff."

"Perhaps the dog?"

"No, no, no! It's human."

"Human, is it? Then it was I."

The farmer's wife *accepts* her bad marriage as a norm. She is powerless to change things, and she can only express her resentment in a destructive, sarcastic way. The bitterness and the antimale feelings of the wife are frequently seen in female humor but occur far less often in feminist humor. Perhaps that is because the entrapped female regards her husband as the inevitable oppressor, whereas the feminist perceives him ultimately as a person who can or who will change (or as a person she can leave). Feminist humor tends to be a humor of hope, female humor of hopelessness. (This is not to contend that bitterness is absent from feminist humor, merely that, compared to female humor, it occurs much less regularly.)

It will not be clear to most readers without an explanation why some humor is feminist. Why, for example, isn't the menstruation humor in "Rhythm Reds" female (rather than feminist) humor? It might have been. If the humor were created with the idea that menses is dirty, smelly, ugly, and shameful (the traditional attitude that society has inculcated), it would have been female humor. Since, however, the underlying attitude is that menses is normally and naturally female; since, moreover, the attitude is that menses is not to be hidden (as shameful) but to be joked about (as normal) or even celebrated (as naturally female), the humor is deeply feminist. Not by explicit statement but by implicit posture, the expression of such humor attacks the unhealthy and oppressing idea cultivated for thousands of years that women's bodies are foul. There is, of course, a great deal of menstruation humor that is female or male rather than feminist, but such humor has been excluded from our collection.

Feminist satire, like other satire, is didactic and often overtly so. No matter how pessimistic it sounds, it seeks to improve us by demonstrating—through devices of irony, of exaggeration, of sarcasm, and of wit—our human folly. It exposes realities not merely out of love for truth but also out of desire for reform. Whether or not reforms are achieved, they are implicit ideals. In this sense, feminist satire, like feminist humor, is founded on hope and predicated on a stance of nonacceptance.

Stereotypes are accepted norms upon which a great deal of mainstream humor is built. Mother-in-law jokes, for example, are understood when the stereotype—that of an interfering and intrusive relative—is conceded. Feminist humor does not respond by creating father-in-law jokes. Since it arises from a subculture that has no patience with stereotyping, especially in relation to sex roles, we should not be surprised at the tendency of feminist humor to avoid stereotypic characters. *Actions,* however, do become stereotyped in feminist humor. There is much material based on typical limitations of the male. Masculine illogic, for example, is a favorite target. In such humor the man may be a doctor or a check-out boy, old or young, educated or not—but his penchant for illogic is not automatically linked to other identifying traits in the way that "interfering" and "overbearing" are linked to mother-in-law. The particular human behavior might be regarded as *typed* behavior, but the character who commits the behavior is not a stereotyped character.

In the early 1970s, it did look as if one feminist stereotype might emerge—the male chauvinist pig (MCP). His existence, however, was relatively short-lived. And he was not universally accepted in feminist circles. (A sizeable minority objected to the "reduction" of man to four-legged animal. Another minority saw no reason to insult the pig.) Characterizations of that brief stereotype can be seen in "The Male Chauvinist Pig Calendar" (1974) by Betty Swords *(see pp. 15, 108, 114, and 131).* Most of the references to the MCP that I came across were, curiously, not from feminists but from men—especially from men in the media. The journalistic practice of reducing feminist issues to slogans and catch-words has done much to trivialize complex issues raised by the women's movement. MCP served that purpose. It appealed to the imagination of males in the media: "I used to be an MCP," or (on interview shows with a feminist guest), "Do *you* think I'm an MCP?" Readers will find only a few MCP references in our collection. The male chauvinist pig actually derives from the protest rhetoric of the 1960s. The "pig," the visible oppressor, frequently a policeman, became MCP when rebelling feminists tried to show their fellow male protestors that oppression of women was a fact of life in everyday radical politics. The MCP is definitely a derived stereotype rather than an original creation. We note his demise with no sorrow.

An unwarranted expectation of stereotypes accounts, I believe, for the nervous response of many men to the term "feminist humor." They have assimilated the misogyny of male humor, and with some guilt they expect that feminist humor will return their treatment in kind. Let us be clear about how the female is treated in mainstream (male) humor. It has taken many centuries to produce the stereotypical female of male comedy. By A.D. 101, in Juvenal's "Sixth Satire," the female stereotype is firmly defined as nasty, lying, vicious, pretentious, emasculating, garrulous, aggressive, vulgar, nymphomaniacal, gluttonous, dishonest, shameless, greedy, selfish, quarrelsome, impertinent, and disgusting. Notably absent in Juvenal is the idea of woman as stupid and ineffectual. Instead, she is offensively intelligent—the legitimate castrating bitch. When we add stupidity and ineffectuality to the Juvenalian list, we have a fairly complete picture of the stereotypical woman targeted by male humorists.

Many men assume incorrectly that feminists have created, as a counter or opposing stereotype, a nasty and oppressive male as repulsive and disgusting as their stereotypic female. That assumption is perhaps founded on an unacknowledged belief on men's part that women are, after all, just like men and that we will act exactly as they do when we attain positions of power. But we do not have historical precedent for determining how women in power will act. The exceptional women who have "ruled" (Elizabeth I of England, Catherine the Great, Golda Meir) nonetheless functioned in traditionally patriarchal worlds. They dealt not with an assortment of men and women, they dealt not with other women, but they dealt mostly or even exclusively with men committed to established hierarchical power systems. The idea that a single woman can ignore or change the entire patriarchal social order is ludicrous, but it is an argument that antifeminists are quick to offer. It is, therefore, interesting to see that given the freedom to go in our own direction, women do so. Feminist humor is NOT the obverse of male humor. If it is true that people are revealed through their humor, our collection is an important document that testifies to a difference, if not between female and male, at least between feminist female and mainstream male. Feminist humor and satire demonstrate that *culturally* we have not been doing what the male does. It may be that politically our ways will also be our own.

Even more than humor, satire tends to rely heavily on stereotypical characters. In "New Discoveries Hailed as Birth Control Breakthroughs," Jane Field satirizes behavior, not an individual. Virginia Woolf in *Three Guineas* (perhaps the most sustained and elegant piece of sarcasm in the English language) does not approach the terrain of stereotype. In Una Stannard's sophisticated burlesque, "Why Little Girls Are Sugar and Spice and When They Grow Up Become Cheesecake," a parody of the entire process of history and of scholarship, the stereotyping so natural to burlesque (compare Dostoevski's "The Crocodile") is not even a factor. In each of these feminist works behavior is satirized and stereotypical men are not invented to commit the objectionable behaviors. Quite to the contrary. Virginia Woolf wittily examines the statements of British philosopher C. E. M. Joad, a real figure rather than a contrived stereotype. Una Stannard quotes the poet Byron rather than invent a foolish statement to put into the mouth of an available stereotype.

Feminist humor and satire are not new. Perhaps the best-known example of both dates from the 5th century B.C. In Aristophanes' *Lysistrata*, the women of Athens and Sparta force the men to make peace by withdrawing sexual favors from their husbands, whose desires for sexual activity ultimately overpower their desires to make war. The play presents men as incompetent in their roles as leaders of state and reveals women as having a more valid social perspective. Women are not idealized. They also have their pugnacious side, and they are ready physically to do battle with men. When the Chorus of Old Men attempts to smoke the striking women out of the Acropolis, a counter-Chorus of Old Women appears, and there is a fight between the men with the burning torches and the women with pitchers of water. When the men's torches are extinguished, they complain to the magistrate: "Besides their other violent acts, they threw water all over us, and we have to shake out our clothes just as if we'd leaked in them."[*]

The Mastermind

© R/M HURLEY 1974

"WHEN I WANT YOUR OPINION I'LL TELL YOU WHAT IT IS."

In the comic tradition, women battle with household supplies, no one gets hurt, and responsible social action follows. Mother Jones's labor-organizing activity comes from that tradition. In "How the Women Mopped Up Coaldale," a chapter of her autobiography, she recounts how she organized a female force armed with mops and brooms. The women faced a militia whose colonel threatened to charge with bayonets. The scene was worthy of Aristophanes, but the union struggle was no prewritten play with a guaranteed safe outcome. Mother Jones used humor to defuse a situation in which danger was terribly real. In the Coaldale battle (which she described as "a great fight"), she led her army to the militia's headquarters and had them eat the soldiers' breakfasts. Like Aristophanes, she was a master of comic irony—he the writer, she the practitioner.

Mai Zetterling, in her film *The Girls* (1968), again focuses feminist attention on Aristophanes' *Lysistrata*. Not only does she invoke and reinforce Aristophanes' themes, but she also addresses contemporary feminist issues satirically. The film presents an acting group on tour with Aristophanes' play. Zetterling shows the twentieth-century audience (at the time of the Vietnam war) to be still unreceptive to

[*]tr. Charles T. Murphy, *Ten Greek Plays*, ed. L. R. Lind, Cambridge, Mass.: Riverside Press, 1957, p. 381.

the antiwar sentiment of *Lysistrata*. Turning to modern issues, she treats contemporary sexual relations with dry wit. In a hotel bedroom, for example, a touring actress asks her businessman-husband about his mistress, who is physically present as a mannikin. As the husband stuffs the mistress-mannikin into a large trunk (with the wife watching), he insists there is no other woman. The trunk-stuffing involves much physical contact between husband and mistress (compared to no contact with the wife). The sequence, which is well executed, is funny as plain slapstick. But it also implies that he regards the mistress entirely as object (in *that* sense, there really is no other woman). The visual treatment of woman-as-object has never been done more imaginatively. With subtlety Zetterling also suggests that the wife and the mistress share similar problems (vis-à-vis men) as well as a common humanity. There is a magical sympathy between them. We see the wife as a person of civilized complexity, the husband as superficial and farcical. To treat farce, which is based on crudely obvious exaggeration, with such complex subtlety is fine and rare art.

Between Aristophanes and Zetterling there is a space of more than two millennia. It is not an empty space. A history of feminist humor is in order, but that is far beyond the space and the scope of my introductory remarks. It will require a volume of its own. To comment only on the recent past in the United States, we note that the suffrage movement created its share of platform wits—Anna Howard Shaw, Sojourner Truth, Susan B. Anthony, Lucretia Mott, Harriot Stanton Blatch, and Elizabeth Cady Stanton, to mention a few. Marietta Holly (who is not in our collection) and Fanny Fern (who is included) wrote as declared feminist humorists. Their issues are today's issues. Although the tradition of feminist humor continued into the twentieth century, the current movement, which emerged in the '60s and has produced so much humor and satire of its own, seems to have lost touch with the earlier feminist humor tradition. We are largely unaware of the wit of the early suffragists as well as the "new suffragists" of our own century. We don't remember the feminist wit that flourished in the flapper age, and much of the work of the '30s and '40s, such as Ruth Herschberger's "Josie Takes the Stand" (1948), Dorothy Sayers' "The Human-Not-Quite-Human" (1947), and even Virginia Woolf's *Three Guineas* (1938), is not widely known. Although our collection is a highly selected sampler, not an anthology that can be used to reconstruct a history of feminist humor, perhaps it will inspire such an effort.

Feminist humor is richly various, but a dominant undercurrent is the pickup, an obvious reversal of the putdown. In some cases pickups happen in response to putdowns ("A woman's place is in the home" generates "A woman's place is *every*place"). Some pickups are extended. The last sentence of Gabrielle Burton's "No One Has a Corner on Depression But Housewives Are Working on It" is a calculated pickup. Naomi Weisstein closes her long standup-comic routine, "The Saturday Night Special: Rape and Other Big Jokes," with a deliberate pickup. Such humor is a healthy contrast to mainstream humor, most of which seems to knock people down—or to laugh at people who are already down. Laughs come from a perceived superiority of the hearer or reader to the character ridiculed. Pickup humor, however, is based on equity. Through it, we do not laugh *at* people, we bond *with* them.

One of the best and most popular pickups of the movement is Flo Kennedy's remark, "A woman without a man is like a fish without a bicycle." Our society has asserted and reinforced the idea that no woman is complete until she finds her "other half" and unites in heterosexual marriage. Society says, "You are half." Kennedy says, "You are whole." It is interesting (but not surprising) that many men take this powerful and clever pickup of women to be an indictment of men as both unnecessary and worthless. Rather, it defies a system that tells woman she is singly incomplete; in a larger sense it is a revolutionary celebration of woman alone. It ignores rather than attacks men.

The selections in *Pulling Our Own Strings* were made chiefly on the basis of quality, but there were other major criteria. We were unable to get permissions for all of the material we wanted to use. Limitations of space forced us to reject other good material, including some of our favorite pieces. Although we did try to give a sense of the variety of forms, of approaches, and of subject-matters, we cannot offer a comprehensive sampler that fairly represents the rich variety of both feminist humor and feminist satire. Our selections have been deliberately weighted toward the humor at the expense of the satire—not because feminist satire is less interesting or less distinguished, but because we feel that at this moment in its history, the feminist movement needs to share its humor even more than its satire, which has already found an audience through print.

Feminists are not simply angry women. As persons, we are complex: we are as likely to explode with laughter as with anger; we are as likely to write satirical essays as to circulate petitions; and we value all aspects of our feminism—our street actions and our scholarship, our poetry and our doggerel, our anger and our laughter.

The world is always humor-poor. There is never enough of it. Yet, without humor we cannot survive. Our world is too relentlessly cruel, too callous, too uncivilized, and feminists who contemplate it will die of depression or lapse into cynicism and inaction without our humor. By joking, we rehumanize, recivilize ourselves. By joking, we remake ourselves so that after each disappointment we become once again capable of living and loving.

CHAPTER ONE

Periodic Hysteria

The First Tampon
by Claire Bretécher

Becoming a Tampax Junkie
A PERFORMANCE

IVY BOTTINI

Ivy Bottini

I'd like to talk to you about something that all women share. I was about eight years old. I was sitting in our kitchen, while my mother brushed my hair and drank coffee. *(Brush! Brush! Slurrrrp!)*

She said *(brush! brush! slurrrp!),* "Ivy, you're a girl."

"Yeah, Ma, I know that."

"Any day now *(brush! brush! slurrrp!)* you'll be getting something."

This one morning, she was brushing *(brush! brush! brush! brush!),* out of control, so I knew something was up. Finally she said, "You will be getting something *(brush! brush! slurrrp!)* that we call *(brush)* men- *(brush)* stra- *(brush) (slurpation).* And when you get it, you will have to wear a Ko- *(slurrp, brush),* because you will be *(slurp, slurp, brush! brush!)."*

I didn't hear *the* word. You know what I thought she said I was going to get? MEN'S TREASURE!

And when I finally got it, at age eleven, in the middle of a baseball field, in a pair of white shorts, I thought, "Men's treasure! Listen, fellas, you can have it back! Or at least, let's share."

When I went to school at age eight, I carried a large purse with six Kotexes—*all super.* When the teacher asked me why I was never without my purse, I told her it was "my lunch"! I was never without six Kotex—*all super.*

I would sneak into the little girls' bathroom between classes, close the door, and nail it shut. And there, on the back of the door, was the sign (probably printed more than the Bible) that we all know so well. You can say it with me: DO NOT FLUSH SANITARY NAPKINS DOWN TOILET. USE DISPOSAL BOX. But my mother never told me about the disposal box. Did your mother ever tell you about the disposal box?

But then I discovered something totally freeing and liberating—TAMPAX! Oh Great Tampax! Now I could get twelve in my purse—*all super.* I became a tampax junkie. I had them stashed all over. Under the couch cushions in the living room, in case I got it there. In the refrigerator for those hot summer days. I'm never without them. In fact, when I walk into a room where the women know me, they all relax—because they know I've got them covered!

How many of you women have some form of sanitary protection with you right now? (About two-thirds of the audience raised their hands.) Look at all those hands! Next question—how many of you are actually having your period? (About half of the raised hands go down.)

Look at that! We don't have penis envy! We have a tampax fetish!

Ragtime

A doctor pointed out that estrogen (the female hormone) is at its lowest level during the menstrual cycle. So at our "worst," we are most like the way men are all the time.

(from Chicago North Suburban NOW Newsletter)

Question: How do you know when an elephant is on the rag?

Answer: You find a dime on your dresser and your mattress is missing.

A ten-year-old boy went to a drugstore with fifty cents to spend. He spent a lot of time looking and finally chose a box of Tampax.

"Are you *sure* that's what you want?" the druggist asked.

"You bet!" the boy said. "The box says that with these you can swim, ride, or play tennis, and up to now I haven't been able to do any of those things."

Periodical Bea

E. M. BRONER

For no good reason on this earth, Bea still fertilizes. Being an imprecise person, Bea cannot possibly follow exact tampon directions. She cannot make decisions between:

> a. placing one foot on the toilet or chair, or
> b. sitting on the toilet seat with knees apart, or
> c. squatting slightly with legs apart
> whichever seems most natural and comfortable for you.

None did, none was. Poking with that cardboard Tootsie Roll between bladder, rectum, vagina, hoping, as in some dimestore game, to fit rolling object into right hole, she invariably ended up leaving in the cardboard and pulling out the cotton. Or she would end up with bloody fingers and the tampon floating inaccurately in a sea of blood.

Those careful explanations of what to do with grasping thumb and forefinger, aiming directly at the small of the back, removing the forefinger to free the withdrawal cord, all of that required an engineering student, a mechanical genius, or someone less shy about poking into cavities, like a dental assistant.

Bea sidles up to the drugstore counter, trying to avoid the gray-haired man behind the cash register, trying not to stand near the male customers in line. She has selected her napkin, her dinner napkin, her breakfast napkin, her man-sized napkin, not folded next to her plate, not folded under her chin, not folded in her lap, her neat napkin folded between her legs.

She can have Stayfree and run, like the black-haired beauty in gossamer dress, through green fields. In gossamer dress? Nowhere under that transparent material can Bea make out belts, pins, metal tips, wads of cotton batting.

Bea, all of her life, has failed the menstrual ads. They were so discreet, they whispered. She would never, if she heeded them, be inconvenienced by bleeding, backaches, nausea, bad circulation in feet and hands, twitching of leg muscles, chills, or cracked lips. The girls in the Land of Magazine Menstruation, the girls with periods in the periodicals leap immediately into the water, wearing tight swimsuits or, in short, crisp, white, swinging tennis skirts, there they were out on the court!

Bea was taking mincing steps from bed to bathroom, bed to teakettle. Not those girls who won blue ribbons at horse meets, who attended balls gowned in Modess.

At the store she bought boxes, daintily marked like handkerchief or stationery boxes. Soon all sanitary products would be sold in stationery stores. On each napkin would be the wearer's initials. Have them monogrammed for your best friend!

She carries these boxes home proudly, not in the old brown paper bag. Her Stayfree goddess trips through a blur of green. On each box, flora, fleurs-de-lis, green mint leaves, Kotex-blue roses. The boxes vie for euphemism and fantasy. Tear along the perforated edge for a visual experience of napkins backed in green or pink. Smell them. They are perfumed. Wear them as edgings on cashmere sweaters. Wear them as earmuffs in cold weather.

Bea wonders if she is normal, if she has ever really menstruated in her life. Perhaps it is all psychology and if she were less neurotic, she, too, could roll in dewy flowers, jump hurdles with her stallion, or dive from the highest board.

(from Her Mothers, *1978)*

Splat

MARILYN FRENCH

[Mira reminisces about an early discussion among female students at Harvard University.]

What kept coming into her mind was a scene in Lehman Hall a week or two ago, when Val had embarrassed her horribly. A group of them were sitting around talking about the months, or year, or two years ago when women had not been permitted in Lamont Library, or in the main dining room of the Faculty Club.

"It was a problem," Priss was saying, "because there are classrooms upstairs in Lamont, and female teaching assistants still couldn't use the front door, they had to go in the side entrance and climb the back stairs to teach their classes. Like in Rome, you know, slaves teaching the children of the freeborn."

"The same thing happens at Yale," Emily said. "Mory's is such an institution they hold committee meetings there, but no women are allowed to eat there, so they have to go in a back way and climb a back staircase to where the meetings are held."

"Well, that won't last long," Val said dryly. "God, the whole world's going to pot. I mean, once they let women in, heaven knows what will come next! It's a terrible degrading of standards. I mean, you have to consider the real reason they keep women out. You know, they say to let women enter med school, or Harvard, or whatever, means lowering their standards, but you know as well as I that women do better than men in high-school grades. So *that's* not what they mean. And women don't mangle books or dirty the card catalog any more than men do, right? So they're just being polite, the men, when they talk about standards. It's a euphemism. They don't want to embarrass us. The real reason is sanitary. You let women through front doors and what will they do? Splat splat, a big clot of menstrual blood right on the threshold. Every place women go they do it: splat splat. There are little piles of clotty blood all over Lamont Library now. There are special crews hired just to keep the place decently mopped down. That's an expense! And they have to put in separate toilets. That's an expense too, and it takes up space! But what can you do? Women *will* do it: splat splat. Just one more example of the decaying standards of the modern world, letting women in. Nobody," she concluded bitterly, "cares about decorum anymore."

(from The Women's Room, *1978)*

A Person Who Menstruates Is Unfit to be a Mother

HADLEY V. BAXENDALE, M.D., Ph.D. *

Q. *Are men and women really different?*
A. Absolutely. Every psychologist instinctively knows this, and Hendrik Hendrikson of Harvard established it conclusively some years ago. In a landmark study,† Hendrikson asked sixty children to construct models of anything they liked. Little boys constructed model penises, thus demonstrating a symbolic interest in guns, warfare, rocketships, and aerosol deodorants. . . . But the majority of girls happily constructed model wombs, revealing their preoccupation with interior decorating . . . .

Women, it turned out, do not perceive a distinction between margarine and the high-priced spread. Men, however, discover the difference at once. On the other hand, men cannot distinguish white from "whiter than white," whereas women unerringly can. . . .

The logical consequence of all this is that the sexes engage in radically different activities. Women menstruate, give birth, scrub tubs, and type letters. Men found empires, fly airplanes, fight wars, and make money. Women, typing letters, become nimble-fingered and attentive to detail. Men, making money, become rich. That these differences have significant implications for women's competence in the professions is undeniable. For the moment, however, let us focus our attention on menstruation, as the archetype of women's ills. . . .

The menstrual process, when taken with the appropriate seriousness, can incapacitate a woman for three weeks out of every four. In the week beforehand, she is hypertense and anxious, biting her nails, counting the days, thinking, "Oh hell, here it comes again." During the week itself, she is smitten and crazed by the "transient stab of dread and loss" that one of our talented girl writers has described so well. At worst, she is also prostrate with incredible contractions, tossing on a couch for seven days, clutching herself, screaming wildly, gagging, panting, mopping the floor, washing the dishes, doing the laundry, lugging great bags of provender home from the supermarket. The next week, she is so relieved and relaxed that she has no motivation to do anything but bake a few cakes, make new curtains, gut some fish, and pluck a duck or two. That leaves one week in which to clean the oven, defrost the refrigerator, and polish the silver. Given all these biologically dictated activities, how is she to find time to *work?* . . .

These biological events bear in an obvious way on women's fitness for jobs—particularly on their fitness for child-rearing, the most noble and important job there is. Motherhood is a full-time profession, calling for a mature, dependable person, willing to stay at work, without sick leave or vacation, for 20 years or more. It requires sound health, an even temperament, great energy, and two or more Ph.D.s. . . .

One point emerges with startling clarity from the preceding discussion, indeed from all discussions on this subject. This point—which the zealots and bra-burners of Women's Lib consistently evade—is that *a person who menstruates is unfit to be a mother.*

Child-rearing is too important and complex a job to be entrusted to unstable, untrained neurotics, who can be thrown off balance by the merest biological event. . . .

(from Are Children Neglecting Their Mothers? *1974)*

*Hadley V. Baxendale—psychoanalyst, husband, and father of three—is a caricature invented by Joyce Wood for her book, *Are Children Neglecting Their Mothers?* (Doubleday, 1974). Ostensibly a collection of sexist psychoanalytic essays, the book is published under Baxendale's name.

†*Am. J. Masoch. Bugg.* (Sept. 1966), pp 346-85.

A Crowd of Commuters

MARY ELLMANN

. . . when Bruno Bettelheim characterizes the male mind as *expansive* and *exploratory* and the female mind as *interiorizing,* it is ludicrously clear that he envisages a mental copulation between the two. . . . So too when Louis Auchincloss characterizes several American women novelists as *conservers* or *caretakers.* And when Norman Mailer pronounces that "Temples are for women." The female mind is repeatedly seen as an enclosed space in which what other and (as we always say) *seminal* minds have provided is stored away or tended or worshipped.

When the uterus-mind is seen as conservative or nutritive, it is praised. When it is seen as claustrophobic, it is blamed. By sexual correlation, all energy or enterprise is customarily assigned to male thought, and simple, accretive expectation to female thought. The one breaks through, the other broods. An immobility is attributed to the entire female constitution by analogy with the supposed immobility of the ovum. This imaginative vision of the ovum, like a pop art fried-egg-on-a-plate, is dependent of course upon a happy physiological vagueness. In actuality, each month the ovum undertakes an extraordinary expedition from the ovary through the Fallopian tubes to the uterus, an unseen equivalent of going down the Mississippi on a raft or over Niagara Falls in a barrel. Ordinarily too, the ovum travels singly, like Lewis *or* Clark, in the kind of existential loneliness which Normal Mailer usually admires. One might say that the activity of ova involves a daring and independence absent, in fact, from the activity of spermatozoa, which move in jostling masses, swarming out on signal like a crowd of commuters from the 5:15.

(from Thinking About Women, *1968)*

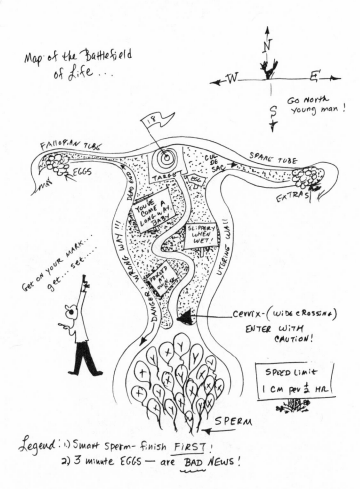

Map of the Battlefield of Life . . .

N
W — E
S
Go North young man!

FALLOPIAN TUBE
MAN EGGS
SPANG TUBE
CUL DE SAC
EGG
18
DEAD END
TARGET
WRONG WAY!!!
YOU'VE COME A LONG WAY, BABY
SLIPPERY WHEN WET!
UTERINE WALL
DANGER
PROCEED WITH CARE
EXTRAS!
Get on your mark . . . get . . . set . . .
CERVIX—(WIDE CROSSING) ENTER WITH CAUTION!
SPEED LIMIT 1 CM PER ½ HR
Y Y Y Y Y Y Y X Y X X X X X X X X X X X
SPERM

Legend: 1) Smart Sperm- finish FIRST!
2) 3 minute EGGS — are BAD NEWS!

If Men Could Menstruate

★ ★ ★ ★ ★ ★ ★ ★ ★ ★ ★ ★ ★ ★ ★ ★
A   P O L I T I C A L   F A N T A S Y

GLORIA STEINEM

A white minority of the world has spent centuries conning us into thinking that a white skin makes people superior—even though the only thing it really does is make them more subject to ultraviolet rays and to wrinkles. Male human beings have built whole cultures around the idea that penis-envy is "natural" to women—though having such an unprotected organ might be said to make men vulnerable, and the power to give birth makes womb-envy at least as logical.

In short, the characteristics of the powerful, whatever they may be, are thought to be better than the characteristics of the powerless—and logic has nothing to do with it.

What would happen, for instance, if suddenly, magically, men could menstruate and women could not?

The answer is clear—menstruation would become an enviable, boast-worthy, masculine event:

Men would brag about how long and how much.

Boys would mark the onset of menses, that longed-for proof of manhood, with religious ritual and stag parties.

Congress would fund a National Institute of Dysmenorrhea to help stamp out monthly discomforts.

Sanitary supplies would be federally funded and free. (Of course, some men would still pay for the prestige of commercial brands such as John Wayne Tampons, Muhammad Ali's Rope-a-dope Pads, Joe Namath's Jock Shields—"For Those Light Bachelor Days," and Robert "Baretta" Blake Maxi-Pads.)

Military men, right-wing politicians, and religious fundamentalists would cite menstruation ("*men*-struation") as proof that only men could serve in the Army ("you have to give blood to take blood"), occupy political office ("can women be aggressive without that steadfast cycle governed by the planet Mars?"), be priests and ministers ("how could a woman give her blood for our sins?"), or rabbis ("without the monthly loss of impurities, women remain unclean").

Male radicals, left-wing politicians, and mystics, however, would insist that women are equal, just different, and that any woman could enter their ranks if only she were willing to self-inflict a major wound every month ("you *must* give blood for the revolution"), recognize the preeminence of menstrual issues, or subordinate her selfness to all men in their Cycle of Enlightenment.

Street guys would brag ("I'm a three-pad man") or answer praise from a buddy ("Man, you lookin' *good!*") by giving fives and saying, "Yeah, man, I'm on the rag!"

TV shows would treat the subject at length. ("Happy Days": Richie and Potsie try to convince Fonzie that he is still "The Fonz," though he has missed two periods in a row.) So would newspapers. (SHARK SCARE THREATENS MENSTRUATING MEN. JUDGE CITES MONTHLY STRESS IN PARDONING RAPIST.) And movies. (Newman and Redford in "Blood Brothers"!)

Men would brag about how long and how much

Men would convince women that intercourse was *more* pleasurable at "that time of the month." Lesbians would be said to fear blood and therefore life itself—though probably only because they needed a good menstruating man.

Of course, male intellectuals would offer the most moral and logical arguments. How could a woman master any discipline that demanded a sense of time, space, mathematics, or measurement, for instance, without that in-built gift for measuring the cycles of the moon and planets—and thus for measuring anything at all? In the rarefied fields of philosophy and religion, could women compensate for missing the rhythm of the universe? Or for their lack of symbolic death-and-resurrection every month?

Liberal males in every field would try to be kind: the fact that "these people" have no gift for measuring life or connecting to the universe, the liberals would explain, should be punishment enough.

And how would women be trained to react? One can imagine traditional women agreeing to all these arguments with a staunch and smiling masochism. ("The ERA would force housewives to wound themselves every month": Phyllis Schlafly. "Your husband's blood is as sacred as that of Jesus—and so sexy, too!": Marabel Morgan.) Reformers and Queen Bees would try to imitate men, and *pretend* to have a monthly cycle. All feminists would explain endlessly that men, too, needed to be liberated from the false idea of Martian aggressiveness, just as women needed to escape the bonds of menses-envy. Radical feminists would add that the oppression of the nonmenstrual was the pattern for all other oppressions. ("Vampires were our first freedom fighters!") Cultural feminists would develop a bloodless imagery in art and literature. Socialist feminists would insist that only under capitalism would men be able to monopolize menstrual blood . . . .

In fact, if men could menstruate, the power justifications could probably go on forever.

If we let them.

"If he had a period, we'd have grant money for menstrual research."

Walking the Knife's Edge

OR

BLUE BALLS IN BIBLELAND

LISA ALTHER

The first time I ever saw "the Sparkplug of the Hullsport Pirates," as the sportscaster of WHPT referred to Joe Bob Sparks, he came flying through a paper portrait of a snarling pirate who had a black patch over one eye and a knife between his teeth and a bandanna around his head. Joe Bob led with one cleated foot, his elbows extended and his shoulder pads hunched up around his maroon helmet. Number thirty-eight he was, halfback and captain. I had of course heard of him. He was an area legend by this time. But I had never seen him close up, only on distant athletic fields, because he lived in a housing development on the opposite side of town and we had gone to different elementary schools.

The cheerleaders were leading the packed stands in a frantic yell: "Sparky! Sparky! He's our may-un! If he cain't do hit, Dole cay-un!" (It seemed unlikely to me then, from the fierce good looks of Joe Bob, that there was *anything* he couldn't do. Being all palpitating pudenda, I hadn't yet realized that the ability to think did have its occasional uses.) Then Doyle charged through the deflowered paper hoop. The cheerleaders in their white and brown saddle shoes spun wildly, their full maroon and gray skirts swirling up around their waists to reveal maroon body suits. I spun, too, twirling my flag.

I could see Joe Bob in the middle of the field as I did so. He was prancing in place like a horse in the starting line at the Derby. Once the team had all established that they could leap through the hoop, Head Coach Bicknell appeared, surrounded by his assistants like a Mafioso by his bodyguards. All the players removed their helmets and tucked them under their left arms. The cheerleaders and I stood at attention, me with my flag shouldered like a rifle. The band blared through its unrecognizable rendering of "The Star-Spangled Banner," and I watched with approval as Joe Bob placed his huge right hand over his breast and stared reverently at Old Glory, while most of his teammates fidgeted and flexed. Then the team formed a tight circle, their eyes closed, and Joe Bob's most intently of all. Coach Bicknell led them in a prayer for good sportsmanship and teamwork, and, as an afterthought, victory.

Then the cheerleaders led our packed stands in welcoming the Sow Gap Lynxes: "Our game is rough,/ Our boys are rowdy./ But we send Sow Gap/ A great big howdy!"

The Kinflicks of that first heady game, which Mother was shooting from the front row of the bleachers, show me in a variety of prescribed poses: I remove my plumed helmet and do cartwheels as though the rotation of the earth depended on it; I grab up the cheerleaders' megaphone and shriek fervently toward the bleachers, "Y'all yell, ya hee-yah?"; I fall to my knees and raise my eyes to the heavens, pleading for a touchdown; after our first touchdown, I skip through an allemande left with the seven cheerleaders while the band blasts out its unique drum-dominated version of the school song to the tune of "Stars and Stripes Forever." And in one sequence I prophetically savor each letter as, after his first touchdown, we spell out "Sparky." (People around school called Joe Bob "Sparky," though I always preferred the more dignified "Joe Bob.") "Gimme an Ess!" "Ess!" "Gimme a P!" "P!" And so on. "Whaddaya got?" "SPARKY!"

We watched the clock on the scoreboard and counted down the last thirty seconds in a roar. Joe Bob had scored three touchdowns and had led the Pirates to a crashing victory over the Lynxes. He was carried from the field on the shoulders of fans who spilled from the stands. The entire town attended all the high school athletic matches. Meets with neighboring towns brought out all the latent intertown hostilities. It was as though each town were a warring city-state, and the high school teams were the town heavies.

A victory dance was held in the school gym, which was decorated with maroon and gray streamers and fierce pirates on poster paper. I stood in my short shorts and go-go boots with a couple of the cheerleaders and watched my classmates milling around. Occasionally, I'd flash a smile at a familiar face, a smile too enthusiastic for credibility, and would offer the ritual Hullsport High greeting: "Say hey!"

I was distracted by the presence a few feet away of Joe Bob Sparks himself, changed into a neat plaid sports shirt and slacks, his light brown crew cut still damp from the shower. People kept clapping him on the back and saying, "Great game, Sparky!" Joe Bob would smile his moronic smile and look at the floor with a modest shrug.

Then, as though in response to my yearnings from the sidelines, he sauntered up to me, fans falling away from him on every side like from Christ on Palm Sunday, and introduced himself. Or rather, he presented himself, since he correctly assumed that everyone already knew who *he* was.

"Say hey!" he said with his dopey smile, which smile I tried to overlook the whole time I dated him. It was a smile in excess of any possible stimulus. In fact, now that I think about it, Joe Bob's smile was usually unrelated to external stimuli and generally appeared at the most unlikely or inappropriate times. This smile (I dwell on it so obsessively because, like Mona Lisa's, it embodied his very essence) contorted his entire face. Most people smile from their noses downward. But not Joe Bob. His smile narrowed his eyes to slits, raised his cheekbones to temple level, wrinkled his forehead, and lifted his crew cut. And in spite of the exaggerated width of the smile, his lips never parted, probably because of the omnipresent wad of Juicy Fruit gum, which he minced daintily with his front teeth. In short, Joe Bob's smile was demented. But I managed to overlook this fact almost until the day I left him because I wasn't remotely interested in the state of his mind.

It was his remarkable body that occupied virtually all my thoughts. I loved the way he had no visible neck, his head being permanently stove into his shoulders from leading with it in blocking and tackling. I worshiped his chipped front teeth and mangled upper lip from the time he'd dropped the barbell on his face while trying to press 275 pounds. I adored the Kirk Douglas cleft that made his chin look like an upside-down heart, which cleft was actually a crater from an opponent's cleat. I admired the way his left eye had only half an eyebrow from once when he had hit the linesman's stake after being tackled. Joe Bob was evidently indestructible—a quality of incalculable appeal for someone like me, who was braced for disaster around every corner. But most of all, I loved that sunken valley down the middle of his spine, with the rugged ranges of muscle upon muscle rising up on either side. I loved to hold them, one hand on each ridge, as we danced.

Joe Bob didn't talk much. He preferred to be known by his actions. But when he did talk, his voice was soft and babyish; he would grin and open his mouth much wider than necessary and make flapping sounds. In retrospect, I realize that he had a speech defect, but at the time at Hullsport High a soft baby talk in imitation of

Big Sparky was all the rage. His favorite expression, and hence the favorite expression of the entire school, was "Do whut?" He said "Do whut?" punctuated by his demented grin every time he didn't understand what someone had said to him, which was often. It was an all-purpose question, the equivalent of "I beg your pardon?"

For example, after saying "Say hey!" to me at the victory dance, he next asked, "Why haven't ah seed you around before?" As though it were his personal prerogative to approve each student at Hullsport High.

"I'm a sophomore," I explained faintly, dazzled to be the sole focus of his attention. The music was so loud that it drowned me out.

Joe Bob grinned and tilted his head down and said, "Do whut?"

"A sophomore!" I yelled. "I'm a sophomore!"

He nodded, still grinning. "Wanna dance?"

And so we performed those mating rituals called the boogaloo and the chicken scratch. We circled each other slowly with carefully calculated flailings of arms and legs, with coyly disguised thrusts of hips and profferings of breasts. Joe Bob's movements lagged behind by about half a beat due to the five-pound canvas-covered wrist and ankle weights he was wearing, shackle-like, to build up his arms and legs. As though they needed any more building.

Occasionally, unable to tolerate the mounting tension, one of us would whirl off and, back to the other, writhe in narcissistic isolation, eventually spinning back around, restored, to face the other and resume our invocation of the muse of adolescent lust.

And then the reward: a slow song. "Why does my heart go on beating?/ Why do these eyes of mine cry?/ Don't they know it's the end of the world?/ It ended when you said good-by." The heartbreak of the song merely increased Joe Bob's and my delight at having found each other in a world in which, so Skeeter Davis assured us, the only certainty was loss. Joe Bob wrapped his muscled arms around me as though enfolding a football for a line drive, his wrist weights clanking together behind my back. I shyly put my arms around his waist and first discovered those two delightful ranges of rippling muscle down his back.

We didn't really dance. In fact, we scarcely moved, swaying in time to the adenoidal wailings with only enough friction between us to give him an erection, which prodded my lower abdomen. Not knowing then what an erection was, I assumed that this strange protuberance was the result of yet another football injury, a hernia or something. I politely pretended not to notice, as I'd pretended not to notice his moronic smile, though I did wonder at the reason for his chagrined glances down at me.

I must confess at this point that, in spite of having been flag swinger for Hullsport High and girl friend of Joe Bob Sparks and Persimmon Plains Burly Tobacco Festival Queen, I hadn't always been beautiful and gifted. There was a time, when I was thirteen, when I wanted nothing but to be a defensive left tackle for the Oakland Raiders. That was before I learned the bitter lesson that women led their lives through men. In short, that was before I became a flag swinger on the sidelines of Joe Bob's triumphs. I must have suspected what was cooking, deep in the test kitchens of my unconscious, because my football playing had the desperation of the doomed to it. My tackles were performed with the fervor of a soldier making love on the eve of a lost battle. My blocks were positioned with the loving precision lavished on daily routines by terminal cancer patients. Something in me knew that I would never be an Oakland Raider, that I would never even be a Hullsport Pirate, that I would have to pull myself up by my training bra straps into some strange new arena of combat at some unspecified point in the near future.

That point turned out to be the messy morning my first menstrual period began. My family may have been into death in a big way, but they definitely weren't into sex. So unprepared was I for this deluge that I assumed I had dislodged some vital organ during football practice the previous afternoon and was hemorrhaging to death. Blushing and stammering, averting my eyes to Great-great-aunt Hattie's epitaph on the wall, Mother assured me that what was happening was indeed horrible—but quite normal. That bleeding like a stuck pig every month was the price exacted for being allowed to scrub some man's toilet bowl every week.

"That's life," she concluded. She concluded many of her conversations with the phrase, like a fundamentalist preacher's "Praise the Lord." When she said it, though, the implication was not that one should accept the various indignities of corporeal existence with grace, but rather that one should shift one's focus to the dignities of the dead.

"No more football," she added offhandedly. "You're a young woman now." I knew at that moment what Beethoven must have felt when informed that his ears would never hear music again.

No more football? She might just as well have told Arthur Murray never to dance again. How was I to exist without the sweet smack of my shoulder pads against some halfback's hips, without the delicious feel of my cleats piercing the turf? I went upstairs, and as I exchanged my shoulder pads for a sanitary pad and elastic belt, I knew that menstruation might just as well have been a gastrointestinal hemorrhage in terms of its repercussions on my life.

But before long, I learned that the same body that could butt a blocking machine down a football field could be used in ways more subtle but just as effective. For example, it could be made to twist and twirl and prance. Its hips could swing and slither with the same skill required to elude enclosing tacklers. Its budding breasts, heretofore regarded as a humiliating defect that distorted the number on my jersey, could be played up to advantage with a Never-Tell padded bra. In short, I was transformed from a left tackle into a flag swinger, into the new girl friend of Joe Bob Sparks. *I* got to be the one to bear his abuse for giving him blue balls, and eventually *I* got to be the one to give him hand jobs at the Family Drive-In.

(from Kinflicks, *1977)*

Mosquitoes and Menses

Pennyroyal is a pungent herb that can bring on menses or repel insects. At a spirituality conference in the Midwest, the participants (who were feminist witches) decided to try it as an insect repellent. Thousands of mosquitoes had laid prior claim to the outdoor conference site. Now, when witches gather they do not run down to the local drugstore for bug dope. So they mixed a bland oil with oil of pennyroyal, sniffed the results, and passed it around. Each one anointed herself, thinking no doubt of frustrated mosquitoes and not of menses.

The pennyroyal repellent worked—far better than anticipated. There were no mosquito bites. But also, on the next day every woman had her period! (The pennyroyal had been absorbed through the skin into the bloodstream.) And thus occurred the Mass Menstruation of the Midwest.

"She would like to have just one pup!"

New Discoveries Hailed as Birth Control Breakthroughs

JANE FIELD

PUDENDA, KANSAS, Oct. 10—An entirely new method of birth control has been discovered by Dr. Lura Merkin of the Merkin Clinic. A tiny folded umbrella is inserted in the penis and opens automatically when it has reached the apex of the shaft. The underside of the umbrella contains jelly (hence, the name "umbrelly") which causes the sperm to undergo a chemical change rendering it incapable of fertilizing the egg. Dr. Merkin said that the "umbrelly" can be inserted in the penis without an anesthetic, and with very little discomfort to the male. Thus, it can be done in a matter of minutes, in any soundproof doctor's office.

Experiments on a thousand goats (whose sexual apparatus is said to be closest to man's) proved the sperm umbrelly to be 100% effective in preventing pregnancy and eminently satisfactory to the female goat since it does not interfere with her rutting pleasure.

Dr. Merkin declared the "umbrelly" to be statistically safe for man. "Out of every hundred goats, only two died of intra-penis infection; only twenty experienced painful swelling in the unerected member; sixteen developed cancer of the testicles; and thirteen were too depressed to have an erection."

Dr. Merkin pointed out that early cancer detection is a feature of the Merkin Clinic. Removal of one or both testicles is now considered a simple operation and has very little effect on a goat's sexual prowess. Only one out of a thousand goats had to have a radical penisectomy—that is, removal of the penis as well as the testicles. "But it is too rare to be statistically important," Dr. Merkin said. Other distinguished members of the Women's College of Physicians and Surgeons agreed that the results far outweigh the risk to individual men.

(from Majority Report, *October, 1972)*

Superpower Sought on the Contraceptive Front

CAROL TROY

First, we just kissed. A state of true contraception. Then we almost went all the way, a hazy mode of contraception, at best, especially with the boys that promised "just the tip, just the tip." Then came that miserable state of affairs known as *coitus interruptus,* which was a dumb thing to do.

Then we made love and used nothing, because if we were in love, God would watch over us. God often took the liberty of sending us on dark drives to Philadelphia doctors' offices and lightening our pockets of $500.

Rubbers came after love. First, just rubbers were enough. Then they were supposed to be thin and sensitive, like a young English poet. Some of the more sophisticated girls, hearing the Fugs in Tompkins Square Park in New York City, sent their boyfriends out for Saran wrap. Their older sisters told them Scott towels made just as much sense.

Then suddenly everyone had a diaphragm. They came in different sizes, 65, 75, 85, but we soon learned not to compare sizes. I bought a zippered bag large enough to conceal the bulge of the ugly plastic compact until a fashionable friend of mine sniffed at it and showed me the Provençal cotton case she had found in a Village store. She could take it anywhere, she told me. The very afternoon I bought my $18 hand-batiked case from Bali, the news came on all three networks that the world had gone on a Pill standard.

First, Pills were all pretty much the same, white and round. Then they blossomed into an entire range of colors, like confetti, set in rectangular, square, circular dispensers, clicking us from day to day, regulating our rhythms. Boy, this was it. No more worries. Free love.

But then one day I went into the ladies' room at the office, clicked my pill container, and the woman at the next sink asked me why, if I was planning on killing myself, did I have to do it in a public facility? Pills were out.

Coils were in. Soon many women were observed on tables equipped with stirrups. A coil was the only way we could keep up with our Pilly playing around and avoid ferocious arguments about a steady diet of Ortho-Novum being worse than taking up with Richard Speck. Sure, the coil hurt that first day, but not much more than getting punched in the stomach. Anyway, going off the Pill was said to make one jolly and slim. True. But our beds, despite our happy, thin, new selves, were disconcertingly empty. We realized that making love, like taking the Pill, was another fad that seemed to have slipped into disfavor, along with wrinkled work shirts and acid rock. Finally, a man of the world took me aside one

- PHARMACY -

"It's the next best thing to a male birth-control pill. By the time you're done struggling with the safety cap, you're too tired for sex."

night on my king-size bed and told me that, in his experience, making love with a woman wearing a coil felt about as pleasant as nuzzling an emery board. The coil was out.

I got refitted for a diaphragm by a twenty-year-old Spanish-speaking paramedic at the Women's Clinic. And now I know I have finally done the right thing at the right time. Just a few months ago *Cosmopolitan* and *Ms.* said the diaphragm was back. Then *Vogue* followed with *their* diaphragm article.

But it's not easy keeping up with all this. Just the other week, I forgot to bring my diaphragm to my vacation house (I'd long ago given the $18 batik case to the Planned Parenthood Thrift Shop), and my lover called to say he'd be out for the night. I biked down to the local drugstore on my new Italian ten-speed and asked the pharmacist to give me a diaphragm. "Diaphragm?" he said, sneering. "We don't *stock* them anymore. Don't you know everyone's on the Pill? I can put one on order—three, four days." (He obviously had not read *Cosmo, Ms.,* and *Vogue.*) I biked home, racking my brain for a blast from the past. The Pill? No, not enough time for that one, either. A coil? Getting into a doctor's office usually takes seven weeks and three days.

My lover arrived late that night. I tell him I've forgotten my diaphragm. The drugstore is closed. We get into his Honda Civic and drive down to the

local gas station, remembering that rubbers were once sold in just such places for an ancient mating ritual called backseat love. A grown woman, I wait in the car blushing. He returns with a fifty-cent red, white and blue Bicentennial prophylactic packet clearly marked FOR NOVELTY USE ONLY. But it's '76 and novelty is passé.

We're back to basics. So, listen, God. We're in love, remember that. Watch over us, okay?

Jumbo, Colossal and Supercolossal

Barbara Seaman, at hearings before the Select Committee on Population (March 7–9, 1978), testified: "We also think—and I'm sorry, gentlemen, if this disturbs any of your egos—that condoms should be marketed in three sizes, because the failures tend to occur at the extreme ends of the scale. In men who are petite, they fall off, and in men who are extremely well-endowed, they burst. Women buy brassieres in A, B and C cups and pantyhose in different sizes, and I think if it would help condom efficacy, we should package them in different sizes and maybe label them like olives: jumbo, colossal, and supercolossal, so that men don't have to go in and ask for the small."

To the Editor

(In response to an anti-choice article by Hugo Carl Koch in Playboy Magazine)

There is only one way to get through to Hugo Carl Koch, and I'm working on it. Just as soon as I've developed my powers of witchcraft, I will turn him into a middle-class mother of three preschoolers. And on his/her very worst day, when the washing machine has conked out, she's had a fight with her husband, she's received an overdraft notice from the bank, the three year old has flushed his fire truck down the toilet (which is now spilling over into the hall), after tossing her glasses into the garbage disposal, the two year old has smeared his feces all over the living room wall and the baby has been crying and vomiting down her back all day--then, I will give her a missed period.

Shirley L. Radl
Palo Alto, California

The Natural Masochism of Women
(EXCERPTS)

HADLEY V. BAXENDALE, M.D., Ph.D. *

In the last several years, as women have become more and more militant and sophisticated, obstetricians have begun to report a disturbing phenomenon. Increasingly, in the delivery rooms of our nation's great hospitals, disappointment is being expressed. Women in childbirth are asking, over and over: "You mean this is *it?*"

Masochists by nature, women spend their days in a relentless quest for miserable experiences. Beckoned into motherhood by Biblical promises of travail and "sorrow" (Genesis 3:16), they feel bitterly short-changed by the actual experience. With birth only moments away, women suddenly realize that they have suffered greater agonies in their everyday lives.

"Housework is much more degrading than this," a woman in labor told me angrily. "If I'd only realized that the nasty tasks I perform every day are the *ultimate* in misery, I wouldn't have wasted my time getting pregnant. I can't wait to go home." Or, as a Ph.D. file clerk with twins put it, "Being denied a job because you're a woman is much more frightening and humiliating than lying in a labor room alone for ten hours."

In short, the pain and ill-treatment women may experience in childbirth does not begin to compare with what many suffer at home, in love, and on the job. This truth is carefully concealed from women until it is too late. For if motherhood were not sold in terms of martyrdom and ultimate self-sacrifice, if anyone were to admit that there is actually pleasure and joy in rearing children, then women might refuse to become mothers. The human race would die out. "It wasn't nearly painful enough to suit me," one traumatized new mother told me. "I'm not going through it again."

(from Are Children Neglecting Their Mothers? *1974)*

*Pseudonym for Joyce Wood. See footnote p. 24.

Revolutionary Contraceptive

ROBERTA GREGORY

Because of a minor medical emergency, a super-cool dyke finds herself seeking the services of a male gynecologist.

"I need to ask a few questions," he says. "What is your method of birth control?"

"My present method is Norma."

"I haven't heard of that—is it an oral contraceptive?"

"Well, sometimes."

(from Dynamite Damsels, *1976)*

"Mom, I've got a date tonight. Can I borrow your car and the Pill?"

The Perfect Job for a Pregnant Woman

After the Supreme Court ruling that women have no legal right to disability pay for pregnancy, Representative Patricia Schroeder (Democrat from Colorado) addressed the National Press Club in Washington, D.C.

"One of the best jobs in the world for a pregnant woman," said Schroeder, "would be a position on the Supreme Court. The work is sedentary, and the clothing is loose-fitting."

A Few Words About Breasts

NORA EPHRON

I have to begin with a few words about androgyny. In grammar school, in the fifth and sixth grades, we were all tyrannized by a rigid set of rules that supposedly determined whether we were boys or girls. The episode in *Huckleberry Finn* where Huck is disguised as a girl and gives himself away by the way he threads a needle and catches a ball—that kind of thing. We learned that the way you sat, crossed your legs, held a cigarette, and looked at your nails—the way you did these things instinctively was absolute proof of your sex. Now obviously most children did not take this literally, but I did. I thought that just one slip, just one incorrect cross of my legs or flick of an imaginary cigarette ash would turn me from whatever I was into the other thing; that would be all it took, really. Even though I was outwardly a girl and had many of the trappings generally associated with girldom—a girl's name, for example, and dresses, my own telephone, an autograph book—I spent the early years of my adolescence absolutely certain that I might at any point gum it up. I did not feel at all like a girl. I was boyish. I was athletic, ambitious, outspoken, competitive, noisy, rambunctious. I had scabs on my knees and my socks slid into my loafers and I could throw a football. I wanted desperately not to be that way, not to be a mixture of both things, but instead just one, a girl, a definite indisputable girl. As soft and as pink as a nursery. And nothing would do that for me, I felt, but breasts.

I was about six months younger than everyone else in my class, and so for about six months after it began, for six months after my friends had begun to develop (that was the word we used, develop), I was not particularly worried. I would sit in the bathtub and look down at my breasts and know that any day now, any second now, they would start growing like everyone else's. They didn't. "I want to buy a bra," I said to my mother one night. "What for?" she said. My mother was really hateful about bras, and by the time my third sister had gotten to the point where she was ready to want one, my mother had worked the whole business into a comedy routine. "Why not use a Band-Aid instead?" she would say. It was a source of great pride to my mother that she had never even had to wear a brassiere until she had her fourth child, and then only because her gynecologist made her. It was incomprehensible to me that anyone could ever be proud of something like that. It was the 1950s, for God's sake. Jane Russell. Cashmere sweaters. Couldn't my mother see that? *"I am too old to wear an undershirt."* Screaming. Weeping. Shouting. "Then don't wear an undershirt," said my mother. "But I want to buy a bra." "What for?"

I suppose that for most girls, breasts, brassieres, that entire thing, has more trauma, more to do with the coming of adolescence, with becoming a woman, than anything else. Certainly more than getting your period, although that, too, was traumatic, symbolic. But you could see breasts; they were there; they were visible. Whereas a girl could claim to have her period for months before she actually got it and nobody would ever know the difference. Which is exactly what I did. All you had to do was make a great fuss over having enough nickels for the Kotex machine and walk around clutching your stomach and moaning for three to five days a month about The Curse and you could convince anybody. There is a school of thought somewhere in the women's lib/women's mag/gynecology establishment that claims that menstrual cramps are purely psychological, and I lean toward it. Not that I didn't have them finally. Agonizing cramps, heating-pad cramps, go-down-to-the-school-nurse-and-lie-on-the-cot cramps. But, unlike any pain I had ever suffered, I adored the pain of cramps, welcomed it, wallowed in it, bragged about it. "I can't go. I have cramps." "I can't do that. I have cramps." And most of all, gigglingly, blushingly: "I can't swim. I have cramps." Nobody ever used the hard-core word. Menstruation. God, what an awful word. Never that. "I have cramps."

The morning I first got my period, I went into my mother's bedroom to tell her. And my mother, my utterly-hateful-about-bras mother, burst into tears. It was really a lovely moment, and I remember it so clearly not just because it was one of the two times I ever saw my mother cry on my account (the other was when I was caught being a six-year-old kleptomaniac), but also because the incident did not mean to me what it

meant to her. Her little girl, her firstborn, had finally become a woman. That was what she was crying about. My reaction to the event, however, was that I might well be a woman in some scientific, textbook sense (and could at least stop faking every month and stop wasting all those nickels). But in another sense—in a visible sense—I was as androgynous and as liable to tip over into boyhood as ever.

I started with a 28 AA bra. I don't think they made them any smaller in those days, although I gather that now you can buy bras for five-year-olds that don't have any cups whatsoever in them; trainer bras they are called. My first brassiere came from Robinson's Department Store in Beverly Hills. I went there alone, shaking, positive they would look me over and smile and tell me to come back next year. An actual fitter took me into the dressing room and stood over me while I took off my blouse and tried the first one on. The little puffs stood out on my chest. "Lean over," said the fitter. (To this day, I am not sure what fitters in bra departments do except to tell you to lean over.) I leaned over, with the fleeting hope that my breasts would miraculously fall out of my body and into the puffs. Nothing.

"Don't worry about it," said my friend Libby some months later, when things had not improved. "You'll get them after you're married."

"What are you talking about?" I said.

"When you get married," Libby explained, "your husband will touch your breasts and rub them and kiss them and they'll grow."

That was the killer. Necking I could deal with. Intercourse I could deal with. But it had never crossed my mind that a man was going to touch my breasts, that breasts had something to do with all that, petting, my God, they never mentioned petting in my little sex manual about the fertilization of the ovum. I became dizzy. For I knew instantly—as naïve as I had been only a moment before—that only part of what she was saying was true: the touching, rubbing, kissing part, not the growing part. And I knew that no one would ever want to marry me. I had no breasts. I would never have breasts.

My best friend in school was Diana Raskob. She lived a block from me in a house full of wonders. English muffins, for instance. The Raskobs were the first people in Beverly Hills to have English muffins for breakfast. They also had an apricot tree in the back, and a badminton court, and a subscription to *Seventeen* magazine, and hundreds of games, like Sorry and Parcheesi and Treasure Hunt and Anagrams. Diana and I spent three or four afternoons a week in their den reading and playing and eating. Diana's mother's kitchen was full of the most colossal assortment of junk food I have ever been exposed to. My house was full of apples and peaches and milk and homemade chocolate-chip cookies—which were nice, and good for you, but-not-right-before-dinner-or-you'll-spoil-your-appetite. Diana's house had nothing in it that was good for you, and what's more, you could stuff it in right up until dinner and nobody cared. Bar-B-Q potato chips (they were the first in them, too), giant bottles of ginger ale, fresh popcorn with melted butter, hot fudge sauce on Baskin-Robbins jamoca ice cream, powdered-sugar doughnuts from Van de Kamp's. Diana and I had been best friends since we were seven; we were about equally popular in school (which is to say, not particularly), we had about the same success with boys (extremely intermittent), and we looked much the same. Dark. Tall. Gangly.

It is September, just before school begins. I am eleven years old, about to enter the seventh grade, and Diana and I have not seen each other all summer. I have been to camp and she has been somewhere like Banff with her parents. We are meeting, as we often do, on the street midway between our two houses, and we will walk back to Diana's and eat junk and talk about what has happened to each of us that summer. I am walking down Walden Drive in my jeans and my father's shirt hanging out and my old red loafers with the socks falling into them and coming toward me is . . . I take a deep breath . . . a young woman. Diana. Her hair is curled and she has a waist and hips and a bust and she is wearing a straight skirt, an article of clothing I have been repeatedly told I will be unable to wear until I have the hips to hold it up. My jaw drops, and suddenly I am crying, crying hysterically, can't catch my breath sobbing. My best friend has betrayed me.

"No, being flat-chested doesn't make me feel inferior. Does being flat-chested make _you_ feel inferior?"

She has gone ahead without me and done it. She has shaped up.

Here are some things I did to help:
Bought a Mark Eden Bust Developer.
Slept on my back for four years.
Splashed cold water on them every night because some French actress said in *Life* magazine that that was what *she* did for her perfect bustline.

Ultimately, I resigned myself to a bad toss and began to wear padded bras. I think about them now, think about all those years in high school I went around in them, my three padded bras, every single one of them with different-sized breasts. Each time I changed bras I changed sizes: one week nice perky but not too obtrusive breasts, the next medium-sized slightly pointy ones, the next week knockers, true knockers; all the time, whatever size I was, carrying around this rubberized appendage on my chest that occasionally crashed into a wall and was poked inward and had to be poked outward—I think about all that and wonder how anyone kept a straight face through it. My parents, who normally had no restraints about needling me— why did they say nothing as they watched my chest go up and down? My friends, who would periodically inspect my breasts for signs of growth and reassure me— why didn't they at least counsel consistency?

And the bathing suits. I die when I think about the bathing suits. That was the era when you could lay an uninhabited bathing suit on the beach and someone would make a pass at it. I would put one on, an absurd swimsuit with its enormous bust built into it, the bones from the suit stabbing me in the rib cage and leaving little red welts on my body, and there I would be, my chest plunging straight downward absolutely vertically from my collarbone to the top of my suit and then suddenly, wham, out came all that padding and material and wiring absolutely horizontally.

Buster Klepper was the first boy who ever touched them. He was my boyfriend my senior year of high school. There is a picture of him in my high-school yearbook that makes him look quite attractive in a Jewish, horn-rimmed-glasses sort of way, but the picture does not show the pimples, which were air-brushed out, or the dumbness. Well, that isn't really fair. He wasn't dumb. He just wasn't terribly bright. His mother refused to accept it, refused to accept the relentlessly average report cards, refused to deal with her son's inevitable destiny in some junior college or other. "He was tested," she would say to me, apropos of nothing, "and it came out a hundred and forty-five. That's near-genius." Had the word "underachiever" been coined,

she probably would have lobbed that one at me, too. Anyway, Buster was really very sweet—which is, I know, damning with faint praise, but there it is. I was the editor of the front page of the high-school newspaper and he was editor of the back page; we had to work together, side by side, in the print shop, and that was how it started. On our first date, we went to see *April Love,* starring Pat Boone. Then we started going together. Buster had a green coupe, a 1950 Ford with an engine he had hand-chromed until it shone, dazzled, reflected the image of anyone who looked into it, anyone usually being Buster polishing it or the gas-station attendants he constantly asked to check the oil in order for them to be overwhelmed by the sparkle on the valves. The car also had a boot stretched over the back seat for reasons I never understood; hanging from the rearview mirror, as was the custom, was a pair of angora dice. A previous girl friend named Solange, who was famous throughout Beverly Hills High School for having no pigment in her right eyebrow, had knitted them for him. Buster and I would ride around town, the two of us seated to the left of the steering wheel. I would shift gears. It was nice.

There was necking. Terrific necking. First in the car, overlooking Los Angeles from what is now the Trousdale Estates. Then on the bed of his parents' cabana at Ocean House. Incredibly wonderful, frustrating necking, I loved it, really, but no further than necking, please don't, please, because there I was absolutely terrified of the general implications of going-a-step-further with a near-dummy and also terrified of his finding out there was next to nothing there (which he knew, of course; he wasn't that dumb).

I broke up with him at one point. I think we were apart for about two weeks. At the end of that time, I drove down to see a friend at a boarding school in Palos Verdes Estates and a disc jockey played "April Love" on the radio four times during the trip. I took it as a sign. I drove straight back to Griffith Park to a golf tournament Buster was playing in (he was the sixth-seeded teen-age golf player in southern California) and presented myself back to him on the green of the 18th hole. It was all very dramatic. That night we went to a drive-in and I let him get his hand under my protuberances and onto my breasts. He really didn't seem to mind at all.

"Do you want to marry my son?" the woman asked me.
"Yes," I said.
I was nineteen years old, a virgin, going with this woman's son, this big strange woman who was married to a Lutheran minister in New Hampshire and pre-

tended she was gentile and had this son, by her first husband, this total fool of a son who ran the hero-sandwich concession at Harvard Business School and whom for one moment one December in New Hampshire I said—as much out of politeness as anything else —that I wanted to marry.

"Fine," she said. "Now, here's what you do. Always make sure you're on top of him so you won't seem so small. My bust is very large, you see, so I always lie on my back to make it look smaller, but you'll have to be on top most of the time."

I nodded. "Thank you," I said.

"I have a book for you to read," she went on. "Take it with you when you leave. Keep it." She went to the bookshelf, found it, and gave it to me. It was a book on frigidity.

"Thank you," I said.

That is a true story. Everything in this article is a true story, but I feel I have to point out that that story in particular is true. It happened on December 30, 1960. I think about it often. When it first happened, I naturally assumed that the woman's son, my boyfriend, was responsible. I invented a scenario where he had had a little heart-to-heart with his mother and had confessed that his only objection to me was that my breasts were small; his mother then took it upon herself to help out. Now I think I was wrong about the incident. The mother was acting on her own, I think: that was her way of being cruel and competitive under the guise of being helpful and maternal. You have small breasts, she was saying; therefore you will never make him as happy as I have. Or you have small breasts; therefore you will doubtless have sexual problems. Or you have small breasts; therefore you are less woman than I am. She was, as it happens, only the first of what seems to me to be a never-ending string of women who have made competitive remarks to me about breast size. "I would love to wear a dress like that," my friend Emily says to me, "but my bust is too big." Like that. Why do women say these things to me? Do I attract these remarks the way other women attract married men or alcoholics or homosexuals? This summer, for example. I am at a party in East Hampton and I am introduced to a woman from Washington. She is a minor celebrity, very pretty and Southern and blond and outspoken, and I am flattered because she has read something I have written. We are talking animatedly, we have been talking no more than five minutes, when a man comes up to join us. "Look at the two of us," the woman says to the man, indicating me and her. "The two of us together couldn't fill an A cup." Why does she say that? It isn't even true, dammit, so why? Is she even more ad-

dled than I am on this subject? Does she honestly believe there is something wrong with her size breasts, which, it seems to me, now that I look hard at them, are just right? Do I unconsciously bring out competitiveness in women? In that form? What did I do to deserve it?

As for men.

There were men who minded and let me know that they minded. There were men who did not mind. In any case, *I* always minded.

And even now, now that I have been countlessly reassured that my figure is a good one, now that I am grown-up enough to understand that most of my feelings have very little to do with the reality of my shape, I am nonetheless obsessed by breasts. I cannot help it. I grew up in the terrible fifties—with rigid stereotypical sex roles, the insistence that men be men and dress like men and women be women and dress like women, the intolerance of androgyny—and I cannot shake it, cannot shake my feelings of inadequacy. Well, that time is gone, right? All those exaggerated examples of breast worship are gone, right? Those women were freaks, right? I know all that. And yet here I am, stuck with the psychological remains of it all, stuck with my own peculiar version of breast worship. You probably think I am crazy to go on like this: here I have set out to write a confession that is meant to hit you with the shock of recognition, and instead you are sitting there thinking I am thoroughly warped. Well, what can I tell you? If I had had them, I would have been a completely different person. I honestly believe that.

After I went into therapy, a process that made it possible for me to tell total strangers at cocktail parties that breasts were the hang-up of my life, I was often told that I was insane to have been bothered by my condition. I was also frequently told, by close friends, that I was extremely boring on the subject. And my girl friends, the ones with nice big breasts, would go on endlessly about how their lives had been far more miserable than mine. Their bra straps were snapped in class. They couldn't sleep on their stomachs. They were stared at whenever the word "mountain" cropped up in geography. And *Evangeline,* good God what they went through every time someone had to stand up and recite the Prologue to Longfellow's *Evangeline:* ". . . stand like druids of eld . . ./ With beards that rest on their bosoms." It was much worse for them, they tell me. They had a terrible time of it, they assure me. I don't know how lucky I was, they say.

I have thought about their remarks, tried to put myself in their place, considered their point of view. I think they are full of shit.

May, 1972

by Kristin Lems   Mammary Glands

1. Do you want to pay to take a peek
   At what drives men insane?
   Well they're in anthro books galore and
   I'm just sure that you'll adore 'em
   Even cave women have the same two simple

   chorus

2. The men decided that a certain shape
   Stands out more than the rest;
   They made such a major issue
   Women stuff their bras with tissue,
   Throw shoulders back to look their best!
   show off their

   chorus

3. Well if you're more than 36 you are desirable
   So don't be shy, they'll pay
   For once you finally sold out
   You may get a center foldout--
   They dig your dugs, you're on the way!
   with famous

   chorus

4. It's a multi-million dollar enterprise
   But no one knows what it's about
   If we think before we'd try it
   We'd bust the myth, we would defy it
   And we might stand up and shout:
   they're ONLY

   chorus

   coda: a natural mammalian sight!

What Do You Say When a Man Tells You, You Have the Softest Skin

MARY MACKEY

do you say
it's progesterone, progesterone makes it soft?
when he says
you have big brown eyes
do you say
of course
I'm nearsighted?

my body grew in rings
like a tree trunk
at the center I'm always 10
at the center I'm always wearing
pink plastic glasses
braces
wire wrapped around my head
a mouth full of rubber bands
I have buck teeth I can spit through
corrective shoes
pimples
no legs
no butt

no breasts
one day my mother buys me falsies
overnight I grow from 28AA to 36D
I look down and notice I can't see my feet
I feel like a fork-lift
I imagine they are realies

in gym the girls steal my bra
and throw it in the pool
my rubber breasts float away

like humpbacked whales
I dive for them
over and over
I dive for my breasts
and come up flat

what do you say when a man tells you
you're beautiful?
do you tell him,
"I'm still fishing
I'm still fishing for my body."

Keeping Abreast
of What Men Want

MARY KAY BLAKELY

A few weeks ago a Fort Wayne teacher was criticized by her principal because she allegedly showed up at school without the appropriate female cover-up—a bra. Now there is criticism of Miss America contestants for showing up on the runway with too much camouflage—padded bras. We seem to be at a nexus on the issue of breasts and how they should be worn.

The controversy rages wherever the issue of breasts pops up: *National Geographic* magazine was banned from a Southern school because it contained full-color pictures of African women wearing their breasts untrammeled. A local TV station manager read a letter from a viewer asking the status of a certain newswoman's breasts during her broadcast—were they in a bra or not? Two otherwise dignified reporters went bananas on the air one day over a story about Miss Colt and her Forty-Fives.

Fort Wayne officials agonized over just what constituted an obscene violation of breast-wearing. And Morris Greenblatt of Chicago, whose business it is to fit Miss Americas into their swimsuits, stated that, in all his forty years, he has seen only six sets of perfect ones. (Each woman in the 98-percent category has been believing all this time that she was the only imperfect one.

A great myth has been unmasked here, if anyone is interested.)

Breast-owners are confused. Intent on discovering the correct way to wear them, women have turned to the experts. Madison Avenue has braless mannequins to demonstrate how to wear clothing over bare breasts. Fashion magazines advise that if you can hold a pencil under your breast, you need to wear a bra at all times. But if a teacher shows up at school braless, she is likely to lose her job. She either pleases the experts on Madison Avenue or she pleases her boss.

Breast-owners have looked to the judiciary for an answer. There, Archie Simonson, the recalled Madison, Wisconsin, judge, implied that it really didn't make any difference what individual breast-owners did with their own breasts: If any woman is doing something questionable with hers, all women are responsible. Simonson did not indicate that all men were responsible when one man used his anatomy irresponsibly. We don't know why communal guilt applies only to women.

Mixed messages about breasts have the owners asking themselves, to paraphrase Freud, "What do men want?"

One man, Karlis Adamsons, Chief of Obstetrics and Gynecology at Women and Infants Hospital in Rhode

bülbül © 73

SEX OBJECTS

Island, thinks that "ideally it would be best to remove breasts surgically," but that it would be a "hard concept to sell in this society." Indeed. Breast-owners— even those in Morris Greenblatt's imperfect 98 percent, would, I hope, strenuously object.

Certainly, the men who pay to see breasts would be forced to find a new hobby. Hugh Hefner would be out of business. Employers might be in trouble because they wouldn't be able to tell who gets the lower paycheck. It just isn't a practical solution.

Perhaps some Breast Legislation is in order. It wouldn't be simple—there would be a Cleavage Lobby, no doubt. And probably a Crossed Heart Faction. Later, we may have to accept some ridicule from effete political historians who might uncover our Breast Legislation. When we hear students snickering over the stupidity of nineteenth-century legislation regulating the wearing of women's ankles, necks, and upper arms, it does give one pause about Breast Legislation.

Perhaps there is no simple solution. What we are left with, I'm afraid, is that breast-owners are going to have to decide for themselves how they are going to wear their breasts.

The non-owners on Madison Avenue and school principals and TV station managers and even, maybe, Morris Greenblatt will be upset. Some women will, undoubtedly, continue to wear them inappropriately, because men will pay them to. Other women will pretend that they don't even have breasts, because other men will pay them more if they don't.

Some women may give up their bras altogether and paste them into *National Geographic* magazines for Southern schoolchildren. A few women, who own large ones and who no longer use purses, may decide to carry their pencils there. Another group, Miss Americas included, may continue to put foam pads and wires into their swimming suits to avoid the scorn reserved for the 98 percent.

Whatever happens, it is only fair to suspend judgment on the breast-owners. The message about how to wear them, gentlemen, is unclear.

CHAPTER TWO

Untying
the Mother Knot

STRATTON

". . . in this show, the daddy goes to work every day and the mommy stays home with the kids. That's why it's called a situation comedy."

On Sleeping with Your Kids

ALTA

there were so many who grew up with their mom in their bed. she would sleep with the kid instead of the husband. when i was a child, that seemed particularly perverse to me. & i kicked mom out when she tried it. but so many of the women in her generation refused to sleep with their mates (4 years ago my brother called "hey! i just heard this great idea! joan baez (i think) said women should refuse to screw soldiers & then the war would end!" i answered, "i got an even better idea. women should refuse to screw men & then sexism would end!" i did quit, too, but after that mess with the *babe* i could hardly believe in revolutionary feminism so now i take whatever i can get.)

another part of what i saw as our mothers' perversion was that so many slept with their sons. but last week i think i may have figured out why. i was mad at angel & didnt want to go to bed since he was in it, so when i got tired i went to the other bed, which had the kids in it. i lay down next to them & watched them sleep for a while, which always overwhelms me with love since nobody is doing a no no & they look so lovely, & i thot "too bad i cant sleep in here. if it wouldnt give the girls a trauma, i would. then angel could eat his heart out all night heh heh." then i listened to what i'd said & all the women who slept with their kids flashed thru my head. all but one have been with the same husband all their lives. divorce is out of the question, evidently. how to effectively divorce yr husband but still get room & board? sleep with the kids. he cant accuse you of adultery cause yr not doing it. he cant raise hell, it would traumatize the children. he cant accuse you of desertion cause youve only walked across the hall. & he cant fuck you in front of the kid. all he can do is lie there lonesome while you rest comfortably, undisturbed by his horny lil cock.

(*from* Momma, a Start on All the Untold Stories, 1974)

The Day's Work

If I gave up the dog, it would be one less thing to feed, one less dish to wash, one less scrap of attention to hand out.

BARBARA HOLLAND

After the first year, husbands don't put the seat back down any more. However, there are compensating advantages. I forget their names.

He slinks out into the dawn before the rest of us get up. He kisses me as I lie there fighting off the day with a pillow over my head. In fact, that's almost the only time he kisses me now. Maybe I look safer asleep. Maybe horizontal with my eyes shut I still look like a woman. As soon as I stand up I run around like a battery toy; push a button and it smacks the kids and burns the stew, screaming. So, for all the good it does us at that hour, he kisses me and is gone.

The alarm rings and I turn it off. Children come stand in the doorway, cautiously, and then go away whispering, "She's still asleep." I hunch under the covers, ripe with potential rages, a great rumpled sulky Gulliver. How did I get here? Can I leave? Am I held prisoner by little whispering people?

I am.

What brown eyes all my children have. It seems to give their stare a kind of weight. My sisters and brothers are all blue-eyed, and my mother; I have left a family where people's looks were light and clear and translucent, and found one where they stare at me opaquely, like chocolate drops; my life has dropped into an ominous key. They have been sent to get me.

They eat enormous breakfasts. When I was a child I suffered tortures over breakfast. A single bite of toast stuck in my chest like a fist all morning. Liquids gagged me. I whined, vomited, anything. I swore that my own children would never have to eat breakfast, not even juice.

They bang their spoons and call for oatmeal, eggs, toast, bacon, milk, juice, sausages, fruit. I run back and forth. "More juice!" they cry. "Can I have another egg?" "Is there any grapefruit?" "She's eating my toast!" "Well, you weren't eating it." "I was too!"

"Hush up, all of you!"

"But she took a big bite of my toast. I want another piece." "All right, give him another piece, I'll finish this one." "Mommy, I said I want oatmeal!"

"Shut up or I'll slaughter you! I mean it! I will!"

I talk like that a lot, and it worries me. I don't think parents should say things like that to their children.

The kitchen looks as if armies had fought in it. Oh, quick, quick, the hairbrush, where is it? I zipper jackets and give each child an extra hug because of shouting at them. Am I forgiven? I can't see through their brown eyes. Do they hate me? Do I frighten them? Worse, are they hardened, callous, and insensitive?

Guilt, the Mommy's monster.

They leave. Silence in the ears chiming like an overdose of quinine.

I make the bed, our bed, battleground and flower garden and sanctuary; it is my one concession. I always make the bed. Having made it I feel efficient. Good housekeeper. Wife. Mother. Advertising person. Shower. Dress. The dog whines: is it never my turn? Brother,

I feel so much stronger and braver at work, where I know what I'm doing.

can you spare a pat? A kind word? A harsh word, even? No. Look at the clock, the clock, the clock. Oh, boy, am I late.

The kitchen. Could I simply drop a bomb on it? Or have I already? Some of the mess is stale mess, yesterday's mess, looking much worse, more reproachful, than fresh mess. I could clean up. I'm so late already I might as well.

I do the frying pans and put the dog into the backyard. Backyard. Hah. Back toilet, dog latrine. This weekend I have to do something about it, scoop it all up. Unless I do something about the kids' rooms. No, forget it, Allie and Chris are coming for dinner; I have to do something about the living room. In my mind I always call it vaguely "doing something," which doesn't commit me to actually cleaning. Something; anything. Pick up the newspapers and take the children's sneakers off the mantelpiece.

I walk to work. Six and a half blocks of peace and noise. I stare around politely at the buildings. We know each other, they wish me a happy day. Whatever the weather I love this walk. Transition between home and office, lovely filthy streets full of blowing trash about which I need do nothing. Just passing through, just browsing, thank you. Passive, I browse like a cow on traffic and shop windows and plastic geraniums in window boxes.

I like my office too, especially when I first come in and see my desk waiting for me like a patient child. I feel so much stronger and braver at work, where I know what I'm doing. Competent, like a man, an executive, glancing at papers and crumpling them up and tossing them toward the wastebasket. Real difference between men and women, home and work: here, if I miss the wastebasket, someone else must ultimately pick the papers up. Exhilarating.

"Dorney was looking all over for you." Ellen's secretary. "He was burned up. I said you'd gone to the little girls' room, but Art told him you weren't in yet."

"What did he want?" Why can't they simply get used to my being late? Why can't I get used to it? Then we could all stop fussing about it. There's no way, *there is absolutely no way* I can be here by nine; can't we all resign ourselves to it?

I leave early too. I always have. They can't get used to that either, and keep looking for me, in desk drawers and file cabinets after I'm gone.

Begin on a stack of radio commercials for a menswear shop.

Peace is an office.

Whistle without attempting a tune. Commercials proceed automatically from brain to fingers, without thought. Time was, back when I was a skittery slip of a lass in a ponytail, I used to have to time the things. Whisper them to myself, e-nunc-i-a-ting clearly, watching the second hand on the clock. Now the shapes of a sixty-second commercial, thirty-second, ten-second spot have sunk down into the dream-deep centers of the folded brain and seeped from there to the finger muscles. I am never wrong. Curious things we pick up on the Road of Life. Not like a rolling stone but like rolling Play-Doh; junk embedded forever, the names of the Presidents, and how to make paper airplanes, and what to do for croup.

"Mr. Dorney wants you in his office."

Wants me in his office, does he? Wants my fair white body? Bent backward over the duplicating machine, "Ooh, Mr. Dorney, please, somebody might come in!" Down, down, to the soft white carpet with that irritating abstract pattern like inkblots. "Mr. Dorney, you're tearing my dress!"

Nope. Not me, not Mr. Dorney. He's younger than I am and a whole lot dumber and we worked together once years before, at Mayburn & Atherton, when he was just a pockmarked kid and I was already somebody. Now he's a very large deal and I'm still just somebody. Story of a life. A lady's life.

He'll be bald as a stone, though, before he's forty-five.

"I want to talk to you about your hours. Now, I realize you have other responsibilities. . . ."

Oh, why not bend me over the duplicating machine instead? Who taught you to talk that mush-mouth executive stuff? Me, that's who.

". . . certain responsibilities to us here."

Jerk.

"Like to give you some additional, uh, status around here. To tell you the truth, we have a new account coming in, not absolutely firmed up yet, keep this in strictest confidence. . . requires more, uh, punctuality on your part. . . ."

"I'm afraid I can't promise anything, Jack, I mean, Mr. Dorney. I move as fast as I can. And I don't think you have any complaints about my work once I get here."

I hitch my bottom rudely onto the corner of his desk, which he hates, he wants people to stand at attention, that's why the chairs are kept way over in the corners unless a client comes in. I slunch comfortably. Lovely feeling. This is the other side of the lady's life. I

Nobody has chairs for visitors; if you chat, he thinks you're not working.

am irreplaceable at the nasty salary he pays me. Go on, fire me. Give my job to two guys and an English major. Besides that, I'm married. My husband works. Look at me cross-eyed, you jumped-up junior bookkeeper, and I can be gone before lunchtime. Just let me get my boots from the bottom drawer. Write your own commercials.

In a way you have to feel sorry for the married men around here. Take Art. He never misses a chance to double-cross me, but I can't blame him. He doesn't make much more than I do and his wife doesn't have a job, and they have two kids and a bouncing-baby mortgage, and when Mr. Dorney talks to *him* about being late he sweats pints of pure blood.

"Really would like you to take this on, sure you could handle it. However, it would mean. . . ."

"No way." I smile cheerfully at him. He really hates me sometimes. I go out of my way to be pally with him and it drives him berserkers.

"Quite a substantial increase in salary."

Isn't it lovely to be grown up finally, after all these years? To know what you want, to say no? Oh, there used to be a time: ecstasy, praise, raise, he thinks I can do it! I can, I can, just try me, chief! And oh, horrors, despair, I was late again this morning, what can I do? Maybe if I got up at five instead of six. Or four, or three, or never went to bed at all . . . .

"Nope. I don't need more responsibility any more than I need more money."

". . . make a decision just now, want you to think it over; by the way the series for the Bluebell account. . . ."

"You'll have it by two. Scout's honor." And I leave without being dismissed, switching my tail at him.

Back to work. Occasionally people come in to chat, and sit on *my* desk, not because I hide the chairs but because Jack Dorney doesn't like chatting. Nobody has chairs for visitors; if you chat, he thinks you're not working. We aren't, of course, but I told him to try to think of it as interdepartmental communications and he'd like it better. I believe he tries, but it's not easy, we giggle a lot.

The phone. Curses, oh, curses, the school nurse. Childish impulse to disguise my voice, pretend to be dead or somewhere else.

"Spots?" I say. All innocent, as if spots were as normal to my child as to any leopard's, any giraffe's kid.

"You don't seem to have returned the medical certificate, and we were wondering if he had had his measles vaccination. . . ."

I join her in wondering. Somebody did, but I think it was Number 2; I remember cornering her under the examining table, and she bit the doctor. Unless that was tetanus.

We're old buddies, me and the nurse. I send my kids to school on a *stretcher* if necessary. She calls me a lot.

So I have to consult, this time with Ellen, avoiding Dorney. Ellen is the underboss.

"But you *can't*, not today. Mr. Warren is coming in at two-thirty about the Bluebell series. You'll just have to get someone else to take care of the child."

"Who? You?"

She laughs. "A neighbor or someone. There must be *someone.*"

People always think that. People's ideas of child care are frozen in the rural nineteenth century, when there were all those servants and helpful neighbors and resident aunts and decaying cousins, and dear old nursie up in the attic sewing smocks. It is hard for people to realize that nowadays there is *no one to take care of that child but you.* It's hard for me to realize too.

"You'll have to bring him here, then."

"But he's *sick.*"

"Which one is it? 3-B? Sure, bring him in; I haven't seen the twins in ages." Childless Ellen. "Not since they had flu. They were great fun that time."

They sure were. You should have heard Dorney on the subject, after what they did to the adding machine.

Although in a way the twins do seem to belong to the office. They were born on a Friday (I took the day off) and popped into incubators, and on Monday I came in to work. It was pretty childish, a gag, and they were horrified. I brought cigars, and said it was two boys and my husband was resting comfortably. "But we sent you a *card,*" Dorney's secretary kept wailing. "I just mailed it last night. To the *hospital.*"

Ellen says, "I don't see how you manage without a housekeeper. Or a cleaning woman, or anything. I think it's fantastic."

Shrug modestly. Nothing, really. I can walk on my hands, too, and whistle the overture to *Call Me Madam.*

"I don't know what I'm going to do without mine. She quit last week, simply walked out and never even said she was leaving; and the house is a perfect shambles. Howard and I have been eating out every night. I've been interviewing like mad, but it isn't easy to find someone these days."

Poor lamb.

"Did Dorney talk to you about the new account?"

In my mind I always call it vaguely "doing something," which doesn't commit me to actually cleaning.

"I turned it down. I haven't got the time."

"But there would be a raise," she cries, genuinely upset. "You know, with more money, you could hire someone to help around the house. You wouldn't have to work so hard."

I blush dark red at the real concern on the nice lady's face. Sister. Sister, kind sister, you don't understand, that's you but not me. Household help feels to me like three more children and another dog: someone else to bump into and apologize to. Someone with problems to hear. Someone to try to explain to, how I want things done, choking with guilt at having her do them when I could, and then not telling her after all. Someone to remember to praise: "Gee, that's nice, the way you dusted that cabinet. Really looks nice." Someone to notice where the syrup spilled on the kitchen shelf, a new relative with a husband who beats her and no-

Because of their raging hormonal imbalances, wom\en\make better mothers than men.

good kids.

Ellen is different, she enjoys command.

In the taxi, I inspect 3-B.

"Is it measles?" he asks eagerly.

I try to peer at the spots with professional interest. Your really proper mother these days is supposed to be a kind of barefoot doctor with shoes, shaking down thermometers and administering mouth-to-mouth at every turn. I'm not very good at it. Even my Band-Aids fall off, and when I look into somebody's sore throat all I can see is the soft palate and a couple of silver fillings.

"Is it?"

"Looks like mosquito bites to me. How do you feel?"

"Fine."

Oh dear. If he's sick, really sick, with a fever, he will sit quietly in the art department and play with Magic Markers all day. If he isn't. . . .

"If it's measles, how long do I get to stay out of school? Can I come to the office every day?"

I groan. A week? *Two weeks?* And then feel guilty. Did he have his shots? Oh, my poor neglected babies, my motherless lambs. I grab him and lay my cheek against his silky rumpled unwashed hair and he fights free. "Will they let me use the duplicator if I draw some pictures?"

All the women are glad to see him. Something about a kid in the office brightens up the ladies because it scares the men. Help, help, a child, anarchy and unreason, random destruction and tears, the opposite of what men hope for from their offices. What I hope for too, I guess.

He sits on Ellen's lap itching to get his hands on the interoffice phone.

"How are you doing in school, 3-B? My, you've certainly grown since I saw you last. You know how long it's been since you've come in to see me?"

If she catches measles from him, can they fire me for it, do you think?

"Now listen to me, young man." His eyes drift to the water cooler, how can he listen to me? My voice is a roaring sound in his world, like traffic. I drop it to a whisper: *"Ecoutes-moi, mon petit."* He hears; the head turns.

"I have to go to a meeting and I don't know how long it's going to last. You are going to sit here, *right here at my desk,* and draw me some pictures. If you draw a specially nice one, maybe we can put it through the duplicator. But don't touch anything else. Are you

We're old buddies, me and the nurse. I send my kids to school on a stretcher.

listening?"

"Can I get a drink from the water cooler?"

"Just one."

I have a morbid obscure passion for meetings. How *important* we all feel, with all those sharpened pencils and the phones shut off, and the awful twaddle we talk. I talk it too. As long as I don't lose my temper. Dorney keeps watching me, fiddling with his pen. Trouble with having all those children: tendency to haul off and holler at clients as if they'd forgotten to hang up their jackets.

Attention floating away a little. Tune out the client, tune in to the partition and sounds beyond. Art, far away, shouting "Stop ringing my phone!" Oh, dear. Well, I don't see how he can *hurt* the phones, and even if he does the phone company fixes them free. I think.

Dorney loves a meeting too. "According to statistical research obtaining optimum saturation of the area, readership-wise," he says. "Median per capita income as per the demographic charts."

A muffled crash. Out in the streets maybe? No. Better wind this up quick. No, no way, not with Dorney off and running, not when he sinks his teeth into per capitas, and drags out *Standard Rate and Data* and starts reading us percentages. Poor baby, we all like to feel smart. What the hell could that crash have been?

Muffled sound of running feet.

"Maximize the potential," says Dorney.

My eyes glaze over, I fidget uncontrollably. Two thirds of me rushes into the other room to whack my kid.

The client unrolls himself, says, "Well," and "Let's keep our eye on the ball here," and it's *his* turn to be important. Blast, I've been drawing spiderwebs on my note pad again. Guiltily write "Eye on ball."

Over at last.

Water oozing out of my office to greet me, water and the sound of tears. Dorney's secretary mopping, mopping furiously, and lots of curly chunks of broken glass. Ellen comforting 3-B, who is soaked, bloody,

I brought cigars, and said it was two boys and my husband was resting comfortably.

weeping. One of the big spare jars for the water cooler, tipped over to crash and smash. But why? And how? Those things are heavy.

Soppy litter of paper cups half-opened to make boats. Water creeps toward file cabinets, closer, closer; desperate mopping. Those are the temporary files, made of cardboard. Dorney's precious records, how he loves them, paid printing bills from 1962, carbons of letters saying "Enclosed please find proofs of your ad of January 11, 1971."

"He's hurt," says Ellen. She's glad to see me, offers me 3-B in a lump like wet laundry.

"Serves him right." 3-B howls convincingly. Ah, the poor chick, of course he's unruly and wicked, his mother works.

I step on a curl of glass and it wraps around my foot to pierce stocking and flesh. Blood. The world floats in tears. Why do I do it, why do I live like this? I can't do it any longer. I can't, nobody could. *It isn't fair.* I won't, I cannot go on any longer like this. Apologize, apologize, apologize to 3-B for bringing him here, apologize to Dorney for bringing him here. Sorry, the sitter was late. Sorry, darling, dinner isn't ready. Sorry, lambs, you have to wear yesterday's socks. Sorry, Mrs. McHenry, I couldn't come to school for the conference. Sorry, sweetie, I missed the class play. Not tonight, honey, I'm *so* tired. Sorry, Ellen, I have to leave early, I won't be in till noon, I can't make the sales meeting.

I won't do it any longer. I will not live this way.

My typewriter is buzzing angrily; its keys are jammed. I turn off the switch. Move stiffly, limping; say nothing. My phone is off the hook and its red lights twitch like nerves.

3-B's wounds are slight. He can hurt himself worse than that lying flat in bed.

Down in the elevator. 3-B nervous; I don't usually say nothing. "Are you mad? Mom?"

"I think I must be."

But he enjoys the walk home. We stop for coffee and peanut butter and at the drugstore for notebook paper, three-ring. It is trash day, the sidewalk is heaped with treasure, wealth beyond the dreams of avarice dribbles from every can, shining like emeralds. 3-B collects a broken hand mirror, a headless doll, a publicity shot of a television actor in a cowboy hat, most of a string of beads. "Wait, wait! Mom!" 3-B loves his world. For him life's an Egyptian tomb waist-deep for wallowing in curious and precious things.

Our own street. Alley, really. Our own neighbor, Mrs. Cavallo, who waits daily to take the bloom from my homecoming, lurking to spring. She has a petition for me to sign.

"It's a menace to health, that's what it is, and I've called city hall and called them, and the police too, and they absolutely refuse to do anything about it. All those

GIRLS, I'D LIKE TO TALK TO YOU ABOUT GROWING UP TO BE MOMMIES.

GROWING UP TO BE A MOMMY IS ONE OF THE MOST WONDERFUL THINGS A LITTLE GIRL CAN WANT TO DO. **BUT**... THERE ARE OTHER THINGS IN LIFE SHE CAN DO AS WELL...

FOR INSTANCE, SHE CAN WORK HER HEAD OFF AND SHOW ALL THOSE ARROGANT BOYS THAT SHE'S JUST AS **CAPABLE** AND **INTELLIGENT** AND **CREATIVE** AS ANY LITTLE STUD AROUND!

YOU'RE A "LIBBIE", AREN'T YOU, MS. CAUCUS?

YOU BET, HONEY.

dogs doing their business here in our street where decent people live and pay taxes, too, and what for? Just to step in some dog's business? I was watching out the window this morning and that girl came by again, the one I spoke to, with the Great Dane, and let him do his business right smack in front of my house. There it is right there.''

Exhibit A, buzzing with flies.

"Well, they have to go somewhere," I say weakly. "It's because it's a side street. They take them off the main drags, where there's so much traffic."

"I want every single person on this street to sign this, and then just let them try to laugh it off. I want *police action."*

A squadron of our finest, sirens moaning, revolvers drawn, holding a poodle at bay. "One step closer, dog!" I sign, though.

"I should think you'd be angry especially, and you with them kids." There's a threat in her voice. I had just better be angry, or maybe she'll report me too. What kind of a mother am I?

What kind of a mother am I?

"Mrs. Cavallo, I'm too busy to be angry. Excuse me. Come on, kiddo."

There are cereal bowls all over the table and I forgot to put the milk away. The dog sobs with joy to see us. What is there in the freezer that will melt in time for dinner? I put the wash in the dryer and turn it on. Another section of the day begins, and miles to go before I sleep.

In five minutes they'll be home, all of them, a solid block of noise saying, "Mom, listen, I have to have a new gym suit and I have to have it by tomorrow, shut up, *I'm* talking, my teacher *said*—". . . "and I hate school and I'm never going back!" "Can I have a cookie? Can Rob come over and play? Can you walk him over? Can I call him?" "One hundred on the spelling test and I was the only one in the room!" "Look, I made it in Art, you're not *looking!"*

They close in on me, pulling at bits of my flesh and clothing for attention. One of these days I will come apart in their hands, and each child will have a little scrap of me to shout at.

I won't do it any more. I can't live like this.

Dinner. Sometimes little bits of dinner, burned or raw or still in the cracked saucers from the refrigerator, but on time; sometimes, guiltily, a real dinner, seasoned and sauced, made from recipes that mysteriously stretch out longer and later until my husband has a headache and the children quarrel and drowse over

"Common aspirin cures my headaches if I follow the directions on the bottle—Keep Away from Children."

their plates. But always dinner.

The red marks on 3-B's chest fade peacefully.

My husband says, "Why do you insist on reading them a story every night? You're tired, you have all the dishes to do. Can't they watch television instead? You're just making more work for yourself."

"My mother always read to us."

Who'd believe we *owned* so many dishes? If I smashed half of them, would life be easier?

I can't live this way. He's right, I'm making work for myself, I have built myself into a *completely impossible situation.* I won't do it any more. Am I a victim of the Protestant work ethic? Am I trying to sweat off some buried guilt and in the process knocking more and more guilt down on my head? Am I that disgusting new word they keep using, a workaholic? I will stop it.

Stop what?

What is there to give up? I stare wildly around me, and see the dog. He sees me seeing him, from the floor, close to my ankles. If I gave up the dog, it would be one less thing to feed, one less dish to wash, one less scrap of attention to hand out. His ears flatten to his

51

Which of my brown-eyed children shall I stop putting Band-Aids on?

head and he slaps his tail on the floor; this was what he was waiting for, all day, me to look at him. It is enough, he says. Just see me, every two or three days. I'll wait. My throat chokes with sentimental tears. Give up such inexpensive love?

Not the dog. What, then? Which of my brown-eyed children shall I stop putting Band-Aids on? Give them all away to passing strangers, maybe Ellen? Or shall I give up my husband, the other adult around here, whom I greet occasionally as we pass each other in the shouting chaos, signal to, like people passing in a fire or a shipwreck?

The job, then. Stay home, make do, watch from the windows for dogs to poop? No, the job is mine. I clutch it fiercely, it is the thing I do for *me,* the place where I feel grown up and nobody calls me Mom; it is my self-indulgence, my bubble bath. They pay me money and call me a human being, and I spend the money and no man may question it, or say it was extravagant, buying those ice skates for Number One. It was extravagant, *my* extravagance. I won't give up my job, I need not to be Mom sometimes.

I could hire someone to clean the house. But the house is my flesh and blood, my second skin. Would I hire someone to wash my neck? I want to be alone here with my bellowing horde, my private mess. Remember that nurse I had for the 3's, she scared the liver out of everyone, including me; Number 2 sleeps with a light on since then.

There is nothing to give up. *All* these things are self-indulgences. Even the brown-eyed kids, even the dirty dishes. I do them for me, because I want to.

I stop stirring tomorrow's orange juice and look at the wall with my mouth open. For a moment it seems so terribly simple. Tomorrow it will seem complicated again, but for this instant I seem to see it so clearly. I can have everything, do everything I want. All I have to do is work, and it seems for one blinding moment such a small price to pay for such a lovely life; seems such a simple thing to do.

bülbül © 73

The Pee-In

SHEILA BALLANTYNE

Here we are about to enter the health food store; I have just thrown my cigarette in the gutter. They go crazy if you smoke in there. Ruth Ann still has a school note pinned to her sweater; she looks like a refugee. My little trip made me late for Damon, left them all standing around sucking their thumbs, wetting their pants, wondering if their mother had died. It touched off the usual round of questions on the subject.

"We thought you died."

"No, no; I didn't die." (See, here I am!) *I did my best, but it seems they wanted a dog this time.*

"I don't want to die," said Scott, after a pause I had hoped meant the end of the discussion. Now it's my turn again.

"Why?"

"Because I haven't died before and I don't know how it feels." Well, I understand your reluctance, Scott; we all worry about the unknown, but you can't let that hold you back. There's a first time for everything, know what I mean? *Where is this bitterness coming from? What kind of mother are you?*

They're throwing sesame cookies in the basket while I pick through these apples, trying to find some without worms. I am buying the groceries. I will put them in the house. But I do not plan to be home tonight when he gets back from work. ("I can run from you, I can"—Little Gingerbread Man, p. 5.) Just take the kids to McDonald's and sit around with all the other just-divorced or about-to-be-divorced, getting the feel of what separation is going to be like. All parents succumb eventually to McDonald's, but it is a special haven for the divorced and separated. It eases the transition you have to make from comfortable family meals—however chaotic they may have been—to sitting home alone with the children, trying to ignore the empty place and staring into your coffee, holding back tears.

Someone is standing next to me, humming a song I heard on the radio recently. There are some people whose presence next to you in stores you scarcely notice, and some whose presence you can't shake. I take a peek out of the corner of my eye, taking care not to move my head. I have very good peripheral vision, all paranoids do. She's standing there watching me pick out apples, tapping her foot as she hums. About fifty, but small as a bird, and dressed as an Indian. Her grey, uncombed hair hangs down straight beneath her head-band. Why does it bother me that she's forgotten the feather?

> There is nothing worse than trying to discuss your child's problems with an expert while the child is pulling on your skirt (loaded with snot, sweat, tears), or otherwise clearly indicating that you do not give him the attention he needs.

She swings away from the apples now and does a dance, a little shuffle, lousy rhythm, with the moccasins, toward the refrigerator where the yoghurt and fertile eggs are kept. And there she breaks into full song, just as Ruth Ann comes over and stares rudely, with her mouth hanging open.

"Mommy, is that a real Indian?" she asks, loudly.

"No, honey; it's a lunatic impersonating an Indian," I whisper.

"'I'm the train they call the City of New Orleans . . .'" she sings, reaching for the yoghurt. "Good night, America, how are ya? Say, don't ya know me? I'm your native son . . . .'"

"Mom, I have to pee." The clerk is popping a Vitamin E and washing it down with a half pint of kefir. Looking at his complexion makes you think of something that just crawled out from under a rock.

"Excuse me. Could my son use your bathroom?"

"Sorry, we're not allowed to do that. There's a gas station down the block." I think he's the owner's son. There's a quality about both of them that reminds you of overcooked cabbage.

There's a sweet clerk who works here part-time, on Tuesdays and Thursdays. He'd let Damon use the bathroom, because he's in love with me. His name is Tomaso Ruggiero. He's dark and young and the veins in his arms are alive with nervous fish. He's Italian, and he doesn't give a shit about things like who uses the bathroom. His eyes are so beautiful they make you want to rip off his green apron and jump in some river with him at midday, if you could find one. When it's not crowded, we lean on the counter and shoot the breeze. He knows I'm a "housewife," but it doesn't bother him at all. He says things like: "See that counter full of pills? They should throw them in the street! It's *food, pure* food that makes you feel alive! You know, it makes me glad that *you* don't waste your money on pills. Your body is strong and slim—has grace!—because you get your energy from the *source!*" And I think: Well, actually, it's more from pushing the vacuum around and from nervous tension than from those things; and actually, I buy an awful lot of the poisoned crap down at Pay and Save, I just come here for the produce. But of course I don't say these things to Tomaso. If he's got an image of me as slim and graceful, it's all right with me; I've often said illusions are crucial to the maintenance of life functions, and I wouldn't want to do anything to jeopardize his. He said to me once, "You know, Norma,"—he rolls it: Norrrma, like an aria—"you shouldn't smoke. It *robs* you of vitality! Our bodies are meant to *breathe,* to *move,* to . . . ." That was it, because some woman was drumming her fingers on the counter. I'll never know if he was about to say "celebrate life," in which case I would have vomited, or

"come together," which would have been O.K.; but either way, there was a look in his eyes that left no doubt as to the sexual implication. He gives off a sexual energy that has to be experienced first-hand to be believed. And I thought it significant from the beginning that he has the same first name as Albinoni; I can't explain why I've never mentioned that to him. *Because more than likely he'd throw his head back and laugh. He'd fail to see the significance.* ("Albi-*noni?* Who's-a he? I know him? You gotta *nother* Tomaso? *Non è possibile!* I die! I go drink Coca-Cola!")

Damon is jumping up and down, clutching himself. As for me, I've had it with stores that want your business but won't let your children use their bathrooms.

* * NOTICE * *
MOTHERS
Tired of your children wetting their pants
in stores that refuse the use of their
bathrooms?
Come: Saturday, June 16. *Bring Your Children!*
PEE-IN
Jenson's Natural Foods   21449 Coronado Avenue
(from Norma Jean the Termite Queen, *1975)*

Fairyland Nursery School

SHEILA BALLANTYNE

Norma Jean pulls up in front of Fairyland Nursery School. She is ten minutes late. All the other mothers have arrived on time, fetched their children, and gone. She opens the door, anticipating the unspoken message in the eyes of the teacher: you're late. Again. Damon is anxious. Damon wonders if you have died. Damon is wondering if he has been abandoned by his mother.

"I'm sorry I'm late, Miss Rogers. The lines at Pay and Save were terrible." It's a weak excuse, and she knows it. Why do I have to feel apologetic all the time, about

everything?

"You're late, Mommy," Damon says, from behind the book table. How terrible and alone he looks in the empty room. "Damon, you know Mommy always comes for you . . . eventually."

"Mrs. Harris," *Oh, here it comes, just as I always knew it would . . . eventually,* "I've been meaning to speak to you about Damon. Now that you're here, and the others have gone, this might be a good time, if it suits you."

"Well, I do have another hour and a half before the car pool delivers Scott from his nursery school, Miss

Rogers." And another hour and a half before Ruth Ann comes home from school. *A life measured out in hour and a half portions, five days out of seven, week after week, month, year.* Miss Rogers is looking at her in a peculiar way. Not unusual for Miss Rogers, but under these circumstances Norma Jean is clearly on the defensive, in the wrong, the weaker of the two, and recognizes these facts.

"Yes, this is a good time," she says.

They sit down; Damon is given permission to play with the fire truck. All to himself, no rivals, he accepts the bribe, to Norma Jean's great relief. There is nothing worse than trying to discuss your child's problems with an expert while the child is pulling on your skirt (loaded with snot, sweat, tears), or otherwise clearly indicating that you do not give him the attention he needs.

"Well, Miss Rogers. What is it about Damon?"

"I trust you are aware, Mrs. Harris, of his imaginary playmate?"

"Yes," she begins, cautiously. "All kids have them, don't they? Yes, I'm aware he sometimes has imaginary conversations." *Don't we all?*

"Yes, Mrs. Harris. But are you aware of his... this figure's *name?*"

"Oh. Yeah. Well, I guess you couldn't be referring to anyone else but Fokey. Sure, Fokey I think he calls him."

"I mean his full name, Mrs. Harris. This is rather difficult for me, but I can't believe you haven't heard Damon refer to him by his full name, and that is what concerns me."

The jig is up. She means Fokey Fuckerhead. "Yes, Miss Rogers, I'm aware he has an imaginary companion named Fokey Fuckerhead." Miss Rogers is getting red. It's hard to tell whether it is menopause or Fokey. Norma Jean knows. It's Fokey. Good old Fokey Fuckerhead; if the real kid doesn't get you, the fake one will ...eventually.

(from Norma Jean the Termite Queen, *1975)*

Have you got a doll that plays like Billie Jean King, thinks like Margaret Mead, and talks out like Barbara Jordan?

Molly's Beginnings

RITA MAE BROWN

I didn't know anything about my own beginnings until I was seven years old, living in Coffee Hollow, a rural dot outside of York, Pennsylvania. A dirt road connected tarpapered houses filled with smear-faced kids and the air was always thick with the smell of coffee beans freshly ground in the small shop that gave the place its name. One of those smear-faced kids was Brockhurst Detwiler, Broccoli for short. It was through him that I learned I was a bastard. Broccoli didn't know I was a bastard but he and I struck a bargain that cost me my ignorance.

One crisp September day Broccoli and I were on our way home from Violet Hill Elementary School.

"Hey, Molly, I gotta take a leak, wanna see me?"

"Sure, Broc."

He stepped behind the bushes and pulled down his zipper with a flourish.

"Broccoli, what's all that skin hanging around your dick?"

"My mom says I haven't had it cut up yet."

"Whaddaya mean, cut up?"

"She says that some people get this operation and the skin comes off and it has somethin' to do with Jesus."

"Well, I'm glad no one's gonna cut up on me."

"That's what you think. My Aunt Louise got her tit cut off."

"I ain't got tits."

"You will. You'll get big floppy ones just like my mom. They hang down below her waist and wobble when she walks."

"Not me, I ain't gonna look like that."

"Oh yes you are. All girls look like that."

"You shut up or I'll knock your lips down your throat, Broccoli Detwiler."

"I'll shut up if you don't tell anyone I showed you my thing."

"What's there to tell? All you got is a wad of pink wrinkles hangin' around it. It's ugly."

"It is not ugly."

"Ha. It looks awful. You think it's not ugly because it's yours. No one else has a dick like that. My cousin Leroy, Ted, no one. I bet you got the only one in the world. We oughta make some money off it."

"Money? How we gonna make money off my dick?"

"He followed me home. Do I have to keep him?"

"After school we can take the kids back here and show you off, and we charge a nickel apiece."

"No. I ain't showing people my thing if they're gonna laugh at it."

"Look, Broc, money is money. What do you care if they laugh? You'll have money then you can laugh at them. And we split it fifty-fifty."

The next day during recess I spread the news. Broccoli was keeping his mouth shut. I was afraid he'd chicken out but he came through. After school about eleven of us hurried out to the woods between school and the coffee shop and there Broc revealed himself. He was a big hit. Most of the girls had never even seen a regular dick and Broccoli's was so disgusting they shrieked with pleasure. Broc looked a little green around the edges, but he bravely kept it hanging out until everyone had a good look. We were fifty-five cents richer.

Word spread through the other grades, and for about a week after that, Broccoli and I had a thriving business. I bought red licorice and handed it out to all my friends. Money was power. The more red licorice you had, the more friends you had. Leroy, my cousin, tried to horn in on the business by showing himself off,

but he flopped because he didn't have skin on him. To make him feel better, I gave him fifteen cents out of every day's earnings.

Nancy Cahill came every day after school to look at Broccoli, billed as the "strangest dick in the world." Once she waited until everyone else had left. Nancy was all freckles and rosary beads. She giggled every time she saw Broccoli and on that day she asked if she could touch him. Broccoli stupidly said yes. Nancy grabbed him and gave a squeal.

"Okay, okay, Nancy, that's enough. You might wear him out and we have other customers to satisfy." That took the wind out of her and she went home. "Look, Broccoli, what's the big idea of letting Nancy touch you for free? That ought to be worth at least a dime. We oughta let kids do it for a dime and Nancy can play for free when everyone goes home if you want her to."

"Deal."

This new twist drew half the school into the woods. Everything was fine until Earl Stambach ratted on us to Miss Martin, the teacher. Miss Martin contacted Carrie and Broccoli's mother and it was all over.

(from Rubyfruit Jungle, *1973)*

The Christmas Pageant

RITA MAE BROWN

The Christmas pageant was an enormous production. All the mothers came, and it was so important that they even took off work. Cheryl's father was sitting right in the front row in the seat of honor. Carrie and Florence showed up to marvel at me being Virgin Mary and at Leroy in robes. Leroy and I were so excited we could barely stand it, and we got to wear makeup, rouge and red lipstick. Getting painted was so much fun that Leroy confessed he liked it too, although

boys aren't supposed to, of course. I told him not to worry about it, because he had a beard and if you had a beard, it must be all right to wear lipstick if you wanted to because everyone will know you're a man. He thought that sounded reasonable and we made a pact to run away as soon as we were old enough and go be famous actors. Then we could wear pretty clothes all the time, never pick potato bugs, and wear lipstick whenever we felt like it. We vowed to be so wonderful in this show that our fame would spread to the people who run theaters.

Cheryl overheard our plans and sneered, "You can do all you please, but everyone is going to look at me because I have the most beautiful blue cloak in the whole show."

"Nobody's gonna know it's you because you're playing Joseph and that'll throw them off. Ha," Leroy gloated.

"That's just why they'll all notice me, because I'll have to be specially skilled to be a good Joseph. Any-

way, who is going to notice Virgin Mary, all she does is sit by the crib and rock Baby Jesus. She doesn't say much. Any dumb person can be Virgin Mary, all you have to do is put a halo over her head. It takes real talent to be Joseph, especially when you're a girl."

The conversation didn't get finished because Miss Potter bustled backstage. "Hush, children, curtain's almost ready to go up. Molly, Cheryl, get in your places."

58

When the curtain was raised there was a rustle of anticipation in the maternal audience. Megaphone Mouth said above all the whispers, "Isn't she dear up there?"

And dear I was. I looked at Baby Jesus with the tenderest looks I could manufacture and all the while my antagonist, Cheryl, had her hand on my shoulder digging me with her fingernails and a staff in her right hand. A record went on the phonograph and "Noël" began to play. The Wise Men came in most solemnly. Leroy carried a big gold box and presented it to me. I said, "Thank you, O King, for you have traveled far." And Cheryl, that rat, says, "And traveled far," as loud as she could. She wasn't supposed to say that. She started saying whatever came in her head that sounded religious. Leroy was choking in his beard and I was rocking the cradle so hard that the Jesus doll fell on the floor. So I decided two can play this game. I leaned over the doll and said in my most gentle voice, "O, dearest babe, I hope you have not hurt yourself. Come let Mother put you back to bed." Well, Leroy was near to dying of perplexity and he started to say something too, but Cheryl cut him off with, "Don't worry, Mary, babies fall out of the cradle all the time." That wasn't enough for greedy-guts, she then goes on about how she was a carpenter in a foreign land and how we had to travel many miles just so I could have my baby. She rattled on and on. All that time she spent in Sunday School was paying off because she had one story after another. I couldn't stand it any longer so I blurted out in the middle of her tale about the tax-collectors, "Joseph, you shut up or you'll wake the baby." Miss Potter was aghast in the wings, and the shepherds didn't know what to do because they were back there waiting to come on. As soon as I told Joseph to shut up, Miss Potter pushed the shepherds on the stage. "We saw a star from afar," Robert Prather warbled, "and we came to worship the newborn Prince." Just then Barry Aldridge, another shepherd, peed right there on the stage he was so scared. Joseph saw her chance and said in an imperious voice, "You can't pee in front of little Lord Jesus, go back to the hills." That made me mad. "He can pee where he wants to, this is a stable, ain't it?" Joseph stretched to her full height, and began to push Barry off the stage with her staff. I jumped off my chair, and wrenched the staff out of her hand. She grabbed it back. "Go sit down, you're supposed to watch out for the baby. What kind of mother are you?"

"I ain't sittin' nowhere until you button your fat lip and do this right."

We struggled and pushed each other, until I caught her off balance and she tripped on her long cloak. As she started to fall, I gave her a shove and she flew off the stage into the audience. Miss Potter zoomed out on the stage, took my hand and said in a calm voice, "Now ladies and gentlemen, let's sing songs appropriate to the season." Miss Martin at the piano struck up "O Come All Ye Faithful."

(from Rubyfruit Jungle, *1973)*

"It's eleven o'clock. Do you know where your children are?"

Needle-and-Thread Envy

SHEILA BALLANTYNE

Breakfast is over, but I'm still here in the kitchen, putting the finishing touches on my contribution to the block-party supper later this afternoon. They just started having the Fourth of July block party here last year; we were on vacation then and missed the first one. So I have mixed feelings, don't know what to expect. After this is done, I'll go back in the garage and work until party time. *You should get a nap in somewhere.* It's strange, but I'm not that tired. In fact, I feel regenerated. *By the way, did you thank Martin for offering to take the children swimming while you work?* No, I did not thank him. If I thanked him every time he did something with the children, emptied the garbage, picked up after himself, it would just strengthen his illusion that he's just doing it all as a *favor* to me; and we all know about favors: they're intermittent, sporadic, and unreliable.

Norma Jean shuts the garage door behind her and switches on the overhead light. No sooner has she removed the cloth and immersed herself halfway to the elbows in clay, than she hears Martin's voice. She can make out her name, but the rest is unintelligible. Better go out there, meet him halfway; can't risk his coming in here and blowing everything so close to the end.

"Norma! Will you come out of there for a minute? There's a problem here." Norma Jean walks quickly to

There is something about the situation that has my name written on it already, even at this stage.

the house, holding her caked arms in front of her as though in casts. Martin is standing in the kitchen with his arms full of towels; Ruth Ann and Scott languish nearby. Damon is not in the group; so I cleverly conclude that the "problem" concerns Damon. Mothers get so they can tell these things, even with their eyes closed.

"What's the problem, Martin?" I ask, trying to affect nonchalance; there is something about the situation that has my name written on it already, even at this stage. It won't be easy erasing my name and writing in his without the use of my hands, but I suddenly think of a man I once saw in a sideshow, who did these amazing charcoal portraits with his toes, and it gives me strength.

"Listen, that kid" *he must mean Damon* "has a HOLE in his bathing trunks!"

"He does?" I ask, in my most carefully modulated conversational tone.

"How could you not see a thing like that? It's right in the seat of his pants."

"I don't know, Martin. I don't worry about those things very much any more. If it's in the back, it will only show when he bends over. Don't worry about it."

"Don't *worry?* Sometimes I don't understand you at all. You can't let that poor kid go swimming EXPOSING HIS ASS!"

"Oh for Christ's sake, he's just a child. What difference does it make? As long as it doesn't bother *him,* no one else is going to get worked up about a thing like that!"

"I won't *have* it. I absolutely won't have it. No son of mine. . ." Damon enters, stage left. He is grinning in the manner of evil spirits and fanatics everywhere. The reason he is grinning is because he has reversed his bathing trunks, so that the hole under discussion is now in the front. What a coincidence that it should be located at precisely the latitude and precisely the longitude of his penis. It smiles at us, and waves. Damon begins to dance. I start laughing. So do Scott and Ruth Ann. I figure it's either the theater, night clubs, or the nut house for him.

"This is NOT funny," Martin says. Ruth Ann and Scott stop laughing. Not me. It has just occurred to me that the Pleasant Valley Country Club might have been liberated by Damon Harris, if his father weren't such a stuffed-shirt. On the other hand, a second glance tells

you right away that the father isn't fooling around with this business of the hole in the son's bathing trunks. So siree, he's doing a slow, but hot, burn. So we can no longer afford, funny as it is, to take the matter lightly. We can't afford it because already the lines are being drawn, and the issue over which this war is about to be declared is: WHO WILL SEW THE HOLE? I suppose some would see it as a good sign that the father is burning; he would have no need to burn if he were secure in his conviction that it is the mother, and only the mother, who can, should, or will sew the hole. I concede that it's a good sign; but I also know that this is my last stand. Needles and thread is about as far as you can push it. Of course, I intend to give it all I've got; I always do.

"Are you going to sew that poor kid's trunks, or does he have to stay home?" A weak opening, using a pawn; it surprises me. Still, it's well known that things can and do throw the best of players, and there are big stakes riding on this one. Now the question is, do I counter with a weak move myself, ("Gee, my hands are covered with clay!") or do I reduce him to jelly at the very start, with a show of my power? I decide to restate the rules, which could be considered a move in some circles.

"There *are* other alternatives, Martin." He reads me right away; he doesn't even bother to say, "Well, then, where is his other suit?" There's no doubt, this is going to be a short game.

"Oh *no;* unh unh," he says, or something like that, backing off. This is where you have to move fast; it's

I figured, blowing *two* things definitely does *not* add up to a recovery, any way you cut it.

the whole game, right here. Lose them when they first back off and you lose it all.

So I scream. I haven't done that for a while, it startles him. "*You* know how to sew, just as well as I do!" I yell. "When you couldn't even afford the Chinese laundry, you sewed yourself! Before I met you you sewed your own buttons! You were a Boy Scout!" I pause briefly for breath and, when I resume, I am in full control. I speak with a cold-hearted authority from which there is no appeal; it frightens even me. "The needle and thread are in the left-hand drawer of the sewing machine. You can choose your own style: machine or hand. He is *your* son, as well as mine. I'm busy working right now, and you're not; my hands are dirty, yours are clean; you *do* know how to sew; and since it is *you* who is concerned about the hole, it is *you* who will repair the hole. And since it is I who is *unconcerned* about the hole, it is I who will do nothing about the hole." He is silent. And sullen. He is also stunned that I have pulled it off. I am not convinced that I have pulled it off, so just for good measure, as a form of insurance, I say lightly, as I make my way back to the garage, "Nowhere is it written that I must do all the sewing. And at no time did I verbally promise to do all the sewing. Therefore, I shall *not* do all the sewing. And Damon's suit is the very *first* of all the sewing that I shall not do!"

I would be lying if I said I went right back to kneading and shaping. I went back to the garage and had a cigarette and thought to myself: You blew it. Blew it. You went through months of hell, it was in the palm of your hand this morning, and you blew it over a little one-inch hole. Reason tries her best (*I think your argument is basically sound. . . although my Jack never would have stood for it*) but I am unconsolable. Twenty minutes pass this way; and although it crossed my mind in the first five seconds to run upstairs and mend the damned hole, I stayed right there on the stool. I figured, blowing *two* things definitely does *not* add up to a recovery, any way you cut it. Having become familiar with biding my time, I decided to master it now, if it killed me.

There is a strange scraping at the door. Suddenly it swings open and the garage is flooded with light. And standing there smiling are the father and the son—the little one, with the hole. I am thrown off-guard by their sudden appearance, and all that light hitting me in the eyes, but it doesn't take me long to recover. I read the situation in a flash. They're smiling because they are proud of themselves—the father in particular. And they're here because they want my approval. Well, in spite of what you might have thought, I'm not as cold-hearted as I sometimes appear. I'm not all business—not me. I can spot a victory when I see one; and the truly exceptional thing about this victory is that it is

shared equally, three ways. There are no losers.

So I slide off the stool and hug them both. Martin, (can I do this without using war analogies or baseball emotions?) *Keep those man-and-nature images out of it, too.* Well, that just leaves sex. There are any number of things he *likes.* But as for that flush of ecstasy, I don't know; even a triumph at work doesn't fit. There aren't many triumphs at work, and none that produce the flush of ecstasy, that I know of. Sex isn't accurate either, because eventually you roll over and relax. He doesn't relax; he isn't going to come down for a long time. This one is going to go on and on, this sudden mastery and unexpected pride.

"Well. I can't believe it. You *did* it!" I say.

"I did it," he says, feigning modesty.

"See? Dad sewed my hole!" Damon demonstrates, bending over. Sure enough. *Good Lord! Look at that! He did a better job than you do!* Anyone can do a better job than. . . You know, you're right. He really did. You can't even see the stitches. How did he do it? *You sound envious!* Well, there was just a trace, but you couldn't see it without a microscope. I have repressed it already. Just the tiniest trace, very manageable. Needle-and-thread envy. How times change.

(*from* Norma Jean the Termite Queen, *1975*)

Raising Sons

ELIZABETH CADY STANTON

[One son] made a life-preserver of corks, and tested its virtues on a brother about eighteen months old. Accompanied by a troop of expectant boys, the baby was drawn in his carriage to the banks of the Seneca,

"I'll tell you what I don't like about a working mother. . . I don't like the lunches my dad packs."

stripped, the string of corks tied under his arms, and set afloat in the river, the philosopher and his satellites in a row-boat, watching the experiment. The child, accustomed to a morning bath in a large tub, splashed about joyfully, keeping his head above water. He was as blue as indigo, and as cold as a frog, when rescued by his anxious mother.

The next day, the same victimized infant was seen by a passing friend, seated on the chimney, on the highest peak of the house. Without alarming anyone, the friend hurried up to the house-top and rescued the child from the arms of the philosopher.

Another time, three elder brothers entered into a conspiracy and locked up the fourth in the smoke-house. Fortunately, he sounded the alarm loud and clear, and was set free in safety, whereupon the three were imprisoned in a garret with two barred windows. They summarily kicked out the bars, and sliding down on the lightning-rod betook themselves to the barn for liberty. The youngest boy, then only five years old, skinned his hands in the descent. This is a fair sample of the quiet happiness I enjoyed in the first years of motherhood. It was 'mid such exhilarating scenes that Miss Anthony and I wrote addresses for temperance, anti-slavery, educational and woman's rights conventions.

(from History of Woman Suffrage, Vol. II, *1882)*

The Pros and Cons of Motherhood

MARY KAY BLAKELY

Recent statistics on childbirth indicate that young women today aren't choosing motherhood with the same reckless abandon as those of us who married in the '50s and '60s. Today's young women seem to be studying the issue, arrogantly assuming that they have some choice in the matter.

I, for one, applaud their insistence on informed consent, despite pressure from would-be grandparents and friends. As a kind of public service to the women who are thinking it over, I have set down a partial list of facts I have learned concerning motherhood.

On the minus side

1. Most people who insist that they "love babies" have very limited data on which to base this hasty conclusion. Experienced mothers have been known to suggest that a baby's adorable exterior is merely protective coloration for its survival. For example, Elizabeth Adamson once commented that a baby is really "an alimentary canal with a loud voice at one end, and no responsibility at the other." While infants can certainly be winning, even Gerber babies would be hard pressed to keep it up twenty-four hours a day. A close friend of mine said Gerber could curb the birthrate if it would only picture in its advertising what the baby looks like after years of care and feeding—a gangly teen-ager with pimples and a guitar hanging from the shoulder.

2. Do not be deceived into thinking that you are "good with children" because you may have had a successful interaction or two. I, too, thought I was great with children because, like Lucas Tanner, I spent only an hour a week with them.

It is quite risky to assume that your "maternal instincts" will take over once the children arrive. I have not been able to develop any great affinity for diaper pails or sour laundry since becoming a mother. Neither have I been more genetically inclined than my husband to get up at three in the morning to deliver a drink of water to the adjoining bedroom. I once detected in myself a total absence of the flowing maternal juices, when our three-year-old son ran out of paper and applied his magic marker to his younger brother.

3. All efforts to appear rational during early motherhood are futile. Perhaps because of the interrupted sleep, young mothers frequently exhibit aphasia, forgetfulness, lack of continuity: That is the only explanation I can offer for finding my aluminum foil in the refrigerator. Once I caught a reflection of myself in a store window while talking to a friend, rocking and burping the grocery bags I was holding.

Young mothers sometimes operate on automatic pilot (so they can sleepwalk), but there are disadvantages. Another friend, in a state of semiconsciousness, leaned over the shoulders of three luncheon companions and cut all their tomato slices into bite-sized pieces before one of them reminded her that he was old enough to handle a knife by himself.

4. The job description of mother is clearly in need of revision. As it stands, the shifts are twenty-four hours, for a period of approximately 1,825 consecutive days. The benefits are sorely in need of amendment: no vacations, no sick leave, no lunch hours, no breaks. Moreover, it is the only unpaid position I know of that can result in arrest if you fail to show up for work.

5. The cultural attitude toward mothers is hopelessly lopsided. While we are all familiar with the generous platitude, "There is no such thing as a bad boy," society is ready to jump on the case of a bad mother without the slightest hesitation.

Some children have perceived this imbalance and have exercised their option to write books about their mothers after they are dead. Also, you will not be admitted to your children's therapy sessions to tell your side of their "unhappy childhood" stories.

On the plus side

1. For women interested in developing a deep humility, motherhood is an excellent training ground. Notice, for example, that none of the ten most powerful people featured in the *Journal-Gazette* was a mother. The confident portraits did not suggest that any of these individuals had recently lost an argument with a three-year-old. Nor did their distinguished appearances offer even the slightest trace of stained prunes on lapels or Playdough handprints on sleeves. When presidential candidate Carter posed in his hotel room election night with his baby granddaughter, he was clearly unprepared when she stuck the pencil she was holding up his nose. Such humbling acts usually accompany motherhood, not the presidency. A mother is never cocky or proud, because she know the school principal may call at any minute to report that her child has just driven a motorcycle through the gymnasium.

2. Mothers are able, after only minimum training, to recite entire immunization records, carpool schedules, and vitamin programs. Within a reasonable time, they can simultaneously fry an egg, sign a permission slip, and find exact change for the bus. This attention to de-

tail and juggling ability prepares mothers for such responsible positions as den mother and Girl Scout leader.

3. Motherhood offers its own unique bonding experiences. The women who gather in the kitchen at cocktail parties and seemingly begin to communicate instantly, talk not about party politics, not about the Super Bowl, but about mothering—the intricate and consuming project of their lives. The clannish circle, frequently the loudest and most raucous group at the party, is closed to non-mothers, because mothers know that "you had to be there" to understand their humor.

4. Mothers have access to a strong underground network—the secretive support system of mother folklore and intelligence. A wise, seasoned mother once told me her toddlers were entertained for hours by a piece of Scotch tape around their fingers.

The network also offers relief for guilt, as other mothers confess that they, too, almost left the baby in the highchair overnight by mistake. Motherhood offers women a universal experience—and we are learning to share and affirm it.

5. Mothers experience intense pleasure over their children's unparalleled comic routines—those multidimensional scenes that Kodak cannot capture. In a world that teaches us to be stoic and accepting and detached, mothers have come to depend on their children's wonderful excess of emotion.

And mostly, mothers may take pride. They are working under conditions that are impossible, with advice from "the experts" that is full of inexplicable contradictions. Each finding her own way through the maze of rules and sanctions and guilt, mothers learn to love and to nurture, to honor their commitment to their children.

We doubt and we wonder and we are well-practiced worriers. But we wouldn't trade the truths we learn, about ourselves, about relationships. We wouldn't trade the goosebumps that rise when the rushes of affection tell us, however tenuously, that if we had to choose again, we would still, incredibly, choose mothering.

CHAPTER THREE

Clicking, Clunking, and Clowning

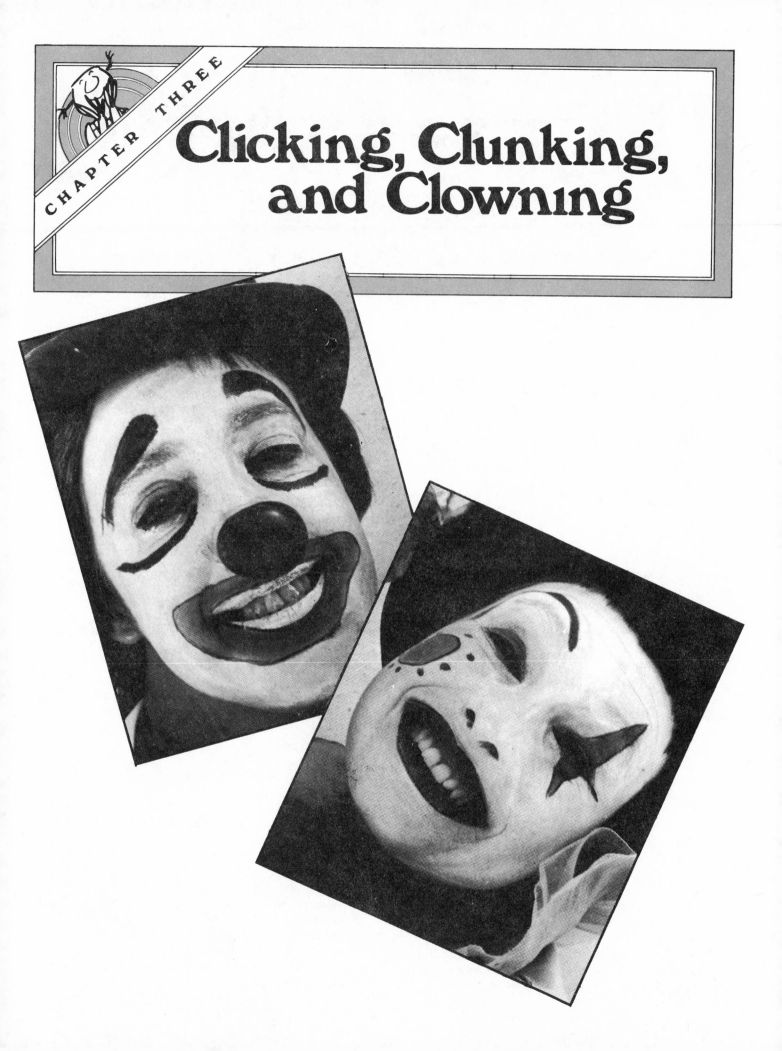

CLICKING

click "klik" *n* **1:** to make a point aptly.
2: to put down someone with style.
3: to teach in a witty manner.

"Age is something that doesn't matter, unless you are a cheese." *Billie Burke*

"Being a mother is a noble status, right? Right. So why does it change when you put 'unwed' or 'welfare' in front of it?" *Florynce Kennedy*

"There are more whooping cranes in the United States of America than there are women in Congress." *Joanna Russ*

"This whole society is like slow dancing—the men get to lead and the women get stepped on."
Lily Tomlin

"You know you're really poor when you have to put water on the corn flakes." *Elaine Boosler*

When Rosalynn Carter walked behind her husband in Jimbo, Saudi Arabia (in deference to local customs), a feminist quipped, "Can you imagine Andy Young walking behind him in South Africa?"

For her part, Rosalynn Carter also knows how to click. At the Houston IWY conference, she was President Carter's envoy, and she said, "*You're* not going to say, 'He sent a woman to do a man's job!'"

When Bella Abzug ran for mayor of New York City, one of her campaign slogans was, "There's more to Bella than meets the ear." A Congressman skeptical about spending money on a woman's IWY conference told Bella that the "girls" would just go to booze and carouse. "I've attended many meetings," returned Bella, "but I've never heard a woman ask for call boys."

"Growing up white and male in this society is like swimming in a salt lake—no matter how rotten you are, it's impossible to sink to the bottom." *Sheila Tobias*

"We live in a male homosexual society—not genital, of course. But we live in a society where men prefer the company of other men." *Phyllis Chesler*

"My husband and I have figured out a really good system about the housework: neither one of us does it." *Dottie Archibald*

"My husband is very open. He says, 'Honey, you can have an open relationship with anyone you want. As long as it's not mental. Or spiritual. Or physical. Or emotional.' If the person's in a coma, I can be totally open, just hang out." *Lotus Weinstock*

"I think the Democratic [party] emblem should be changed from a donkey to a prophylactic. It's perfect. It supports inflation, keeps production down, helps a bunch of pricks and gives a false sense of security when one is being screwed." *Robin Tyler*

"It seems that in order to be the kind of woman who's strong enough to live with a man, you tend to become the kind of woman no man wants to live with." *Lotus Weinstock*

"I have five sons and therefore have to go out a lot." *Jean Kerr*

****

In 1972, Liz Carpenter, the former White House staff director for Lady Bird Johnson, unexpectedly met Arthur Schlesinger, former aide to President Kennedy. Carpenter's book, *Ruffles and Flourishes,* reminiscences about the L.B.J. White House, prompted Schlesinger to remark, "I liked your book, Liz. Who wrote it for you?"

Carpenter replied, "I'm glad you liked it, Arthur. Who read it to you?"

A Bargain with the Judge

FLORYNCE KENNEDY

When women began wearing pants there was a tremendous backlash. I can remember—I was still practicing law at that time—going to court in pants and the judge's remarking that I wasn't properly dressed, that the next time I came to court I should be dressed like a lawyer. He's sitting there in a long black dress gathered at the yoke, and I said, "Judge, if you won't talk about what I'm wearing, I won't talk about what you're wearing," because it occurred to me that a judge in a skirt telling me not to wear pants was just a little bit ludicrous. It's interesting to speculate how it developed that in two of the most anti-feminist institutions, the church and the law court, the men are wearing the dresses.

(from Color Me Flo, *1976)*

Don't You Wish You Were Liberated Too

SHIRLEY KATZ

Once, I had a bosom
Big, stiff, pointed bosom
Filled with silicone and foam
Well, I burned my bra and
    now I'm neat
I can even see my feet, now
Don't you wish that you were
    liberated too!?!

Chorus: Oh, you can be
           Brave and free!
           Oh you can be liberated
           Just like me!

Once, I had a giggle
Ought to see me squeal and wiggle
I would always wear a smile
Now, I ask what's funny
Men don't call me honey
Don't you wish. . . etc.

Once I wore my mini
Shaved my legs and starved me skinny
Never took my face out in the rain
Now I've got my head together
I can march in any weather
Don't you wish. . . etc.

Once, I tried some lovin'
"Somethin' from the oven"
Always satisfied that guy
Then I set my psyche free
Left him the number of the bakery
Don't you wish. . . etc.

Once I sharpened pencils
Fetched the coffee, made neat stencils
Tried to keep my head above water
    in that typing pool
Joined the union yesterday
No more coffee grounds but twice the pay
Don't you wish. . . etc.

Once, I was dodging pinches
slingin' hash and losing by inches
'cause those bill collectors
    were catching up to me
Now I make 10,000 bucks
Pitching garbage in those trucks
Don't you wish. . . etc.

Once, I was no shirker
I was a loyal party worker
Twenty years and never on the
    slate
'Til I said, "You've had your fun
Step back, boys, I'm gonna run!"
Don't you wish. . . etc.

Once, I was a Mrs.
Scrubbed the floors and washed
    the dishes
After I got home from work
Now I'm a superMs with a supermale
He can tote that mop and lift that
    pail
Don't you wish. . . etc.

Gee! It sure sounds good
UNION! NOW! and SISTERHOOD!
S. S. double U. L. C. (that's the
    South Suburban Women's Liberation
    Coalition!)
Let's all shout now
Let's get raucous!
Let's all join the Women's Caucus!
Wow! It's neat that you've been
    liberated too!

           OH, WE CAN BE
           BRAVE AND FREE
           OH, WE CAN BE LIBERATED
           YOU AND ME!

The South Suburban Women's Liberation Coalition Marching Society and Housewives' Revolutionary Band Fight Song

(Don't You Wish That You Were Liberated Too)

Words & Music by Shirley Katz

Once, I had a bosom, big, stiff, pointed bosom

filled with sili-cone and foam. Well, I burned my bra and

now I'm neat! I can even see my feet! Well,

Last verse: Wow!

Chorus

don't you wish that you were li-be-ra-ted
it's neat that you've been li-be-ra-ted

too?! Oh, you can be (you can be) brave and
too! oh, we can be (we can be) brave and

free! (brave and free!) Oh you can be li-ber
free! (brave and free!) Oh we can be li-ber

-a-ted just like me! (just like me!)
-a-ted you and me! (you and me!)

69

The man was right—'Life Isn't Fair'

By ELLEN GOODMAN
© Washington Post Writers Group

BOSTON — It seems hardly possible, but it is more than three years since Jimmy Carter first proclaimed that Life Isn't Fair. Of course, at the time, most of us thought he was describing a condition, not a goal. But, Lord knows, let us give him credit for maintaining one campaign promise.

In the ensuing three years, as a kind of personal kinky celebration of August 26 Women's Equality Day, the anniversary of the passage of the Suffrage Amendment, we have paused in order to give thanks to all of those who have done their best to maintain this Great American Motto.

But enough of these banal generalities. On to the specifics of the third annual Life Isn't Fair awards.

The envelopes please.

The Gone with the Wind award, a working calendar of the year 1843 appropriate for hanging, goes to the Mississippi State Legislature, which this year voted against the amendment granting women the right to vote. So much for The New South.

The You Can Always Get a Woman for Less prize goes to the United States Mint, which succeeded, where all others have failed, in making Susan B. Anthony a lightweight. Now, weighing in at 8.1 grams and wreaking more havoc at the vending machines than she did at the polling booths, Anthony is employed as a figurehead to save the government $25 million a year.

The Outstanding Graduate of Army Tact School plaque goes to those swell guys in the White House who, in the best tradition of displaced hostility, battered Bella instead of Billy. This award, for their elegant dismissal of Bella from the President's Advisory Committee for Women, is a leatherbound copy of "How to Make Friends and Influence People."

> 'The Stand By Her Man prize for ardor in battle goes to the Santa Ana, Calif., woman who sued her ex-husband for alimony payments while he was in a coma. A stone that gives blood will be sent westward shortly.'

The If It Weren't for You I Woulda Been a Star award, stuffed with fading photographs, goes to Michelle Marvin, who proved this year that the cost of free love had inflated to $104,000. To her own catty Ballou goes our annual literary "Say It with Flowers — PLEASE!" award for his courtly letters read publicly during this case. They include the memorable lyric: "Oh baby, I want so much for you please."

The Profiles in Courage badge, once again by popular outcry, is awarded to a Florida state senator. The Man of the Hour is Guy Spicola, who ran, with ERA funds, on a pro-ERA platform only to vote against it. This profile is a silhouette of a chicken.

The He Was Asking for It graffiti goes to the woman who contributed the most in defense of her craft. When a man grabbed her while she was painting a building, she striped him with Day-Glo.

The Boys will be Boys award, a ready-to-assemble pig pen, goes to the New York Yankees who gleefully autographed the bare derriere of an Illinois expressionist.

The Stand By Her Man prize for ardor in battle goes to the Santa Ana, Calif., woman who sued her ex-husband for alimony payments while he was in a coma. A stone that gives blood will be sent westward shortly.

The Biting the Hand that Feeds the Next Generation award, a small but rabid dalmatian, goes to the fire department in Iowa which tried to prevent Linda Eaton from breastfeeding her baby.

The Ayatollah Khomeini Music Appreciation disc goes to Japanese songwriter Masashi Sada, whose hit song, "Your Lord and Master" proclaims: "Keep quiet and follow behind me."

The Power Behind the (Tumbling of the Throne) award, a small knife suitable for back-stabbing, goes to that aging flower child Margaret Trudeau who is truly Beyond Reason.

The Golden Ruler award goes to the U.S. Congress, which remains exempt from its own laws. This year they failed to pass the Udall-Schroeder bill that would prohibit discrimination in the halls and offices of Congress. The Golden Ruler is to be used for self-discipline.

The Why Must A Woman Be Like a Man bumper sticker is sent via satellite to Margaret Thatcher.

To Greta and John Rideout, everybody's fun couple, go the only prizes they truly deserve: Each other. May they take their prizes to the heart-shaped bathtubs of the Poconos. After all kids, why not try again?

The My Kind of Guy button goes to Massachusetts Governor Edward J. King, who replaced the Commission on the Status of Women with the new Commission on the STATUS QUO of Women. This group of conservatives has so far tackled such tough matters as distributing perfume samples.

The Miracle on 42nd St. award, a well-furnished bordello and porn shop, goes to the masterminds of the fashion industry who created that wonderfully subtle and demure style: The Hooker Look.

*"Yes, I did place an ad for a large, friendly male
with red hair, but I was talking about an Irish Setter."*

*"Did you see today's paper? There was an interesting article which reported
that most women today prefer rugged outdoor-type men. vibrant athletic men,
quiet intellectual men, and men who are playful and childlike."*

clunk ''klənk'' *n* **1:** a sharp stab of disappointment or frustration that negates previous visions of idealism and independence; a feminist word. **2:** A backsliding attack that arouses fantasies of a simpler, more protected time for women. See **CLICK:** the reverse state of clunk.

JANE O'REILLY

I am often tired of being a feminist.

I'm not even sure I am a feminist.

Probably I am just tired. I'm tired of earning my own living, paying my own bills, raising my own child. I'm tired of the sounds of my own voice crying out in the wilderness, raving on about equality and justice and a new social order. I wasn't raised to take care of myself. Self-sufficiency is exhausting. Autonomy is lonely.

It is so hard to be a feminist if you are a woman.

Every time I get another layer of my consciousness raised, I find another,

stubborner, layer beneath. Never mind that I know self-sufficiency is the only answer, that I know none of us is going to be taken care of by anyone else. (I remind myself that statistically women have a fifty-fifty chance of being divorced, separated, or widowed by the time they reach middle age.)

Never mind that I have, comparatively, nothing to complain about. I am, truly, grateful that I do not have to work as a waitress. Nevertheless, whenever I read *Vogue,* whenever someone I know buys a house at the seashore, whenever I can't pay my bills, whenever I am not taken seriously, then I want to marry a rich lawyer and work

needlepoint pillows. Clunk.

I have been married. Twice. Marriage doesn't mean not having to work. (Although it can mean not having to work as hard.) And yet, contrary to all experience and observation, the myth lurks just at the line of awareness, tantalizing and demoralizing, something that makes me go out—Clunk.

No wonder we go ''clunk.'' We thought that the pointing out of absurdities and insecurities would result in improvement. That women would begin to get equal pay. We thought that because the majority of people agreed with the Supreme Court decision that abortion is a matter of individual

©1978 NICOLE HOLLANDER

choice, women, therefore, including poor women, would be able to get abortions.

Oh, well, I guess we were a bit naive and trusting. I was willing to skirmish, even to face a battle. But I wasn't really prepared for a siege. So I am sometimes so tired of being a feminist.

And I am so afraid that being tired means I am not a feminist at all.

Clunk.

In my article on clicks, I described the moment when I watched the men in my household ignore the basket of laundry my loving hands had collected, sorted, washed and folded, and finally placed right on the couch by the television set. The family moved it to one side of the couch so they could sit down. I left it there. I put more on the couch. They piled it up. They began to dress off the couch. I began to avoid the television room. At last, guilty and crazy, my nerve failed and I carried the laundry upstairs. No one noticed. Click.

We have all felt that tangible sensation of the tumblers falling into place in our heads, the moment which signals a permanent recognition that the Women's Movement is . . . me. That *I* am one of those people oppressed, embarrassed, enraged, inconvenienced, and generally irritated by attitudes and patterns that the world would be well rid of. It is the click of tiny doors opening in the mind, and they never shut again —even though they may swing a bit in the breeze.

Clicks were enraging and stimulating and tended to strengthen us for the task of making straight the path of reform. The trouble is, we tend to forget that the path is not very well marked. We've been trying—for how long this time? five or ten years?—to right the wrongs of 4,000 years. It seems to me we get unreasonably dispirited and embarrassed by minor failures. Those are the moments when we do not click—we clunk. As in: "I have a wonderful new doctor," says my friend. "Oh?" I say, "what's his name?" "She is a woman," answers my friend. Clunk.

I went down to Washington to cover the women lobbying for the National Women's Agenda. I walked all over Capitol Hill looking for funny political ladies in hats, and in the process I chanced to remark to a colleague: "Gee, some of these women are amazingly well-informed on the issues." There were, by the way, no hats. Clunk.

At lunch with some newswomen I found myself arguing that women's news should only be covered when it

73

deserves coverage. I realized I was defining "deserved" as outstanding, remarkable, and astounding; instead of the run-of-the-mill coverage such as labor or television people get. Clunk.

I try to remember it's better to be a lawyer than to marry one, but, alas, the truth is, there is no one who wants to marry me.

I once wrote that I confidently expected that someone would like me, even love me, as soon as I liked myself. Perhaps I haven't yet reached the necessary liking-myself plateau, but all the men I meet retire from the field murmuring: "I can't handle it."

They can't handle it? How about me? I'm trying to get onto the path of equality and mutuality before the final resolution of such problems as: he has an expense account and I don't. So I insist on paying for my drinks, but I run out of money before the drinking is over. He buys the last round, which spoils the entire effect.

If he does not make some joking remark about the inadequate intensity of my feminism—an observation many men seem too ready to make—the relationship might develop until some night we will find ourselves in bed, and I will feel able at last to express my needs and desires. Then I will fake it in order to reward him for his kindness in listening. A dull thud. A definite clunk.

Does that failure mean I should stop shaving my legs and go back to trying to love my body even if I hate it hairy? Why should shaving my legs be a new source of guilt? Feeling guilty makes me feel guilty. Clunk.

A few more things to feel guilty about: I turned on the television set to watch a soap opera. It crossed my mind that a man would watch an important program. I am assuming that what men watch, and read, and write is nobler than what women watch. Baseball is not nobler. What if it were? So what? Clunk.

Last fall I worked in an office for a few weeks. I loved going out to drink with the fellows after work. I never wondered why the women didn't come along. Should I feel guilty because I never noticed? Guiltier because I never noticed that they worked harder than the men, and then went home to run their houses? Clunk? Yes, clunk. On the other hand, the men asked me out for

"What do you mean remove my wrinkles? I've earned every single one of them!"

drinks and the women didn't. Perhaps they should feel guilty. Maybe they didn't like me and should feel guilty about not liking another woman. Plainly, that is ridiculous. Lots of women are not likable. Especially when the women are twenty years younger and flirting with the man I am talking to at a party.

Clunk.

What if a woman is not only twenty years younger but has just sold the paperback rights to her first novel for $250,000 Is it a clunk if I hate her?

I could sit right here and worry about competitiveness until Christmas, but eventually, if the effort is to be at all useful, I will have to get out of my chair and apply what I think. Theory is not always the best goal. I recently spoke to a woman in Washington whom I admire very much. Her work in the field of family and child care has contributed an enormous amount toward finding answers to a crucial feminist question: "Who will take care of the children?" And yet, she told me that she didn't consider herself part of the Women's Movement, that she didn't like to "join things." She was surprised when I told her she was a leader of the Women's Movement by virtue of her work, her attitudes, her influence.

The worst clunk of all is to worry about clunks too much. Trying to be a perfect feminist, with daily examinations of conscience, is not really a big improvement on trying to be a perfect wife, mother, and lady. Backsliding is undesirable, but giving up because you can't meet the standards is much worse. It helps if you feel a deep impatience with the way the world is presently arranged and try to question any manifestations of the systems that oppress people. But as for standards. . . well, the guidelines are still flexible. Inflexible guidelines are probably antifeminist by definition.

I think narrow discussions of who is and who is not adopting the correct political stance are usually arrogant and excluding. No one is entrusted with the final truth about feminism—because feminism is about autonomy; finding out what we as individuals (not sex roles) really want and can do. There is no oracle, no entrails to yield up their secrets. Dogma is too easy. It is also the death of imagination, and we have a very long span of history for which to imagine an alternative. The cure for clunks—from the minor slip into socialized instincts to the major political error—is imagination, intellectual curi-

osity, experimentation, the continuing attempts to define the personal so as to discover the universal.

It also helps to laugh. There is, after all, a certain inherent humor in being on the cutting edge of a social revolution. It is funny, actually, to be unsure of what you feel more offended by: the guests ignoring your opinions or not complimenting you on your souffle.

****

75

Pandephobium

SUE HELD

"...and who were you before you were married?"

Fear of failure
Fear of success
Fear of allure
Fear of a mess
Fear of flying
Fear of falling
Fear of trying
Fear of stalling
Fear to be lost
Fear to be found
Fear to be tossed
Fear to be drowned
Fear to be loose
Fear to be tight
Fear to deduce
Fear to delight
Fear to be feeling
Fear to be un-
Fear to be dealing
Fear to be done
Fear of youth
Fear of age
Fear of truth
Fear of rage
Fear to be cheerful
Fear to be glum
Fear to be fearful
Fear to be ho hum
Fear to be wrong
Fear to be right
Fear to be strong
Fear to be slight
Fear to be peerless
Fear to be bland
Fear to be fearless
Fear to demand

Fear of sleeping
Fear of waking
Fear of keeping
Fear of breaking
Fear of saving
Fear of wasting
Fear of craving
Fear of tasting
Fear of classics
and graffiti

What are you afraid of,
Sweetie?

Clothes Make the Man

SALLY SERTIN

At six-thirty this morning the alarm rips into my sleep. I stumble into the shower, splash away my warm dream, and step out to discover the hot faucet won't turn off. The water is barely an inch below the rim of the stall. So at 6:45 A.M., wet and naked, I run down to the cold cellar, frantically trace the pipes, and finally find the faucet to turn off the hot water. It's rusted. It won't budge.

I'm not surprised. My whole week has been going this way. You know, every ten minutes—another crisis:

"Sally, they just fired Mrs. Donahue. Her kids are three and five, and her ex-husband won't pay child support. Get her job back. Get her a better job. Get her a good husband."

And, "Sally, this new widow locked herself up in her house. It's ten days since she answered the phone or the door. Get someone to love her. Get a fireperson to break down the door."

And, "Sally, I *know* we don't have money yet for the shelter, but someone has *got* to take Maria in before her husband kills her. How about your living room . . . ?"

And, "Ms. Sertin, let's keep your mother in the hospital another week to be sure that lump isn't cancer."

And then your best friend calls long-distance to say goodbye before she commits suicide.

Untitled

ALTA

```
that chick is SO REVOLUTIONARY
she dresses poor on purpose.
she eschews the boozhwa comforts like
washing machines, male lovers, &
flush toilets.  i mean she is
EVERY KIND of revolutionary!
she'd bum off her friends before she'd work
in a counterrevolutionary government job!
(how come she can afford
   to be so revolutionary?)


i mean, this chick is SO REVOLUTIONARY,
she laughs at housewives, agrees that
we're an inferior breed.
she would never have a kid if she could have
an abortion instead. get it? this chick is
SELF- FULFILLED!
super chick ta daa!
even her period glows in the dark.
```

So that's the way the week is going—every day the same—this week exactly like the week before, and it's adding up, it's getting to me. The worst problems I won't mention, because who likes to complain? But, believe me, the tension runs high.

On top of everything, there's a nagging in my mind—a phone call I haven't returned. The call (as usual) is a call for help—from a transvestite. Now, on an ordinary day the call would be no problem. In Norfolk we are super-prepared. We just take these guys down to our local transvestite center, where they feel right at home and where their problems melt like snowflakes in July.

But I'm not thinking too well. I wonder, what do I say when he asks, "How can a transvestite find happiness in Norfolk, Nebraska?" I ponder the question deeply. I pound at it with my sledge-hammer mind. No go.

I don't return the call.

Instead, I dash off to our Yuletide feminist bash, where once a year we don't discuss issues, don't bring up problems, just relax and reestablish connections. Where affection and support flow free. Just what I need! What luck it's tonight!

I'm not there five minutes when in walks Brian-who-would-rather-be-called-Susanna, asking for Sally Sertin. A thousand hands grab me, shake me: how'd *he* get *here?* (How the hell do I know?—except this proves god is male.)

Now Brian-Sue is far from your archetypal transvestite. The most ordinary thing about him is, he wants to wear dresses. The second most ordinary thing is the way he *does* dress, which is in thin shorts, vertically striped, that look like BVD's but that are mercifully concealed by his survival jacket (it's winter), so only his bare shaven legs are visible. He does have on thin orange knee sox. Well, his legs are not the healthy red response to snow that ordinary white skin puts out. No, they are a dull, pale, greenish blue. So much for his healthy side.

Otherwise Brian-Sue radiates pain, pain, pain and sick, sick, sick. And watch how all these feminists rally around to help me! That's our strong point, right? They all know what tough weeks I've been having, right?

"Touch luck, Sally."

"I've been doing this all day—no more for me!"

"Too bad, kid—you shouldn't have brought him HERE."

As if I went out and kidnapped Brian-Sue because I didn't want to come alone.

So I spend three hours at the party with Brian-Sue because everyone else has already spent her 8-or-10-or-12-hour working day soothing unbalanced transvestites. While he's droning in his long monotone, which I strain to hear below the din of the party (because his voice has the strength of a sick oyster), I think longingly of my plumbing problem. Why didn't I stay home and clean out the shower drain? I'm thinking of the cozy way I started the day, nude and shivering in the basement, stroking the pipes.

But will Brian-Sue allow me the luxury of my memories? No. He wants my ear, my eye, my everything . . .

"Why," he says for the 243rd time, "is it OK for a woman to dress up as a man and not for a man to dress up as a woman?"

A logical question—which I answer in seven different ingenious ways, each one more brilliantly and uncompromisingly antiestablishment. My answers, however, are lost somewhere on the way to his brain. So my real problem is how to help him, or even how to *deal* with him. Why couldn't he be something simple like an invalid, battered wife with four preschool kids and a drunken, unemployed husband? Something ordi-

nary like that—within the range of my competence.

Of course there isn't a solution for *every* problem, but suddenly I feel Brian-Sue is not asking me to cure him. All he wants to do is wear a lousy skirt. The answer comes in a flash.

"Brian-Sue," I say, "I've got just the job for you!"

"Why," he says for the 244th time, "is it OK for a woman to dress up as a man and not for a man to dress up as a woman?"

"You can do it! You can do it," I say. "Listen, Brian-Sue, how about going for Pope?"

"I'm not religious," he says.

I am determined, undefeated: "Federal judge?"

Brian-Sue smiles.

On Stage with Harrison and Tyler

	OPENING		ago, we used to come out in long tight gowns, lots of make-up, teased hair . . . .
	(applause)		
HARRISON:	Thanks for the clap. God knows as women we've had everything else.		
TYLER:	Hey, it's great to be here. Of course we're really dressed funky—the blue jeans, the caps. How many of you like my sequined bowtie? On Liza Minelli it's called cute.	TYLER:	How many of you guys dig make-up? *(Men applaud)*
		HARRISON:	If you dig it, then why don't you wear it!
		TYLER:	Yeah!
HARRISON:	On you it's called drag.	HARRISON:	I'm tired of being a sex symbol.
TYLER:	Well, I dig the way we're dressed. After all, we're feminists . . .	TYLER:	Don't laugh. This woman was very famous. Pat Harrison used to be one of the top high-fashion models in New York City. She was in *Look, Life, Harper's Bazaar* . . . she's done
HARRISON:	and that's not a hygiene deodorant. When we started ten years		

Time.

You want to know why *I* became a feminist? When I was sixteen—I developed breasts. (Laughs)

HARRISON: What's so funny about that? We know how you guys talk about us women.

TYLER: *(Mimicking man's voice)* Ey, ey! Lookit the pair a knockers on that broad!

HARRISON: How would you guys like to go through life as nothing but cock and balls, cock and balls?

TYLER: Society says there are only two kinds of women.

HARRISON: Those that do and those that don't.

TYLER: Right.

HARRISON: If you do, you're a pig—if you don't, you're a dyke.

TYLER: Anita Bryant was offered a booking in Alaska, but she turned it down.

HARRISON: She didn't want to bump into a klon-DYKE.

TYLER: Anita Bryant is to Christianity what paint by numbers is to art.

HARRISON: We don't believe in busing to school. Why send those kids to racist, sexist schools when they can stay on the bus and learn more from each other than in class?

TYLER: We happen to agree with the "right-to-lifers," because—if you don't agree with them . . .

HARRISON: they'll kill you.

TYLER: There's all this preoccupation in this country with the size of women's breasts. So we finally figured it out, gang. Women do not have penis envy.

HARRISON: Men have mammary envy.

TYLER: That's because America is built on sucking. If you guys are going to judge us by the size of our breasts, we're gonna judge you by the size of your "wee-wee's."

HARRISON: And we know all men aren't created equal, don't we?

TYLER: Women have been discriminated against for centuries and centuries, and why?

HARRISON: Because we can't stand up to pee.

TYLER: It's true. *(High voice)* "Mr. Smith, why am I earning forty percent less than Mr. Jones? We do the same job."

HARRISON: *(Deep voice)* "Because you can't stand up to pee, Mary. That's worth at least forty percent."

TYLER: *(High voice)* "So I went home to practice. Boy, it's sure messy."

TWO HOMEMAKERS

(Madge and Marge have been married twenty years. Both are fighting for wages for housework. Tyler plays Marge, Harrison Madge.)

MARGE: Little did I know when I got married and said, "I do," how much I'd have to.

MADGE: I married my Harry for better or for worse. He could have done better, I couldn't have done worse. Do you know how tired I am of standing in the kitchen with that goddamn crown on my head?

MARGE: Doves flying in my kitchen window, shitting all over my kitchen floor.

MADGE: Every evening I see the white knight coming in my dreams. It's the only thing that happens in my bedroom.

MARGE: I don't want to say I'm getting attached to my vibrator, but last Valentine's Day I sent it two dozen roses.

MADGE: You're lucky. Every night for twenty years my Harry has come home and said, "Yoo hoo, come get your daddy's peaches."

MARGE: So?

MADGE: Well, they may be peaches, daddy, but they're sure hanging from a dead limb!

THE SENSUOUS GERIATRIC

HARRISON: *(As an old woman)* Hooray—I'm eighty years old and still sexual! I still have the will—and don't need the pill. You bet I have lots of energy! I don't know why they retire old people. The only place they don't throw you out of after you're sixty-five is jail . . . and Congress.

COMMERCIALS

TYLER: How many of you have time to go to your toilet bowl, lift up the lid, and talk to some dumb guy floatin' around in there?

HARRISON: If I saw a guy floating in my toilet, *flush!*

TYLER: We work night clubs a lot. You work night clubs, they think you're fast.

HARRISON: A guy came over to me and said, "Do you use Pristine?" I said, "Of course I do, darling, twice a day—but I hate the taste."

TYLER: I'm very innocent about those things. I used to think Summer's Eve was a warm night in June.

HARRISON: I had no idea women did that to themselves.

TYLER: On TV, Dirt represents Guilt. If men are so worried about ring-around-the-collar, why don't they wash their necks?

HARRISON: They have a new soap detergent called Fug. The jingle goes:
> *(sings) If Rinso won't rinse it*
> *And Duz won't do it—*
> *Fug it.*

TYLER: When we play campuses, a lot of people do not draw the analogy between racism and sexism. Both are based on the economic need for cheap labor. We always do this commercial for them:
> "You've come a long way, baby, to get where you're going . . ." *(sings whole commercial).*

HARRISON: Or, "Promise her anything, but give her Arpege."

TYLER: And the guys say, "There's nothing wrong with that commercial. We're putting women on a pedestal."

HARRISON: Can you imagine doing that to black people?
> *"You've come a long way, Negro, to get where you're going today.*
> *You've got your own hair spray now, Negro.*
> *You've come a long, long way."*

TYLER: Or, "Promise them anything, but give them a watermelon." They'd kill 'em. But they do it to *us!*

HARRISON: I think the most offensive commercial is the airline's "Fly Me" commercial.

TYLER: How would men like it if a guy got up, dressed in a little blue pilot suit with a little white cap, and said, "Hi, my name is Captain Jack, and I can get it up for you!"

HARRISON: We'd like to do the airline's commercial for you—*our* way.

TYLER: *(Very feminine)* Hi, my name is Priscilla. I'm with Boeing 707, *fly me,* fly worldwide. *(Another seductive voice)* Hi, my name is Janet Francis. I'm with Super 747. *Fly me,* fly worldwide.

HARRISON: Hi, my name is Helga. I'm with Trans Women's Liberation Airlines. You fly me and I'll kick your fucking ass in!

TYLER: Oh, no! You said it—you said the word that begins with F and that ends with K, the word that most men don't want women to say!

HARRISON: They want us to *do* it, but not to say it.

TYLER: Of course, we think there are dirty four-letter words too.

HARRISON: Like "kill," "hate," "rape . . . ."

TYLER: But now that you said that other dirty word, you know what they're going to say about us?

HARRISON: Sure. They'll say we're aggressive—we work like men.

TYLER: They're going to say . . .

HARRISON: "Hey, those chicks . . . ." Where did guys get the word "chicks"?

TYLER: Some guy must have screwed a Cornish game hen and said, "Wow, a chick!"

HARRISON: So the guys are gonna say, "Hey, those chicks have . . . balls!"

(Look between their legs)
TYLER: We don't have balls. Men are preoccupied with balls.

HARRISON: They throw balls, catch balls, chase balls, kick balls. They watch volleyball, basketball, baseball, football . . . .

TYLER: And then do you know what they do?

HARRISON: Sure.

HARRISON & TYLER: They go home, and they BALL!

TYLER:	Did you ever watch guys talk about sex?
	(Harrison and Tyler imitate two men)
TYLER:	Hey . . . *(adjusting zipper)* Hey . . . .
HARRISON:	Hey, hey, hey . . . .
TYLER:	Did you score?
HARRISON:	Of course I scored! Did you score?
TYLER:	Yeah, I got to first base.
HARRISON:	I slid into home plate.
TYLER:	I mean, what is lovemaking to you guys—some kind of game? Man 1. Woman 0.
HARRISON:	So you're going to have to zip up those anxieties, guys.
TYLER:	Yeah—'cause you can't pull the foreskin over our eyes!

CLOSING

HARRISON:	Once when we were playing a nightclub in Los Angeles, a very drunk and rude man got up. The material must have threatened him. You see, when men make jokes about women, it's called funny. But when women make jokes about men, it's called "anti-male."
TYLER:	So this guy got up and started swearing at us, and finally said what is supposed to be the ultimate put-down for a woman, "Are you a lesbian?" And Patti said,
HARRISON:	Are *YOU* the alternative?
TYLER:	We'd like to leave you with one very positive thought. When you go home tonight, try loving yourselves.
HARRISON:	It might be contagious.
TYLER:	And, by the way, if we offended anybody at all, from the bottom of our hearts . . .
HARRISON:	You needed it!
HARRISON & TYLER:	Thank you and good night.

Harrison & Tyler
By doing jokes from a feminist consciousness as early as 1970, Harrison & Tyler made women the "subject" rather than the "object" of humor. They were never self-deprecating, they attacked the myths, and they proved that feminists did indeed have a sense of humor, only this time the joke wasn't on them. Their humor was the "razor-sharp edge of the truth," and through their laughter they helped organize women all over the world. Thus, they made show-business history in the art of stand-up comedy and are credited with pioneering what is now known as "The New Women's Humor."

Pat Harrison
An orphan until the age of six, Pat spend her earliest years in several different homes until she was taken in by the Paul family of Florida. She went from orphanages to fame . . . from rags to riches . . . by becoming one of the most well-known hi-fashion models in New York City in the '60s, before teaming up with Robin Tyler.

Robin Tyler
Canadian-born Robin Tyler studied drama for seven years. By the time she was twenty and living in New York, she was a trouper, having performed since her early teens. She became a singer and worked for six years before teaming up with Pat Harrison. Robin's first solo comedy album "Always a Bridesmaid, Never a Groom" is on Olivia Records.

Clowning with Ivy Bottini

When I grew up and came out, I realized that lesbians have a hard time. For example, you can't buy HERS and HERS towels. And once the word gets out in your neighborhood, the Avon lady stops calling.

But the finest thing, if you're a lesbian—the toilet seat is always DOWN!

Did you ever notice how cancer-prone rats really are? There's nothing you can give those buggers that they don't get cancer from.

I talk about things that are very personal, that have nothing to do with men—like MENstruation, MENopause, GUYnecology, and HISterectomies.

At the gynecologist's office a nurse would take me into that room with the Frankenstein table, stirrups, and no saddle. She'd give me one of those great gowns with the slit in front. If you put the slit in front, you've got two hangin' out—and if you put the slit in back, you've *still* got two hangin' out!

The doctor says, "Nurse, I will now do a pelvic." Doesn't that sound like a sandwich? "I'll have a pelvic on rye. Hold the mustard, please."

"Nurse," he says, "I'm going to do a pelvic, so give me the speculum, please—the metal one, out of the refrigerator."

Applying for a job in an anti-gay climate, where the job application asks for date, put "only men." Down farther, where it asks for sex, put "only with men." And where it asks about reasons for leaving your previous job, to be really safe, so they'll know you're OK, write, "I am a very serious worker, and the atmosphere was entirely too gay."

Look at your diaphragm to see if there are any holes. If there's a blowout in one of their tires, you can fix it in twenty minutes. But a blowout in one of these—it takes twenty *years*.

Monumental Prophylactic

(from The Washington Pits, *Jan. 3, 1978*)

WASH. D.C.—New Year's Day, 1978—Strange sights have appeared "the morning after," but few more extraordinary than the ones which greeted late partyers and early risers who passed the Washington Monument this morning. That venerable edifice was rising out of the bleary winter mist encapsulated from top to bottom in a star-spangled rubber sheath. Lest anyone miss the point, an eight-foot-high sign which read "Down With The National Erection" had been planted on the Ellipse.

Most informed sources believe the condomnation was the work of radical feminists; a minority opinion holds that it was a publicity stunt staged by exiled South Vietnamese rubber bosses trying to win CIA backing for a takeover attempt.

(off our backs, Dec. 1977)

Men: Beware the ATR

The right wing won. The airlines capitulated. They established separate restrooms, which—because of competition—became quite elegant. Even feminists conceded that the new toilets in the skies were far lovelier than the wicked unisex plumbing of old.

Progress, however, took its toll on the more vulnerable sex. John Johnson was a typical case. He was in flight with an urgent need to use the men's room—all of which were occupied.

The flight attendant said, yes, he could use a vacant women's room, "but *don't dare touch* the console unit on the right wall. That is strictly for women and for women ONLY."

Nodding agreement, Johnson rushed inside. After he relieved himself, he examined the console. There were four buttons: WW, WA, PP, and ATR. Overcome with curiosity, he pressed WW. A stream of warm water pleasantly caressed his anus. Right away he pressed WA. Warm air streamed out and dried his bottom. The sensations were unique and distinctly pleasurable.

"These women!" he thought. "They've really got something going, and they want to keep it all to themselves. Well, we'll see about that!"

So John Johnson, feeling both incensed and delighted, pressed PP. Out came a large powder puff and gently patted his thighs and derriere.

"Wow!" he thought. "What more could I ask? What more can there be?"

He gazed at the button marked ATR. Surely that would bring the ultimate in sensual pleasure! He pressed it. Immediately he was struck with a blinding flash of pain, and he lost consciousness.

Johnson awoke in a hospital bed, face to face with an angry nurse. "What happened?" he said. "Where am I?"

"Why did you do it? Weren't you warned?"

He looked at her blankly.

"Don't play dumb," she said. "We've had it with you men who don't follow instructions. The hospital's full of you!"

"What happened?" Johnson repeated.

"You were told not to press the buttons in the women's room, but you went right ahead," she said with much annoyance, "even the ATR."

"Yeah," he said, "and what happened?"

"ATR," she said, "is Automatic Tampon Removal. Your penis is under your pillow."

We Measured 56-480-47-277-30-19, and Now We Measure More!

CHAPTER FOUR

AN "UGLY RUSH!"

Carrie Chapman Catt recorded that to get the vote in the United States, it took "56 campaigns of referenda to male voters; 480 campaigns to get legislatures to submit suffrage amendments to votes; 47 campaigns to get State constitutional conventions to write woman suffrage into state constitutions; 277 campaigns to get State party conventions to include woman suffrage planks; 30 campaigns to get presidential party conventions to adopt woman suffrage planks in party platforms, and 19 campaigns with 19 successive Congresses."

Men may profess interest in us when our measurements are 36-24-36, but 56-480-47-277-30-19 are more satisfactory indications of what we were. And now we measure more!

★★★★★★★★★★★★★★★★★★★★★★★★★★★★★★★★★★★★

When Taxes Are Taxing

Mary Winsor was among the first group of women who were arrested for picketing the White House in the summer of 1917. Although the women, following the direction of Alice Paul, refused to participate in the court proceedings, they were ultimately found guilty and sentenced to pay fines of five or ten dollars or to serve in prison ten or fifteen days. None paid the fine. Mary Winsor said: "It is quite enough to pay taxes when you are not represented, let alone pay a fine if you object to this arrangement."

"I FOUND THE PART WHERE IT ASSURES EQUALITY FOR MEN, BUT I CAN'T FIND THE PART WHERE IT GUARANTEES SEPARATE RESTROOMS FOR WOMEN"

A Consistent Anti to Her Son

*"Look at the hazards, the risks, the physical dangers that
ladies would be exposed to at the polls."*—Anti-suffrage speech.

ALICE DUER MILLER

You're twenty-one today, Willie,
  And a danger lurks at the door,
I've known about it always,
  But I never spoke before;
When you were only a baby
  It seemed so very remote,
But you're twenty-one today, Willie,
  And old enough to vote.

You must not go to the polls, Willie,

Never go to the polls,
  They're dark and dreadful places
    Where many lose their souls;
They smirch, degrade and coarsen
  Terrible things they do
To quiet, elderly women—
  What would they do to you!

If you've a boyish fancy
  For any measure or man,
Tell me, and I'll tell Father,
  He'll vote for it, if he can.
He casts my vote, and Louisa's,

And Sarah, and dear Aunt Clo;
Wouldn't you let him vote for you?
  Father, who loves you so?

I've guarded you always, Willie,
  Body and soul from harm;
I'll guard your faith and honor,
  Your innocence and charm
From the polls and their evil spirits,
  Politics, rum and pelf;
Do you think I'd send my only son
  Where I would not go myself?

(from Are Women People? *1915)*

The Woman Question in 1872

(EXCERPTS)

FANNY FERN

I have been sitting here, enjoying a quiet laugh all by myself, over a pile of newspapers and magazines, in which the "Woman Question" was aired according to the differing views of editors and writers. One gentleman thinks that the reason the men take a nap on the sofa . . . or else leave it to go to naughty places, is because there are no Madame de Staëls in our midst to make home more attractive. He was probably a bachelor, or he would understand that when a man who has been perplexed and fretted all day finally reaches home, the last object he wishes to encounter is a wide-awake woman of the Madame de Staël pattern, pro-pounding her theories on politics, theology, and literature. The veriest idiot who should entertain him by the hour with tragic accounts of broken tea-cups and saucepans would be a blessing compared to her; not that he would know himself exactly what he *would* like in such a case, except that it should be something diametrically opposite to that which years ago he got on his knees to solicit. . . .

One of the sapient advisers of women ridicules the idea of a woman's voting till she has learned to be "moderate" in following the fashions; moderate in her household expenses; moderate in her way of dressing her hair; moderate in the length of her party-robes and in the shortness of her walking costume. Till woman has attained this desirable moderation he declares her totally unfit for the ballot.

Granted—for the sake of argument, granted; but it is a poor rule that won't work both ways. Suppose we determine a man's fitness by the same rule. Let not his short-tailed coats refuse to be sat upon by the fat owner thereof. Let not his pantaloons be so tight that he cannot stoop without danger. Let not his overcoat flap against his heels, because a new-fangled custom demands an extra inch or two. Let not the crown of his hat pierce the skies. . . . Let him smoke "moderately." Let him drink "moderately." Let him drive "moderately." Let him stock-gamble "moderately." Let him stay out at night "moderately."

. . . If "moderation" in smoking were the test of fitness for the ballot-box, how many men do you think would be able to vote?

(from Caper-Sauce, *1872)*

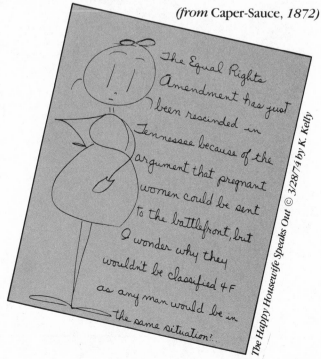

The Equal Rights Amendment has just been rescinded in Tennessee because of the argument that pregnant women could be sent to the battlefront, but I wonder why they wouldn't be classified 4F as any man would be in the same situation!

The Happy Housewife Speaks Out © 3/28/74 by K. Kelly

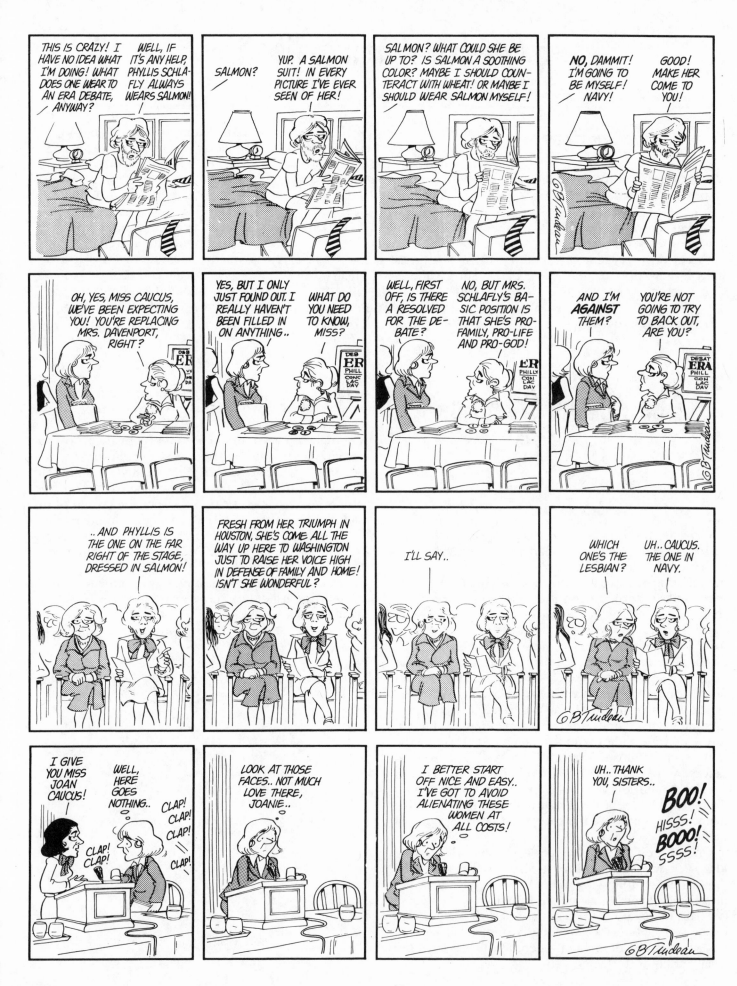

A woman, speaking for the passage of the ERA, was interrupted by a heckler. In a booming voice he shouted, "Don't you wish you were a man?"

"No," she responded. "How about you?"

× ×

Two of the men who had arranged an anti-ERA rally featuring Phyllis Schlafly were talking after the meeting.

"Phyllis was awfully angry. What was she so mad about?"

"Well, she only got four bouquets of flowers delivered over the rostrum after her speech."

"Four?" said the first. "That's marvelous! That's damn good for a political speech!"

"Yeah," the other responded, "but she did pay for seven."

Predictions for 1979

YENTA

Women's Rights

Women's Rights will be won at last in the U.S. but not how you might think. Don't hold your breath for the ERA. What's really going to happen is the Right-to-Lifers will hold a Constitutional Convention and put through an amendment granting fetuses the right to life, liberty, to bear arms and to run for President (if conceived in the U.S.). Thirty-eight states will ratify immediately. There will be some initial confusion over whether fetuses of both sexes or only male fetuses are covered by the amendment, but the Supreme Court will rule that since nobody knows what sex most unborn kids happen to be, female fetuses will have to be given full rights as citizens. Then, around October, in a startling move, Alan Bakke will drop out of med school to champion a lawsuit that will extend unborn rights to the post-natal. He will be suing for equal access to some poor black fetus's placenta. By December, he'll be on the cover of *Ms.*, and the Supreme Court will grant fetuses the right to abort their mothers.

A Flo Kennedy Sampler

They call us militants, but General Westmoreland, General Abrams, General Motors and General Dynamics—they're the real militants. We don't even have a helicopter.

We ought to give the Pentagon budget to the Department of Health, Education, and Welfare, and the HEW budget to the Pentagon. Then we'd have enough money to cure cancer and sickle-cell anemia and muscular dystrophy, and we'd only have telethons for Pentagonorrhea.

If the ass is protecting the system, ass-kicking should be undertaken regardless of the sex, ethnicity, or charm of the ass involved.

There's a little story I've been telling about strategy, and it applies to the church, to the media, to the police, the government, business, everyone. It's the story of a woman who's at the dentist, and she's leaning back in the chair. She's a very square lady, and I don't mean Kimberley knit square, I mean housedress square. So she's leaning back in the chair and the dentist has worked on her for about three minutes, and all of a sudden he realizes that she has managed to obtain a very tight grip on his testicles, and she's squeezing just short of agony. So he stops and says, "What is this?" And she says, "We are not going to hurt each other, are we, doctor?"

Now after five years of feminism and twenty years after the Brown versus the Board of Education decision, I'm urging you to assume the testicular approach, not just in rape but certainly in rape, and recognize that anyone that's close enough to hurt you can be hurt.

(from Color Me Flo, *1976)*

(On the Women's Movement)
If it's a movement, I sometimes think it needs a laxative.

(April 7, 1974, Des Moines Sunday Register)

"Yes, you can keep calling me 'sugar' if you want to, Mr. Chambers, but remember—sugar can make your teeth fall out."

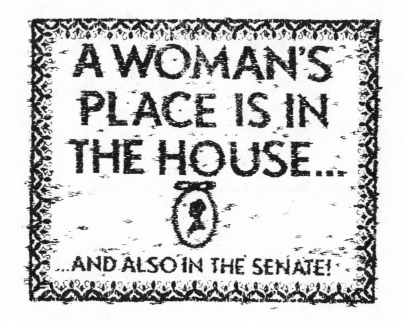

The Lifting Power of Woman

JOAN HONICAN

During the Washington State ERA campaign, a team of pro-ERA women spoke to the Spokane Valley Chamber of Commerce in an attempt to allay the Chamber's fear of equality under the law. The issue of so-called protective labor legislation came up, and one fellow jumped up in a chivalrous attempt to assist the fragile sex.

"Do you realize that women will be required to lift over thirty-five pounds if the ERA is passed?" he demanded.

One of the speakers, a six-foot, 250-pound woman, responded, "Fred, have you already forgotten who carried *you* from your car to your house after that last party?"

Why We Oppose Votes for Men

ALICE DUER MILLER

1. Because man's place is the armory.
2. Because no really manly man wants to settle any question otherwise than by fighting about it.
3. Because if men should adopt peaceable methods women will no longer look up to them.
4. Because men will lose their charm if they step out of their natural sphere and interest themselves in other matters than feats of arms, uniforms and drums.
5. Because men are too emotional to vote. Their conduct at baseball games and political conventions shows this, while their innate tendency to appeal to force renders them peculiarly unfit for the task of government.

(from Are Women People? *1915)*

"THERE'S NO ACCOUNTING FOR TASTE"

ETTA HULME
FORT WORTH
STAR-TELEGRAM

How the Women Sang Their Way Out of Jail

MARY HARRIS JONES

The miners in Greensburg, Pennsylvania, went on strike for more wages. . . .

One day a group of angry women were standing in front of the mine, hooting at the scabs that were taking the bread from their children's mouths. The sheriff came and arrested all the women for "disturbing the peace."

I told them to take their babies and tiny children along with them when their case came up in court. . . . While the judge was sentencing them to pay thirty dollars or serve thirty days in jail, the babies set up a terrible wail so that you could hardly hear the old judge. He scowled and asked the women if they had someone to leave the children with.

I whispered to the women to tell the judge that miners' wives didn't keep nurse girls; that God gave the children to their mothers and He held them responsible for their care.

When they got to Greensburg, the women sang as the car went through the town. A great crowd followed the car, singing with them. . . .

The sheriff said to me, "Mother, I would rather you

Some politicians speak out against the Equal Rights Amendment because they say, "if women were drafted, they might make love to the enemy..." I suppose it would be worse than killing them...

The Happy Housewife Speaks Out © 1/27/74 by K. Kelly

brought me a hundred men than those women. Women are fierce!"

"I didn't bring them to you, sheriff," said I, "'twas the mining company's judge sent them to you for a present."

The sheriff took them upstairs, put them all in a room and let me stay with them for a long while. I told the women:

91

"You sing the whole night long. You can spell one another if you get tired and hoarse. Sleep all day and sing all night and don't stop for anyone. Say you're singing to the babies. I will bring the little ones milk and fruit. Just you sing and sing."

The sheriff's wife . . . used to go up and try to stop them because she couldn't sleep. Then the sheriff sent for me and asked me to stop them.

"I can't stop them," said I. "They are singing to their little ones. You telephone to the judge to order them loose."

Complaints came in by the dozens: from hotels and lodging houses and private homes.

"Those women howl like cats," said a hotel keeper to me.

"That's no way to speak of women who are singing patriotic songs and lullabies to their little ones," said I.

Finally, after five days . . . the judge ordered their release. He was a narrow-minded, irritable, savage-looking old animal and hated to do it, but no one could muzzle those women!

(from The Autobiography of Mother Jones, *1925)*

THE LADIES' ADVOCATE.

MRS. BULL. "LOR, MR. MILL! WHAT A LOVELY SPEECH YOU *DID* MAKE. I DO DECLARE I HADN'T THE SLIGHTEST NOTION WE WERE SUCH MISERABLE CREATURES. NO ONE CAN SAY IT WAS *YOUR* FAULT THAT THE CASE BROKE DOWN."

GIVE ME YOUR SISTERS AND YOUR DAUGHTERS, YOUR GIRLFRIENDS AND YOUR MOTHERS.... GIVE ME YOUR AUNTIES, YOUR GRANNYS, YOUR....

The Human-Not-Quite-Human
(EXCERPTS)

DOROTHY SAYERS

Probably no man has ever troubled to imagine how strange his life would appear to himself if it were unrelentingly assessed in terms of his maleness; if everything he wore, said, or did had to be justified by reference to female approval; if he were compelled to regard himself, day in day out, not as a member of society, but merely . . . as a virile member of society. If the center of his dress-consciousness were the cod-piece, his education directed to making him a spirited lover and meek pater-familias; his interests held to be natural only insofar as they were sexual. If from school and lecture-room, press and pulpit, he heard the persistent outpouring of a shrill and scolding voice, bidding him remember his biological function. If he were vexed by continual advice how to add a rough male touch to his typing, how to be learned without losing his masculine appeal, how to combine chemical research with education, how to play bridge without incurring the suspicion of impotence. If, instead of allowing with a smile that "women prefer cavemen," he felt the unrelenting pressure of a whole social structure forcing him to order all his goings in conformity with that pronouncement.

. . . In any book on sociology he would find, after the main portion dealing with human needs and rights, a supplementary chapter devoted to "The Position of the Male in the Perfect State." His newspaper would assist him with a "Men's Corner," telling him how, by the expenditure of a good deal of money and a couple of hours a day, he could attract the girls and retain his wife's affection; and when he had succeeded in capturing a mate, his name would be taken from him, and society would present him with a special title to proclaim his achievement. People would write books called, "History of the Male," or "Males of the Bible," or "The Psychology of the Male," and he would be regaled daily with headlines, such as "Gentleman Doctor's Discovery," "Male Secretary Wins Calcutta Sweep," "Men Artists at the Academy." If he gave an interview to a reporter, or performed any unusual exploit, he would find it recorded in such terms as these: "Professor Bract, although a distinguished botanist, is not in any way an unmanly man. He has, in fact, a wife and seven children. Tall and burly, the hands with which he handles his delicate specimens are as gnarled and powerful as those of a Canadian lumberjack, and when I swilled beer with him in his laboratory, he bawled his conclusions at me in a strong, gruff voice that implemented the promise of his swaggering moustache." Or: "There is nothing in the least feminine about the home surroundings of Mr. Focus, the famous children's photographer. His 'den' is paneled in teak and decorated with rude sculptures from Easter Island; over his austere iron bedstead hangs a fine reproduction of the Rape of the Sabines." Or: "I asked M. Sapristi, the renowned chef, whether kitchen cult was not a rather unusual occupation for a man. 'Not a bit of it!' he replied, bluffly. 'It is the genius that counts, not the sex. As they say in *la belle Ecosse,* a man's a man for a that'—and his gusty, manly guffaw blew three small patty pans from the dresser."

He would be edified by solemn discussions about "Should Men Serve in Drapery Establishments?" and acrimonious ones about "Tea-Drinking Men"; by cross-shots of public affairs, "From the Masculine Angle," and by irritable correspondence about men who expose their anatomy on beaches (so masculine of them), conceal it in dressing gowns (too feminine of them), think about nothing but women, pretend an unnatural indifference to women, exploit their sex to get jobs, lower the tone of the office by their sexless appearance, and generally fail to please a public opinion which demands the incompatible. And at dinner parties he would hear the wheedling, unctuous, predatory female voice demand: "And why should you trouble your handsome little head about politics?"

If, after a few centuries of this kind of treatment, the male was a little self-conscious, a little on the defensive, and a little bewildered about what was required of him, I should not blame him. If he traded a little upon his sex, I could forgive him. If he presented the world with a major social problem, I would scarcely be surprised. It would be more surprising if he retained any rag of sanity and self-respect.

(from Unpopular Opinions, *1947)*

WHAT WE NEED IN THE MOVEMENT IS SOME SERIOUS, DISCIPLINED THINKING. FOR EXAMPLE,

THE DICTIONARY DEFINES "CHAUVINISM" AS VAINGLORIOUS PATRIOTISM. THUS,

MALE CHAUVINISM IS MALE VAINGLORIOUS PATRIOTISM. AND,

WE ALL KNOW THE PERSONAL IS THE POLITICAL. THEREFORE,

HE UNZIPPED HIS FLY AND PULLED OUT HIS FLAG.

I Laughed When I Wrote It

NIKKI GIOVANNI

the f.b.i. came by my house three weeks ago
one white agent one black (or i guess negro would be
more appropriate) with two three-button suits on (one to
    a man)
thin ties—cuffs in the bottoms—belts at their waists
they said in unison:
    ms. giovanni you are getting to be quite important
    people listen to what you have to say
i said nothing
    we would like to have to give a different message
i said: gee are all you guys really shorter than hoover
they said:
    it would be a patriotic gesture if you'd quit saying
    you love rap brown and if you'd maybe give us some
        leads
    on what some of your friends are doing
i said: fuck you
a week later the c.i.a. came by two unisexes one blond afro
one darker one three bulges on each showing lovely bell-
    bottoms and boots
they said in rounds:
    sister why not loosen up and turn on
    fuck the system up from the inside
    we can turn you on to some groovy
    trips and you don't have to worry

about money or nothing   take the commune
    way and a few drugs it'll be good for you
    and the little one
after i finished a long loud stinky fart i said serenely
definitely though with love
    fuck you
yesterday a representative from interpol stopped me in the
    park
tall, neat afro, striped hip huggers bulging only in the right
place
    i really dig you, he said, i want to do something for you
    and you alone
i asked what he would like to do   for me
    need a trip around the world a car bigger apartment
    are you lonely i mean we need to get you comfortable
    cause a lot of people listen to you and you
    need to be comfortable to put forth a positive image
and digging the scene i said listen i would sell
out but i need to make it worth my while you understand
    you just name it and i'll give it to you, he assured me
well, i pondered, i want aretha franklin and her piano
    reduced to fit next to my electric
typewriter on my desk and i'll do anything you want
he lowered his long black eyelashes and smiled a whimsical
    smile
    fuck you, nikki, he said

(from My House, *1972)*

Feiffer

Liberation of the Yale Divinity School Library Men's Room

★★★★★★★★★★★★ ★★★★★★★★★★★★

CAROL P. CHRIST

At 10:15 on a Thursday morning a contingent of about ten graduate student women walked past the bleary-eyed men students gathered for ritual pipe-smoking and gossip in the library lounge, tacked the letters "WO" on the door of the men's room, claimed possession by placing a bouquet of plastic flowers in the urinal, and sat down. So began the historic "Liberation of the Washroom" at Yale Divinity School. The pipe-smokers awakened as they read the manifesto posted on the wall of the lounge announcing that the Babylonian Captivity* of the facility had come to an end. The women would occupy the washroom for a number of years equal to the number the men had held it, and then it would revert to joint use.

Did the men realize the hardship they would now be forced to suffer? How many times had they smirked in superiority as they watched women colleagues run three flights of stairs separating the women's room from the library lounge, the biblical reference room, the stacks, and the study cubicles? Did they perhaps imagine unknown terrors of silent humiliation when, after spending hours engrossed in an arcane text, and just having discovered the key to some ancient mystery, they would have to answer nature's call with a mad dash up the stairs? Inside the washroom, the women imagined many anxiety-free hours of study that would now be theirs—secure in the knowledge that their own toilet would be only a few steps away.

In recognition of the seriousness of the threat to male dignity posed by the occupation, the men sent a volunteer to test the women's determination. Fearlessly opening the door now marked "Women," he appealed to the occupants with notions of humanism (as opposed to separatism), and declared that he considered the room officially integrated. His oration met a wall of silence, and he cautiously retreated back to the lounge, where he reported he had seen flowers and announced his fear that the urinal would never again see use.

On his withdrawal, the women caucused and sent one of their number out to purchase a lock for the door. Secretly installing the new weapon, they awaited the next assault. It was not long in coming. They braced themselves against the door, suppressing laughter as the male recruits attempted to gain entry, first with pleading words, then with show of force. After a while the attacks subsided, and the women reduced their forces. A revolving contingent of two or three stood guard. They admitted only women throughout the day.

Late in the afternoon, just as the women inside were becoming bored with the escapade, the Dean of Yale Divinity School, sporting a white flag and bearing a peace treaty, rushed down the stairs of the library. The treaty was slipped under the door. Inside, the women noted that he gave official deanly approval to the principle of integration, couched in the liberal Christian language of "common use." He requested only that the users of the room lock the door while inside.

Although the terms did not meet their claim to just retribution for years of humiliation and outrage, the tired women reluctantly accepted the peace treaty. One of them placed the letters "Women and" on the door, and they left. Later they billed the Divinity School $1.53 for the lock. They received prompt recompense from the Dean's "indiscretionary" fund.

To this day the coveted washroom remains integrated. Word has it that the decal letters left by the women have been replaced by an official paint job. The occupation was recorded for posterity on the front page of the New Haven *Journal-Courier*, April 10, 1970, and later in *The New York Times*. Women participating in the action included Carol P. Christ, Francine Cardman, Marilyn Collins, Mary Rose D'Angelo, Margaret Farley, Kit Havice, Margaret O'Gara, Judith Plaskow, and Ann Vater.

Copyright © Carol P. Christ, 1978

*An allusion referring to the sojourn of the Jews in exile in Babylon and to Protestant Reformer Martin Luther's anti-Roman manifesto, "The Babylonian Captivity of the Church."

I SOMETIMES WONDER
IF YOU'RE THE RIGHT ONE
FOR ME TO BE SUBMISSIVE TO

✿ ✿ ✿ ✿ ✿ ✿ ✿ ✿ ✿ ✿ ✿ ✿ ✿ ✿ ✿ ✿

A man was on trial for criminally assaulting his wife. There was a profusion of evidence against him, including two eye-witnesses. Nevertheless, the jury brought back a verdict of innocent.

"What possible excuse can you have for acquitting this man?" asked the judge.

"Insanity, your Honor," replied the foreman.

"All *twelve* of you?" said the judge.

We Need a Name for Bernadette Arnold

(a coffeehouse monologue with audience participation)

JOAN D. UEBELHOER

There is a rumor afoot that I hate men. This musical will not refute that rumor, but it will give me a change to even things out by showing that there are a few women who drive me bonkers too.

Daniel What's-his-name, in a fight for a very important cause, once said: "You know you're out front when you start getting zinged from the rear."

The Rear Zinger! She sounds SO right. And you sound SO crazy. And worse yet, you begin to think that she *is* right, and you *are* crazy. She knows just how to get you, because she's a woman too. She shares your soft spots. She gets you in the age, or in the education, or in the clothes, or in the paycheck, or in the femininity, or in the body shape, or in the sexuality, or in the softest spot of all—the sanity!

We need a name, we need a name, we need a name for HER!

Only sometimes, you think you need a name for you. Because you don't like the unsisterish feelings you have. Sometimes you worry about your own feminism. Sometimes it's hard to remember we have a common enemy. Sometimes you wonder if. . . . Well, my sisters, I think that "ugly outs" are good for the soul. So let's have one. If you will help me, we have song sheets for you. When I say, "Sing A," then you sing:

Sisterhood is powerful, we will not be moved.
Sisterhood is powerful, we will not be moved.
Just like a tree that's planted by the water,
We will not be moved.

When I say, "Sing B," then you sing:

Hey! Won't you play
Another somebody-done-somebody-wrong song?
I feel so all alone, and I think I'm crazy,
And I think I'm crazy.

SCENE 1

You have been working and paining for ten years, dealing with your own liberation and sticking your neck out for women's rights. Your efforts so far have won three denials of the management job in your office. Even though you have a Master's degree, time seniority, and you've been doing the management work for a year, a new man gets the job.

You're discouraged, but then on the way home you hear that the first female Rhodes scholar has been selected. You feel great, because you and other feminists have succeeded in pushing, shoving, kicking open another brand new door for young women. Happily driving along, you sing. . . A.

In the morning you grab the paper and the coffee before the kids are up to grab you, and you read: "Karen Quisling, the first woman to receive a Rhodes scholarship, is not a women's libber, she has never in her nineteen years felt any discrimination because of her sex, and she is sure she was judged completely on her intelligence and her experience."

Sing B.

We need a name, we need a name, we need a name for HER.

SCENE 2

All of the nurses on the staff have been complaining about Dr. Scnott. He has had one of you in tears practically every day this month. At a nurses' gathering, you take the assertive lead and plan to confront him at the next staff meeting. They are all afraid. You are terrified. You tell them to support you by simply nodding their heads—after all, what could he do to the whole staff? The meeting is today. You bolster them all up, you take some deep breaths, glad you wore your slacks to hide your shaking knees. Going into the meeting, you hum. . . A.

You make your speech at an opportune time. You are calm but firm. You are neither strident nor hysterical. You describe what kind of behavior is acceptable between human beings. You tell Dr. Scnott that his behavior of the past will not be tolerated in the future.

There is absolute silence in the room. He looks stunned. Then up gets Bernadette Arnold and says in a high and shrilly voice, "Doctor, some of these girls are new and young. What they don't understand is the tension you're under—making all of those life-and-death decisions. *I* know you don't mean to be cruel—you are just soooooo important!"

He smiles. NOW the other nurses nod their heads.

Sing B.

We need a name, we need a name, we need a name for HER.

SCENE 3

You are at a committee meeting concerning personnel policies for employees. You mention that many women do not take sick days for themselves, but save them for when their children are sick. You suggest amending the sick leave policy to include immediate family members. Some of the women present look up at you. Their eyes are saying, "My God, someone else knows what it's really like." You feel a moment of togetherness. Your heart softly sings . . . A.

Then Mary Male-defined pipes up and squeaks, "Well! I never once had to take a day off for any of my four sick children. If women want to hold down men's jobs, they can't ask for special privileges. Look at me! Look at me! I'm just as good at ignoring my children as any man."

Sing B.

We need a name, we need a name, we need a name for HER.

SCENE 4

You are fifty-six years old. You are back in the job market as a Kelly Girl with your thirty-four-year-old college degree. Your boss is a year younger than your youngest son. He keeps asking you how you feel. The other women in the office seem like a junior-high class on a field trip.

You are the first one in the office each morning. You try to make friends. One Wednesday afternoon, one of the others approaches you and says, "The whole office is going to a party tonight, and . . . ."

"Wow!" you think. "*I'm* going to be included." And your lips begin to hum . . . A.

Then Harriet Hostage finishes, ". . . we're going to eat and drink and dance, so we wondered if you would mind covering for us tomorrow morning. We'll all be too hung over."

Sing B.

We need a name, we need a name, we need a name for HER.

SCENE 5

You are working in an office which requires the women to wear dresses or skirts. The coffee-maker of the week must see that the boss gets his coffee first in the morning. He never makes the coffee. You think the rules might be illegal. You think that his coffee is his own job. During your coffee week, you "forget" him two days in a row. You get a reprimand, but it results in a few of the other women saying what a baby he is. "Maybe . . . just maybe . . ." you hope as you sing . . . A.

On Friday, before you can even NOT make him the coffee, along comes Cathy Copout with coffee for the boss. Miserable in her tight shoes, her head overheated under her wig, and her skirt painfully short, she flirts loudly: "*I'll* get your coffee for you every morning, Mr. Prickness. I swear I don't know what's gotten into that uppity woman. I enjoy being beautiful. I enjoy being a girl. She must be bitter 'cause she's not pretty." Sing B.

We need a name, we need a name, we need a name for HER.

SCENE 6

You have worked as a volunteer at headquarters for years. You have encouraged women to run for public office. You have worked on their campaigns. You have been outspoken in your party in support of the ERA. In the current campaign, there are actually *six* women running. You are proud, and sing . . . A.

When the votes are counted, your county sends its first woman to the state legislature, and she votes against the ERA. The local press reports: "Olivia Off-ourbacks has not felt any discrimination because of her gender, and just wishes to be treated as one of the boys." You are boiling because Joan Gubbins is in her third term in the Indiana legislature asserting that woman's place is in the home, and you sing B.

We need a name, we need a name, we need a name for HER.

So, we bring to a close this "ugly out"—but with a message to the self-made woman, Sally Sellout; with a message to the man-made self, Rosie Ruthless; with a message to Patty Privatesolution, who thinks she made it alone; to Gloria Gamey, who thinks we have to play His game by His rules; with a message to Ethel Eagle, who uses the rights we fought for to stop our progress—to these women, we sing . . . A!

Copyright © Joan Daley Uebelhoer, 1978

"You weigh 119 pounds. Your fortune, however, depends on your own initiative."

On a Different Track

SHARON McDONALD

When it comes to sports, I have always been cordial but distant. As a child, the full extent of my athletic repertoire was the repeated climbing of a single tree, in which I would sit for hours daydreaming of an even less active adulthood. I thought that once I grew up I would be free of the daily pressures to run, sprint, jump, slide, skate, hit, and catch. I fully believed my adult years would be a fruitful time of affairs of the intellect.

Back then, women were allowed, in fact encouraged, to let their muscles atrophy in peace. But right around the time I would have begun living out my happy destiny as a sedentary grownup, the women's movement arrived. At first I naively thought this meant more choices for everybody; I could be either a chemist or a karate champion. What I didn't know then was that while the karate champion would not be expected to study chemistry on her day off, the chemist had better take up some part-time arduous sport to stay in the feminist ballgame. Only the language had changed since childhood. Yesterday's "Get your nose out of that book," had become today's "Get in touch with your body." This is one of the paradoxes of modern feminism that I still find difficult to understand: nobody tells Rosie Casals she has to edit a magazine; why do they tell me I have to jog?

I should at this point explain that I don't dislike sports just because I'm no good at them, though goddess knows that helps. But simple ineptitude is a mere embarrassment that's easily forgotten. What is *not* easily forgotten is a lifetime of sprains, strains, cuts, scrapes, bruises, lacerations, concussions, *and* temporary embarrassments. I dislike sports because I hurt myself doing them, sometimes quite badly. The only time

I can catch a ball that's hurtling straight at my unique and fragile face is when it takes my last two fingers back three inches farther than they were ever meant to bend. I can fall and chip a bone on any type of surface you've got, from grass to concrete. I think it's time for this movement to face the fact that some women were just not meant to totter four inches off the ground on blades, wheels, a foot-long slab of wood, or anything else.

Women whom I would otherwise consider caring friends have tried to get me out there into the danger zone.

"Look at you! You call yourself a dyke? *Look* at that arm, *where's the muscle?*"

"It's in my fingers, I type ninety words a —"

"You've *got* to start thinking about your health!"

"If you really care about my health, then leave me home where it's safe."

"You don't know what you're missing."

"Yes I do: pain."

It doesn't help that Louise is on the side of the athletes in this. One balmy evening, when she and I were in the first glow of newfound love, she chanced to ask what sports I enjoyed. When I said none, that lovely period of idealized romance passed forever into history. Some people are so judgmental.

Louise's childhood had been a whirlwind journey from championship this to championship that. From a modest beginning at prizewinning marbles, she went on to conquer her neighborhood at baseball, ping pong, basketball, skating, and so on. She once remarked to me what an easy transition it had been to go from G.A.A. (Girls' Athletic Association) to G.A.A. (Gay Activist Alliance), without even changing t-shirts.

By now, all I can say is that it's a wonder I have retained my sweet disposition and tolerant, loving, giving, accepting attitude through all this. If in the name of woman-power my lover and friends want to take their level of conversation to the absorption capacities of different brands of sweat socks, I'd be the last person in the world to suggest that it's a step down. I would never imply that there might be a better way to spend their time than chasing a ball and browbeating others into doing the same. I mean, if I let a little disagreement with my sisters over their becoming competitive overachievers turn me into an unsupportive name-caller, well, where would our movement be?

As for Louise and me, we have made a peace of sorts by discovering a physical activity we can do together. Although it is more private than a jog around the local park, I will say that it has satisfied both our wants by providing exercise, sweat, and exhaustion while not requiring a trip to the emergency room. Till something better comes along, this will do just fine.

THE BATHROOM DOOR AT THE LAVENDER LAV
Lesbian Graffiti

Tell me do mixed marriages really work?
—MAXINE FELDMAN

Are you a practicing lesbian?
No, this is about as good as I get!
—STACEY FRANCHILD

If you think lesbians are revolting YOU'RE RIGHT!
—Jes

LIBERATED WOMEN FUCK ~~BEST~~ ~~worst~~ ~~each other~~ WHOMEVER THEY WANT!

Guys don't make passes At girls who love lasses.
LESBIA

Some of my best friends are men.
Yes, but would you want your sister to MARRY one?
—LIZ MOORE

My mother made me a lesbian. If I gave her the material, would she make me one too?

A WOMAN WITHOUT A MAN IS LIKE A FISH WITHOUT A BICYCLE
—FLO KENNEDY

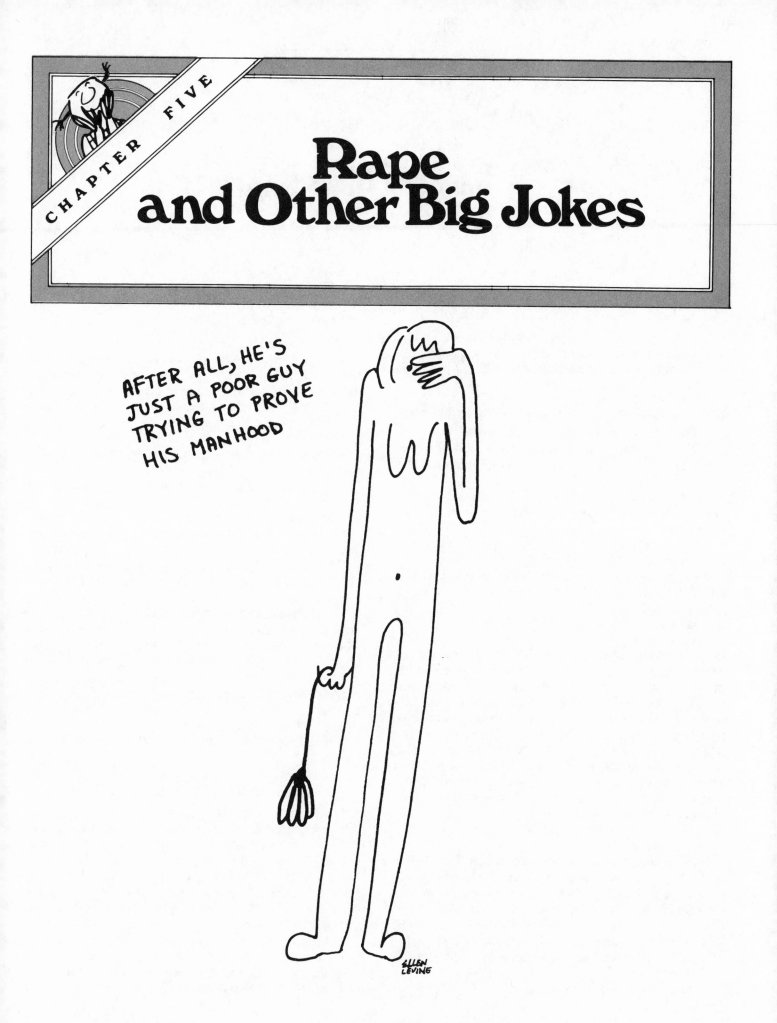

The Saturday Night Special:
Rape and Other Big Jokes

NAOMI WEISSTEIN

Sometimes, I gotta be alone. Play the stereo as loud as I want. Don't have to talk to anybody. Take a nice hot bath. Light the candle, burn the incense . . . .

. . . smoke the dope.
So I'm sitting in the bathtub, eating a bowl of cornflakes and peanut butter and smoking and saying to myself,
"This is okay. This is okay. Pretty soon I'm even gonna fill this tub with WATER" when all of a sudden, I hear
A Creak!
I run to the window, and there's nobody there. Lucky I wasn't wet.
Okay, I'm sitting in the bathtub again when I hear
Another creak!
So I run to the door, and there's nobody there. Then I inch along the wall to the window and I lift a little tiny piece of curtain.
And there's still nobody there.
Do you know why?
Because they're all diving into the bushes, that's why. You see, every rapist in the state of New York is outside my house that night. Tall ones, short ones, ones with undescended testicles, ones with one testicle descended, ones with two, five with three, transplants, prostheses, puss-ridden—Raincoats! You've never seen so many raincoats in your *life*. There are some raincoats without people in them, that's how bad it is. You know, raincoats are usually tan? Well, these are white! And stiff! And they creak when they walk!
And not one of them is wearing pants.
Just black socks, hairy legs, and raincoats.
I gotta take measures.
Lemme see. The door's double-locked, but there's the police lock, and the padlock, and the chain at the bottom, and the two-by-fours one for the top, one for the middle, one for the bottom, and the record of the Doberman, barking, broken glass for the window sills, I'll heat up some cauldrons of boiling water and, and—I'll take the table legs and make a circle of fire outside the house!
I take my bath and go to sleep.

Four o'clock in the morning I hear a creak.
This is a real creak.

This is no doper's creak.
This is a creak for which the creaker should be proud, this is—Shit! Somebody's in my house! So I grab my flame thrower and my Eddie Bauer survival knife and my baseball bat and my teargas bomb and my teddy bear and we run into the living room and
THERE HE IS!
Smegma, the archetypal rapist. Smegma with the shake-and-bake face.
This guy's so ugly, they *make* him wear the nylon stocking over his face.
"How did you get in here?"
He answers me. "Mrrgh grbrnghrmm grwmkjhlkmm mrrghaaa . . . ."
"The chimney? You came in through the chimney?"
Shit! I forgot to stuff the chimney with rags soaked in mustard gas.
They're right. I must've been asking for it. Hence, the Smegma problem. How to get rid of a man in a nylon stocking who got in through the chimney, sounds like a broken dinosaur, can't play chess, and won't watch TV.
I know of only one surefire solution: Drool. Heavy drool.
(Proceed to drool.)
The only thing that'll turn them off: drool on them.

I had a friend who did that once. She used to ride the subway from the beginning of the line in Brooklyn to 241st Street in the Bronx at four in the morning, and nobody bothered her. She'd sit there, rolling her head from side to side and drooling. By the time she got to Manhattan, she'd have the whole car to herself. People would try to jam in at Times Square, but they'd slip and slide on the drool.
But drooling isn't easy.
It's tough.
Your clothes are soaking, and you catch the flu
(To tune of "Old Man River"):

"Your clothes are soaking and you catch the flu
And you've got these drool stains over you. . . ."
(Chorus):
> *But keep on drooling, yes keep on drooling*
> *You must keep drooling, droo droo droo*
> *drooling"*

And you feel like you gotta explain the drool stains to the dry cleaners.

"Oh no, fella, my dog did that. No, honest. Really, it wasn't me, it was my dog. My dog does that to ward off the hounds. I mean the wolves. The hounds *and* the wolves. And the turkeys.

It makes my dog look like a real dog.

3. The Smegma Problem, Part 2

When are they going to make a movie without a rape scene?

My friend called the other night and asked if I wanted to see "The Young Meat Eaters" at Cinemas 6 through 27. I told her no. No rapes on *my* money. Then another friend called and asked if I wanted to see "Les Jeunes Mangeres de Biftek" at the Cinema 28 through 72. Still no. Then I turned on the tube. Guess what was playing?

Chuck Steak.

OK, here's the plot. There's the hero, right, he's lean and mean. Chuck Steak. Chuck Steak. That's his buddy's name, too. And the head of The Division. They're all named Chuck Steak.

And his luck's just run out.
He was a pro.
You're never told at what.
Getting on and off airplanes.
He was the best there was.

He works for an outfit called Bleed, also the best there is. That is, he was working for an outfit called Bleed until his superior, evil Robert Devane, shot him thirteen times in the head, legs, and chest. That was when they were both in Trinidad, you're never told why. He tries to recover in a Port-of-Spain hospital with overhead fans, Chinese orderlies, and a blind cook who knows everything, but it looks rough. He's got gangrene in the head, legs, and chest. He looks *awful.*

He's contemplating stuffing the runoff on his dialysis machine when in walks

sultry and tormented
Shakira Caine,
your all-races native beauty.

She immediately begins to tremble.

"Oh, I am sorry," she whispers. "I bringing mangoes to my mother."

"Don't be frightened," he says, but the chemistry is too much. He has to rape her. It's his last chance for life. For happiness.

At first she struggles feebly. But ecstasy overtakes her. This is what she has been waiting for! An ex-con in a basket without head, legs, or chest! What else could you want? There *must* be a God.

Big rape scene:
Heavy breathing. Glistening skin. Thrashing and moaning.

Drums pulsate in the narrow alleys.
Third world noises: Ayee! Macouba! Quick!
The earth moves for them.
The blind cook breaks an egg over his head.

Then the Mormon Tabernacle Choir begins to sing "Amazing Grace," and—wait—no—what is this? A star? A star in the night sky? Shepherds leaving their flocks? Wise men with gifts?

But now the blinding crimson sun begins to rise. It is morning.

And in the morning—in the morning
The Gangrene is Gone!
The legs are strong!
The chest is strong!

His body is whole!

Chuck Steak has recovered!
Shakira has recovered!
Shakira's mother has recovered!

She is happy! Secrets of her womanhood have been unlocked! Mangoes are strewn on the floor! Tropical birds flutter overhead! Monkeys chatter in the trees! The dialysis machine is wheeled out. You want miracles? Here's miracles!

The rape was a success.

4. The Smegma Problem, Part 3

Big rapes and little rapes. It starts when we're kids. Uncle Solly's looking at you.

He's also drooling. (That's where you picked up the habit.)

And he's saying:

"Cute? Is that one cute? . . . A little angel! Come sit on Uncle Solly's lap, and let him look at you!"

You start out of the room.

"No, come here."

"Uncle Solly, try looking at me from the kitchen."

"C'mon. Come here. Be a good girl."

"I can't Uncle Solly. I gotta go throw up."

5. The Smegma Problem, Part 4

So it starts when we're little girls, and it continues until we die. It probably continues after we're dead. Here's the scene. We're lying in our coffin, and it's the day we forgot to change our underpants, so, just like our mother said, that's the day we're in the fatal car accident.

Cause and effect, right?

"This is State Trooper Nigawski reminding you that— Soiled Underpants Cause Traffic Accidents"

and people are filing by our coffin, tears streaming down their faces, saying,

"Just as I thought. Soiled underpants"

and this turkey leans down, real close, and goes

"(psst) Hey, corpse."

It could happen.

You know what people would say?

"Girlie! Behave yourself! You're dead!"

6. Behave myself? Like it's my fault!

Everything that happens to us is supposed to be our fault. That's what it means to grow up female.

"It's raining."

"I'm sorry."

"You should be."

If some little boy calls you a dirty word, it's your fault. You shouldn't have been wearing your snowsuit. And those mittens? Hot stuff!

Of course, you can't use those words yourself. Most of the words in the English language you can't use when you're growing up female.

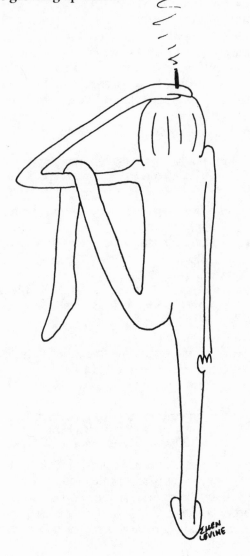

THERE MUST BE A DIFFERENCE BETWEEN
"SHE WAS ASKING FOR IT" AND
"ALL SHE REALLY NEEDS…"

Like——breasts.

That's a really hard thing to say when you're a teenage girl. My mother used to make me go to the butcher shop to get chicken breasts. I'd do *anything* to get out of that.

"I'll wash the dishes?"

"Twice is enough in one day, Naomi. They're probably clean."

"I'll spray the cockroaches."

"Don't do that! It'll make them mad!"

Anything, anything but going for chicken breasts.

The butcher is around the corner. I circle the store for twenty minutes. My friend comes up:

"Hello, Naomi. I see you're in the holding pattern! Chicken breasts for dinner tonight again, huh?"

And when I walk into the store it's high noon. Deserted. After the bomb. Just me and the butcher. The last two people on earth. And the butcher's looking at me.

I have this plan.

I go down the aisles, looking for the swollen cans, the ones with botulism. I pick up the Bon Vivant Vichyssoise. Just as I thought. Swollen. I make a small puncture. It explodes. And as it goes

Pcchhhhhhhh. . . .

I run to the butcher and say, "Gimme four chicken breasts they're not for me they're for a friend."

The butcher says, "Wadja say?"

Oh god. What do I do now?

"Gimme uh um a pound of beef liver. . .one chuck roast. . .twelve lamb chops. . .you got any kidneys? I mean *fresh* kidneys. . .and four uh four uh four. . . four. . .hamburgers! That's it, hamburgers! What? You don't have any hamburger meat? Well. . .grind it up from chicken breasts!"

"Do what?"

"Grind up the hamburger meat from chicken breasts?"

"Chicken breasts!" He begins to smile. I'll always remember that smile. The butcher's benign smile. "Chicken breasts! So you want chicken breasts! Whyn't you say so, honey? What size? Thirty-six D?"

"No, I don't want chicken breasts, I want hamburger meat, 32 A."

7. The Smegma Problem, Part 5

Is there any place you're safe? I used to think you'd be safe in a Jewish delicatessen. I had this fantasy, see. I'm walking down the street, and, as usual, my head's a little bit to one side, because I won't look guys directly in the face or they'll think I want it, and I won't look down at their pants or they'll *know* I want it, so I'm looking at their necks.

So I'm walking down the street, and all these necks are going by.

And this one particular neck is getting closer and closer and closer until finally it's a really close neck,

IF ALL WOMEN SECRETLY
WANT TO BE RAPED,

YOU'RE NOT A REAL WOMAN
IF YOU DON'T WANT TO BE
RAPED.

BUT SINCE
YOU ALWAYS GET
WHAT YOU REALLY WANT,

and this close neck says:

"Nice out."

(Startled) "Aaaaagh! Go away! Aaaagh! Whadja say?"

"Nice out."

This time, I'm cool. I don't answer.

"I said, Nice Out!"

"So?"

"So, I think I'll keep it out."

Then I look slowly from his neck . . . down to his pants, and sure enough, it is out—

"Pigdogcrudprick fascist monkey sexist pig excrescence . . . You Turkey! Put that thing back in your pants or I'm gonna calla cop."

"I am a cop."

"Somebody help me."

"In New York somebody help you? Are you kidding?"

So I start running, he starts running after me, I'm screaming for help, nobody looks up, this one dude in a red velvet caftan joins us for a while, real spacey, saying,

"Far out! Far out! I gotta be *in* this movie" and the three of us are running along, I'm screaming, and then, suddenly—

What is looming up in front of me like the Red Sea parting and Noah sending down a ladder as the floodwaters rise? A Jewish delicatessen! (Sing "Hatikvah.") Safety! Didn't my Lord deliver Daniel? Two thousand years of wandering are over! Who would rape you in a Jewish delicatessen, with the Gefüllte fish, and the Chalveh, and the racks of salami? Why those great phallic salamis hanging there should be enough to humble any man. Not to mention the salami *in slices*.

So you run into the Jewish delicatessen yelling,

"Sanctuary! Sanctuary!"

And these refugees from Nazi Germany working behind the counter pretend they don't hear you because they don't want to get involved.

Finally, somebody says to you,

"Lady, get outta my store. You're scaring away the customers!"

"I'm scaring away the customers? *I'm* scaring away the customers? There's creeps all over this place. They're under the whitefish, on top of the sturgeon, they're crawling out of the pickle barrels, they're doing Tarzans from the salami racks, and you're telling me *I'm* scaring away the customers?"

MAYBE I SECRETLY
DON'T WANT TO BE
A WOMAN.

IF I HAVEN'T
BEEN RAPED,

I'VE GOT TO FIND A SHRINK
TO HELP ME GET RAPED.

105

Early in the women's movement, I was into being really ugly. Not just ordinary ugly: hideous. Grotesque. I wished I had scars all over my face and no hair—except on my lip. I wished I was built like an eight-foot tank (which I still wish)—a spectacular, hairy eight-foot tank with pimples and giant treads. It was about the same time I was taking karate, and yelling,

"Fuck you!"
at hissing men.

I was walking with a friend of mine on Third Avenue and Thirteenth Street, which is a rough neighborhood, but this is the middle of the day, and this guy passes and says:

"Wanna fuck?"

So I get mad. I get mad! What did I expect him to say?

"Why, Doctor Weisstein! What a pleasant surprise to find you here on Third Avenue and Thirteenth Street in the middle of the day!"

"Well, Sir, I don't immediately recognize you—what did you say you do?"

"Pimp! I pimp for the entire neighborhood. Wanna fuck?"

No, this guy cuts out the preliminaries. He just says, "Wanna fuck?" and I turn around and tell him to go fuck himself. Now here's where the magic of words comes in. He's just asked me if I wanted to fuck, and so I turn around and tell him to fuck *himself*.

I'm offering him an alternative.

No, I don't want to fuck but you could always fuck yourself, you know.

I mean, I'm giving him this liberating option. It's a new thing. Fuck yourself, when and where you want it. No embarrassing long silences, no don't touch me unless you love me, no nasty problems with V.D.

So you'd think he'd thank me for this suggestion, which will clearly improve his life, but no, he goes berserk. I used a word reserved for men alone.

So we face off, and he's screaming at me,

"Fuck me? Fuck you. Fuck me? Fuck you. Fuck me? Fuck you."

And I'm standing there thinking: this guy's going to *hit* me, he's going to attack me, and I'm trying to re-

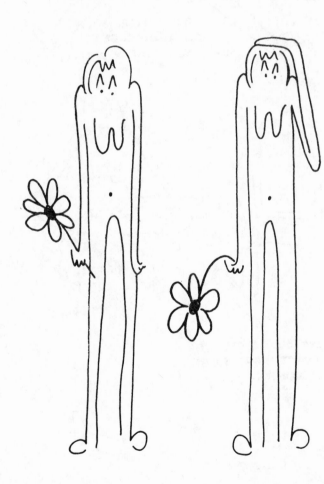

(MAYBE THE COP WAS RIGHT—

THE RAPIST AND I WERE REALLY MADE FOR EACH OTHER.

AFTER ALL, HE'S JUST A POOR GUY TRYING TO PROVE HIS MANHOOD

AND I'M JUST A POOR GIRL WHO NEEDED A GOOD ...)

member what karate position you're supposed to take *(get into karate position)* when your partner hasn't bowed to you first and said a couple of words in fake Japanese.

And while the thought is still going through my head—this guy's going to hit me—I'm already on the ground. I mean, that fast. The problem is, they didn't bring me up to be a Marine, a killer, and two years of karate isn't enough to give you the street reflexes you need to be able to say "fuck you" to passing creeps with impunity.

So I'm on the ground.

My friend starts yelling. I look up. She's got him in a hold. I pick myself off the street and hit him a couple of times. He yells for us to let him go. So this is what we do:

We let him go.

Killers! We're real killers!

Lemme go! Lemme go. Oh, you wanna go? Sure! Here! Go!

He runs about three yards, stops, turns around, faces us again, and says:

"Wanna fuck?"

"No. Go fuck yourself."

Then he does this. . . . He reaches like this. Now, what would you do if you'd just been in a little friendly scuffle, and you had any reflexes at all? I'd tell you what I'd do: I'd get outta there fast. No, we just stood around, jumping from side to side, suggesting liberating alternatives.

What did we think was in his pocket? Kahlil Gibran?

He's going to read to us from *The Prophet.*

Love Thy Neighbor. Wanna Fuck?

He's looking for a dime, that's what he's doing. He's going to call Ann Landers.

"Hello, Hello, Ann Landers? I made a terrible mistake! What can I do to win back her affection and respect? Sincerely yours, Urgent on the Streets of New York."

As you see, I'm still here to tell the tale.

So it wasn't a complete disaster. He went for his pocket, and he took out his comb. And he began combing his hair and strutting off.

"If only my hair had been in place," he's saying to himself, "then they would have wanted to fuck."

9.

I want to end this Saturday Night Special with a little routine on the question of hating men. See, somebody here might have gotten the idea that this was a man-hating routine, and I wouldn't want *anybody* to think such a *terrible* thing about me. When they find out that you're a "libber" and they tell you that they could go along with equal pay if you could *do* a man's job, and, and, anything you women want, but—some of you libbers hate *men* and then a silence like death descends and a few people vomit and the rest pass out because nobody can think of a greater crime against nature than

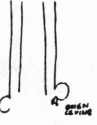

hating men. It's like hating God. It *is* hating God.

It's fine to hate women.

You're manly if you hate women. You can make millions, write for *The New York Times* Sunday Magazine section, be a Great Thinker of the Western World if you really hate them enough. But hating men? A Crime Against Nature.

Whereas, we know that the real crimes against nature are the crimes of violence against women that take place every day in every part of this country. Because you know,

You *know* when you pick up the paper and you see the headline:

Sex Crime! See! Read! This Will Really Disgust You!

You know it isn't some poor, unfortunate six-foot Marine who happened to wander down the wrong street—the one with the women's center on it—and got raped, castrated, and cut up into little pieces, wrapped in newspaper, and stuffed into a garbage can by some small, sincere, man-hating woman.

So, it's a one-sided thing. It's a thing against women. It's not a sex war, it's a rout, we're losing, and we're losing big. And we've got to stop that. We're not exactly advocating turning six-foot Marines into hamburger (or chicken breasts); we're talking about stopping a system that feeds itself on violence, on blood, on our blood.

We're going to stop that system; that's our salute to rape.

How to Avoid Rape

Don't go out without clothes—that encourages men. Don't go out *with* clothes—any clothes encourage some men. Avoid childhood—some rapists are turned on by the very young. Avoid old age—some rapists prefer older women. Don't have a father, grandfather, uncle, or brother—these are the relatives who most often rape young women. Don't marry—rape is legal within marriage. To be *quite* sure, don't exist!

(Saskatoon WL Newsletter, July 1974)

"Now, honey, tell us again about this alleged rape."

CHAPTER SIX

Laboring Under False Assumptions

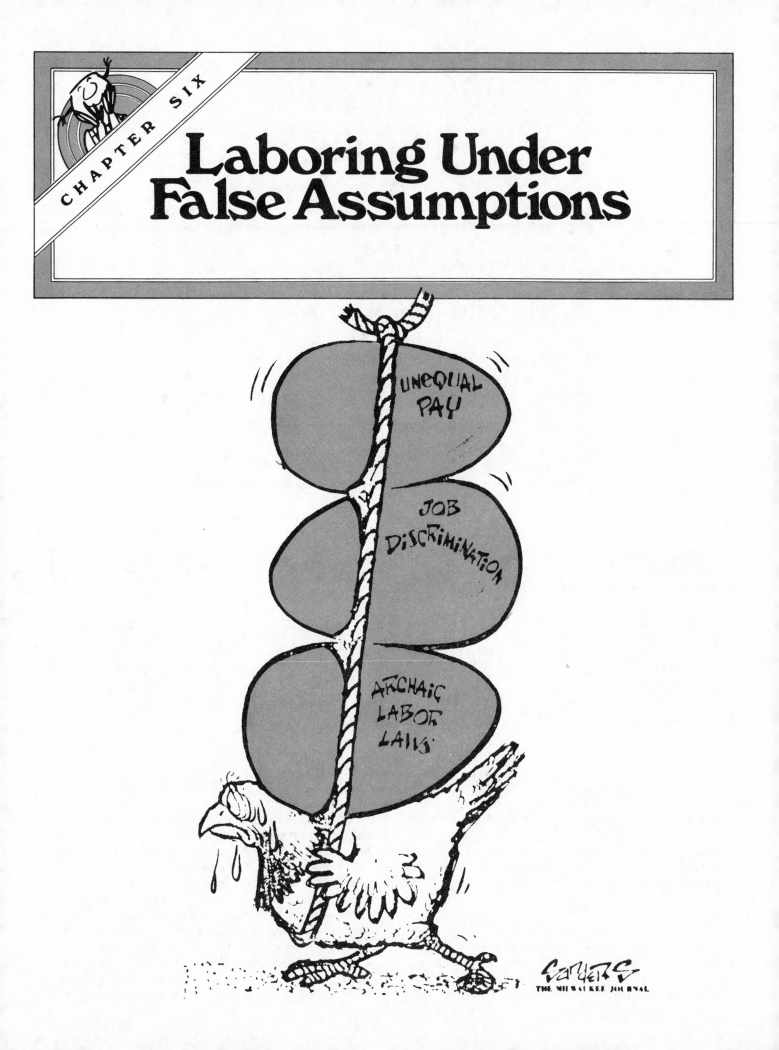

A Great Satisfaction

DOROTHY SAYERS

There has never been any question but that the women of the poor should toil alongside their men. No angry, and no compassionate voice has been raised to say that women should not break their backs with harvest work, or soil their hands with blacking grates and peeling potatoes. The objection is only to work that is pleasant, exciting, or profitable—the work that any human being might think it worthwhile to do. The boast, "My wife doesn't need to soil her hands with work," first became general when the commercial middle classes acquired the plutocratic and aristocratic notion that the keeping of an idle woman was a badge of superior social status. Man must work, and woman must exploit his labor. What else are they there for? And if a woman submits, she can be cursed for her exploitation; and if she rebels, she can be cursed for competing with the male; whatever she does will be wrong, and that is a great satisfaction.

(from Unpopular Opinions, *1947)*

B.C.   by johnny hart

The Aroma of "Miss"

VIRGINIA WOOLF

[The following excerpt from Three Guineas *investigates the reasons why female civil servants are paid less, promoted less, and disappear altogether from top-level administration.]*

. . . it is quite possible that the name "Miss" transmits through the board or division some vibration which is not registered in the examination room. "Miss" transmits sex; and sex may carry with it an aroma. "Miss" may carry with it the swish of petti-coats, the savor of scent or other odor perceptible to the nose on the further side of the partition and obnoxious to it. What charms and consoles in the private house may distract and exacerbate in the public office. The Archbishops' Commission assures us that this is so in the pulpit. Whitehall may be equally susceptible. At any rate since Miss is a woman, Miss was not educated at Eton or Christchurch. Since Miss is a woman, Miss is not a son or a nephew. We are hazarding our way among imponderables. We can scarcely proceed too much on tiptoe. We are trying, remember, to discover what flavor attaches itself to sex in a public office; we

are sniffing most delicately not facts but savors. And therefore it would be well not to depend on our own private noses, but to call in evidence from outside. Let us turn to the public press and see if we can discover from the opinions aired there any hint that will guide us in our attempt to decide the delicate and difficult question as to the aroma, the atmosphere that surrounds the word "Miss" in Whitehall. We will consult the newspapers.

First:

I think your correspondent . . . correctly sums up this discussion in the observation that woman has too much liberty. It is probable that this so-called liberty came with the war, when women assumed responsibilities so far unknown to them. They did splendid service during those days. Unfortunately, they were praised and petted out of all proportion to the value of their performances.

That does very well for a beginning. But let us proceed:

I am of the opinion that a considerable amount of the distress which is prevalent in this section of the community [the clerical] could be relieved by the policy of employing men instead of women, wherever possible. There are today in Government offices, post offices, insurance companies, banks and other offices, thousands of women doing work which men could do. At the same time there are thousands of qualified men, young and middle-aged, who cannot get a job of any sort. There is a large demand for woman labor in the domestic arts, and in the process of re-grading a large number of women who have drifted into clerical service would become available for domestic service.

The odor thickens, you will agree.
Then once more:

I am certain I voice the opinion of thousands of young men

when I say that if men were doing the work that thousands of young women are now doing the men would be able to keep those same women in decent homes. Homes are the real places of the women who are now compelling men to be idle. It is time the Government insisted upon employers giving work to more men, thus enabling them to marry the women they cannot now approach.

There! There can be no doubt of the odor now. The cat is out of the bag; and it is a Tom.

After considering the evidence contained in those three quotations, you will agree that there is good reason to think that the word "Miss," however delicious its scent in the private house, has a certain odor attached to it in Whitehall which is disagreeable to the noses on the other side of the partition; and that it is likely that a name to which "Miss" is attached will, because of this odor, circle in the lower spheres where the salaries are small rather than mount to the higher spheres where the salaries are substantial. As for "Mrs.," it is a contaminated word; an obscene word. The less said about that word the better. Such is the smell of it, so rank does it stink in the nostrils of Whitehall, that Whitehall excludes it entirely. In Whitehall, as in heaven, there is neither marrying nor giving in marriage.

Odor then—or shall we call it "atmosphere"?—is a very important element in professional life; in spite of the fact that like other important elements it is impalpable. It can escape the noses of examiners in examination rooms, yet penetrate boards and divisions and affect the senses of those within . . . .

(from Three Guineas, *1938)*

Marginal Workers

(EXCERPTS)

HADLEY V. BAXENDALE, M.D., Ph.D.*

. . . we men have nothing to fear. Women can't qualify for our good jobs, since we deprive them of the necessary training. The menial jobs most women will be offered are jobs no self-respecting man would want. Feminine breakthroughs will produce upheaval only on the economic margin. The real worry—in short—is that women will take jobs away from dogs.

Already, a great many highly skilled dogs have found themselves out of work. These are dogs who are specially trained to do detective work, to serve as guides for the blind or companions for the old, to help with lab experiments, to function as bodyguards, athletes, shepherds' assistants. Women have displaced them. Indeed, liberated women appear ready to usurp entire career fields traditionally reserved for dogs. Once content with jobs as maids or laundresses, women now train for social work, police work, animal husbandry, and medical research . . . .

They are driving dogs out into unhappiness and unemployment, forcing them to stay idly at home all day—shedding hair and panting softly. In certain communities, the dog layoffs are enormous, and the dogs themselves are increasingly upset. They roam the streets, befoul the sidewalks, invade the supermarkets, paw the lettuces. Some dogs are turning violent, delinquent, even rabid. Guard dogs are attacking their owners and leading bandits to the secret jewels. Courier dogs are intercepting private messages. Saint Bernards are drinking the brandy themselves and leaving babies in the snow.

The tragedy is that dogs need jobs more than women do. Many dogs depend desperately on jobs for their upkeep and status. But above all—and unlike women—dogs *must* have jobs in order to feel that they really belong.

Recently, I conducted a poll of dogs, to add their views on Women's Lib to all the others that have been expressed.

My first subject was Feydeau, four, a suave French poodle and playwright. Feydeau had learned to say twenty words in order to qualify for the support spot on a television talk show. Then the network had hired a woman instead. In our interview, Feydeau uttered all twenty of his words, to wit: "Who is always the first to go when cutbacks occur? The poodle. Who gets clipped at every turn? You said it. The poodle. Who gets kicked? Who gets arf arf arf . . . ."

I subsequently discovered, in meetings with lap dogs, collies and spaniels, that the fate of poodles is typical. I also discovered that Feydeau is not the world's *only* talking dog. (Obviously, this greatly eased my polling task.) "Men prefer to hear us bay and growl," a bloodhound explained, "just as they prefer to hear women giggle and flatter them. That's what

*Pseudonym for Joyce Wood. See footnote p. 24.

"I'm home. . . ."

they want, and that's what they get. But don't think we aren't all capable of something better."

In all of my research, I did not talk to a single dog who favored Women's Lib. A German shepherd complained: "It's unnatural. Women aren't cut out for guard work. Look at them! They've only got two legs! Their sense of smell is terrible."

Dogs resent women deeply. "We used to be treated just like women. We were sent to finishing school, as they were, to learn to serve and amuse our masters. We sat when men said 'sit.' We licked men's hands. We came when they called us. We had the same rights and duties as women. Now, all of a sudden, they think they're better than we are."

A bulldog told me: "We were treated *better* than women. We were taken out every day. There are a lot of men who take their dogs out twice a day, who never take their women out at all."

Reproachfully, a beagle added: "For years, we've been fetching men's slippers, chasing after the silly sticks they throw, fawning, giving them adoring sycophantic looks, catering to all their kinky whims and power complexes. For what?"

It is true that dogs have made extraordinary sacrifices to get ahead. Some have had to sleep with men or give their bodies to science. Women, of course, claim that their experiences are similar . . . .

(from Are Children Neglecting Their Mothers? *1974)*

"Pride, smide, Emerson. For the sake of the firm I suggest you get in line and find out what she knows."

113

There was a rumor that Secretary of Commerce Juanita Kreps was hiring only women. She put the record straight: "We are making every effort to find qualified males." In a pinch, she further directed, "Never mind the standards . . . hire men in more than token numbers."

"This is our experimental physics laboratory, this is
our X-007 data-processing center, and this is our woman."

Letter to the Editor

Joan Daley Uebelhoer, Allen County auditor, responds to charges of "reverse discrimination":

To the Editor:

Wednesday, Jan. 4, the *Journal-Gazette* carried a letter from G. Edgar in which she/he suggested that the auditor's office "has only a few male employees." She/he further stated that "another county office, also held by a woman, has absolutely no male employees."

Because I do not have Mrs./Miss/Mr. Edgar's address, I will respond in the public forum. I welcome the opportunity.

First of all G. Edgar, I must praise you for your attention to the hiring practices of this office and the other county offices. I have, for three years, tried desperately to bring the plight of the clerical workers in the county to the public's attention. It is heartwarming to know there is one taxpayer who has heard my cries for help.

You are right, G. Edgar, there is a paucity of males in the work force of the county clerical offices. We have tried, however. We have had several here but they always move on. One left to be a waiter in a bar; one left to be a telephone operator; one left because his wife was transferred to Philadelphia; one left because his wife was expecting a child; one left because he got married and his wife wanted him to stay home and be a total man. The turnover has been devastating.

I know that, in the interest of affirmative action, we should have a certain percentage of men in our employ in the clerical offices. We do, however, face some problems in finding qualified ones. And our affirmative action plan clearly states that we do not lower our standards to hire them. We have sent notices out through the usual channels to alert groups where they can expect to be found: the Rotary Club, Lions Clubs, the Kiwanis Clubs, the Chamber of Commerce, the Jaycees and the Knights of Columbus. We have posted notices of job openings on the bulletin boards at the Summit Club, in the locker rooms at the country clubs, and at the YMCA. I have interviewed many males, but mostly, G. Edgar, I find that they simply lack the ability to live on $7,000 per year. Most of them, although I know it is dangerous to generalize, expect to be paid for overtime

"Now I found out what they meant by an average 7% raise—clerical workers got 5% and all the others 9%."

hours. Most of them expect to be able to work their way up to being heads of departments. Most of them expect to receive raises each year commensurate with the cost of living increases. Most of them, like this year, for instance, would rather have had the $1,000 raises instead of the 10 percent that all clerical workers received. (And 10 percent of $7,000 is not $1,000.)

We would be glad to offer seminars to help males become adept at the work in clerical positions. We could teach them how to type and how to answer to "girl" or "honey" or "hey, you." We could teach them how to make coffee. We could teach them how to run a copy machine and how to staple their own papers together. We find these skills lacking. And we feel these are learned traits—not genetic deficiencies.

I would like to have a good male secretary...one who would make all those appointments for my children for

"This is an Equal Opportunity machine. It will also work when MEN push the copy button."

the dentist and the doctor. One who would pick out a lovely Christmas present for my husband, one I could take to lunch and tell my troubles to.

Thank you, G. Edgar, for your interest and your concern. We are trying. Perhaps with the new awareness among young people they will be throwing off the old sex roles. Perhaps there will be a time in the future when we will be able to find young men who are trained to live on meager incomes year after year with no upward mobility.

I probably won't see it in my lifetime, G. Edgar, but I am an incurable optimist. With people like you who are concerned—and with the hope of a coming generation filled with humble, submissive young men, I just know that the day of solution and therefore of equality will come. Someday, G. Edgar, I envision county offices filled with men working for $7,000 per year and loving it.

JOAN D. UEBELHOER

A Writer's Interview with Herself

MARY ELLMANN

The general nature of this book was discussed in an interview conducted, several months ago, at the National Institute of Interviews, Lake Norman, New Mexico. It seems convenient now to reproduce the exchange as a reader's guide to all that follows. It also seems convenient to abbreviate Interviewer and my name as: I and ME. M. E.

I.   Do you need any particular environment in which to work?

ME.   I like a room without a view, preferably a closet. Oddly enough, I've never worked in the attic. The front of our attic has a view, you see, and then the back part is jammed with old toys.

I.   Do you need seclusion?

ME.   I wish I could say I'd been locked in a room. It's pedestrian not to have a tyrannical husband. My work is, in this way, deprived of pathetic circumstance.

I.   Never mind, perhaps you have a writer's costume.

ME.   Only a navy blue woolen bathrobe. An effortlessly drab garment, I hate answering the phone in it. But I just don't have any faded dungarees or open-necked sport shirts. They're for men.

I.   They're for men?

ME.   They're for men.

I.   I see. Well, speaking of men, could you explain why you are writing about women?

ME.   I didn't want to overreach. Right from the start I thought: ME, you must limit yourself to *half* of the human race.

I.   Then you were not prompted by feminism?

ME.   Please.

I.   Oh. Feminism is out, isn't it?

ME.   Well, yes, in the way principles all go out before they're practiced.

I.   . . . Now tell me, is your work concerned with the status of American women?

ME.   You make everything sound like a symposium.

I.   Forgive me once again. Nonetheless, a good deal of work has been done on this subject. And it looks as though their status is slipping.

ME.   I applaud this work. I deplore this slipping.

I.   But have you studied the statistics on it?

ME.   You touch on a personal matter which I am of course willing to reveal to the public. My internist has asked me to cut down gradually on my consumption of statistics about American women.

I.   Why?

ME.   It's sort of sad. Say I read that only nineteen American women became orthodontists in 1962. I am humiliated, depressed. I cry easily. It's days before I think to be glad that so few *wanted* to be orthodontists, do you see?

"The lady of the house is out wheeling and dealing."

116

"When I said, 'Go ahead, start a new career,' I had no idea you'd go after my job!"

I.   I think so. You like only statistics of success.

ME.   Perhaps. But I think it's worse than that. I am afflicted by miscomprehension, the failures often seem to me successes. For example, we know exactly how many American women interrupted their husbands' anecdotes at dinner parties in 1966. Quite a few, as a matter of fact—204,648 wives. But of course just to *count* them is to say they have failed at the table. This complicated thing, interruption, is made quite simply bad. And yet all dialogue, like you and me, might be defined as the prevention of monologue. And think of the other guests—how can we hope that they wanted to hear the husbands out? Perhaps these wives are socialists who place the liveliness of the party before their own favor with their husbands.

I.   I think perhaps you might say *Yes* or *No* for a while again.

ME.   Or think of the official successes. I am afraid of the ideal unions toward which counselors propel us. You take an intolerable man and an intolerable woman and put them in an apartment together, and then if they are both *mature,* and each tries to *understand* the other's monstrous nature, a *good marriage* results.

I.   It cannot be wrong to urge understanding.

ME.   No, it must be right in social work. But in nov-

els, say, misunderstanding reasserts itself. Its resilience is apparent, and one feels a grudging admiration for resilience, the admiration one might feel for a viral strain which all the aspirin in the world won't eradicate.

I.   Then really, you relish confusion—or even sore throats.

ME.   I said it was a grudging admiration. There's an enormous number of opinions about women, and I will admit I'm impressed by the regularity and the intensity with which they are expressed. Some are more plausible than others, but their plausibility or implausibility isn't so much the point. It's their *reiteration.*

I.   Perhaps an example.

ME.   With pleasure. In the novel *The Awakening* by Kate Chopin, the woman is annoyed when the man says he won't fan himself because when you stop fanning you're hotter than if you never fanned at all. That sounds like Tennyson, doesn't it? But whether the man is saying something true or not doesn't much matter. It is a tiresome thing to say which some people feel they *must* say. People also say things like *Women have a natural capacity for self-sacrifice* or *Women feel deeply.* Either statement is possibly true, certainly tedious, and evidently irresistible.

Lots of American men say American men don't feel like American men any more. And I'm not trying to speak of other places. I wouldn't dare. What could I say about men and women in India? Food has all the authority in starvation. Sexual politics and sexual opinions, and I suppose sexuality itself, are all fringe benefits of eating.

I.   But in the United States, let's say, you would like to put an end to tedious opinions about women?

ME.   I'm not sure. Imagine the tedium *without* them! Anyway, they're not simply tedious. They're often bold—I mean in their flights beyond embarrassment. I rather like their crazy proliferation too—in that sense, sexual opinions are sexual themselves. They mate with each other and multiply—incessantly! Also, the little ones look like the big ones. I've come to like watching them bob in and out of books—novels, especially. Like those goldfish that go endlessly in and out of their grottoes.

I.   Tell me, do you often think about fish and tides?

ME.   Connect my crabbed little mind with water now, flowing streams and all that. Go ahead. Do me a Molly Bloom. I dare you.

I.   I have neither the time nor the desire to study your mind. I shall only say that you pretend more detachment than I believe you feel.

ME.   Perhaps. But since I am most interested in

women as *words*—as the words they pull out of mouths, I am not pretending to *some* detachment, some is real.

I. And the rest?

ME. What can I say? *[A Gallic gesture here.]* One can imagine an impossibly different world, in which this kind of attention was diverted from women to some other phenomenon. They might like that. A suspension of *belief,* for a change. Or eight sexes instead of two—that would divide all available attention by four.

I. By seven, I think.

ME. We are discussing close attention, I, not short division.

I. But close attention is a compliment, isn't it?

ME. Compliments again! But what if fixed attention and critical attention are the same? Like those love poems where the beloved's ugly hands or crooked teeth turn up in the second stanza. Of course she is presumably loved the more for her defect—but still, there are those damn teeth. Nothing can be looked at very long, that's why lovers fall asleep. And then so much attention is unloving all over. I am thinking of the kind of attention the English newspapers focus on the United States. Or the way people at the zoo stare at cobras or at the outrageous backsides of baboons.

I. We have come a long way now from the topic of women.

ME. On the contrary. We are just beginning it.

(from Thinking About Women, *1968)*

"I'm already involved in a fund-raiser; it's called a job."

Crooked and Straight in Academia

SUSAN J. WOLFE AND JULIA PENELOPE

SCENE: The female humor section at the Modern Language Association meeting. Chicago, December 29, 1977.

SJW: Some lesbian jokes are almost vaudevillian.

JP: Does that mean I have to be the straight man?

SJW: Would you rather be a straight *woman?*

JP: When I joined an English department as an uncloseted lesbian, women faculty members came up at the rate of one a day to announce that they were heterosexual.

SJW: We decided we should post a list in the women's room headed, THE FOLLOWING WOMEN HAVE ANNOUNCED THAT THEY ARE HETEROSEXUAL, so that they could sign in. Then we'd cross their names off and initial them.

JP: One female colleague called me into her office and said, "You know, Julia, I'm different from you," and I said, "Oh, really? How?" She said, "Well, I'm more *conventional.*" I said, "I'm sorry; I don't understand what you mean." "Well, I'm more *conservative.*" I continued, "I still don't understand." She said, "I'm more *traditional.*" I finally said, "I still don't understand. Perhaps you could give me an example of the kind of distinctions you're making." With some hesitation she answered, "I don't teach in blue jeans." I said, "Neither do I." So she haltingly continued, "Well, I'm married," and I said, "That's true." "And," she went on, "I have a child . . . and . . . I'm hetero." Stunned by this announcement, I took a moment to reply, "Well, you know, you needn't suffer anymore. There are doctors who can cure that now."

SJW: This woman announced her heterosexuality as if it were some sort of secret—a confidence. Like, "I'm heterosexual, but don't tell my husband. He doesn't know."

JP: After this rash of declared heterosexuals, I left that department to join the English department at another institution. Shortly afterward, I received a letter from the National Council of Teachers of English explaining that our Committee on Lesbian and Gay Male Concerns in the Profession ought to contain a representative number of "declared heterosexuals." So I called Susan up.

SJW: I knew at once what she wanted. I agreed to serve on the committee, but wondered how I would get to be a "declared" heterosexual. (Most of the people I knew were *latent* heterosexuals.) So I opened the door to the office and screamed into the hallway, "I'm a heterosexual. I admit it!" I didn't want anyone to take this announcement as an invitation, so I quickly shut the door.

The Conference
(EXCERPT)

E. M. BRONER

She goes to the bar. A man with turquoise belt buckle, turquoise ring, black straight hair pulled back with a leather thong, is popping shots of whiskey into his mouth like oysters.

"What is your specialty?" she asks him.

His eyes are turquoise. His smile is greenish.

"Want me to show you?" he asks.

She, the member of the panel, becomes haughty.

"I'm an American Indian from Wounded Knee," he says. "I'm here to buy guns and to fuck women."

She wanders away and is introduced to a Black Lit specialist who is angry that his specialty was not included in immigrant literature. His suit is elegant, more formal than any panelist's. His shirt is silky, his tie an amazement of colors. He talks about his wife in law school, his daughters taking ballet.

"Why are you here?" Bea asks him.

"I'm here to make contacts for my people," he says, "and to fuck me some women."

She is introduced to an Egyptian novelist. He speaks English beautifully, as well as French and Russian, besides his native Arabic.

"Why are you here?" Bea asks him.

"I demand equal time with the immigrant Jews," he says. "There are many Arab-Americans writing also, and they are not represented."

"Then that's why you're here!"

"That, and to fuck some women."

She is introduced to a magazine publisher. He is an angry young Jew. His magazine is angry, young, and Jewish.

"Why have you come?" asks Bea.

"Because I represent the Jew as Eternal Immigrant," says the publisher, "and because I want to fuck some women."

She searches for Professor Harold Stone. He is searching for her. He gives her his arm and escorts her away from the Indian, the Black, the Arab, the Jew.

"Why have you come to this conference?" Bea asks her aged, charming friend.

"To reacquaint myself with old friends," he says, "and to fuck some women."

(from Her Mothers, *1975)*

"I don't know what you chicks are complaining about. We're just trying to protect your feminine mystique."

MLA

MARY MACKEY

early in the morning
the weight of dreams
tears apart the earth
sleep cracks
my bed buckles under me
and I see
the Women's Contingent
from Afkarstan
an imaginary Soviet Republic
and they invite me to come with them to teach

Semyion Semyionovitch
is the Head
(bald)
of the University of Afkarstan
and is known in academic circles
for his Definitive Work on The Comma.
I walk into his office
(it reminds me somehow

of the MLA Convention in Chicago
hotel room interviews for non-existent jobs
and in each room a man sitting on the edge of the bed
saying
you look too young to have a doctorate
saying
what about your husband?
will he come with you?
what about your husband, please?
in Spanish, French, Russian
please
explain.
do you intend to have children?
are you happily married?
what about your husband?
would you leave him to find work?
really leave him?
what about your husband?
and, by the way,
what did you say
you could teach?)

"I take it you've never been examined by a woman doctor before."

"What ever happened to that good old-fashioned girl who could fix anything with a hairpin?"

Anyway
back to the dream
and Semyion Semyionovitch
(from Afkarstan)
suddenly grabs his couch
and spreads its legs
the couch becomes a trampoline
and he does flips
saying
I'm Head of the University
he bounces up and down in front of me
a bald ball
being very impressive
knee-drops, forward rolls
I am, he says,
Chairman of the Department
We are looking for a woman
(he pulls me down next to him on the trampoline)
we are looking for a woman, he tells me,
I'm Head of the Department, he says
I could get you the job
I'm the Head
(he tries to french kiss me
I fight trying to say
Afkarstan is the same as here
another America
why should I leave now?)
we are looking for a woman, he goes on,
at present we only have 2.6
and the .6 woman has only one leg

she has been teaching Freshman Composition
for the last 300 years
for 36 cents per hr.
I could get you a better deal than that
he promises, flipping over on top of me.

this time
instead of his tongue
he sticks
his whole head in my mouth
skull and all
I'm Head of the Department, he reminds me from inside
the voice is a little muffled
like from inside an oil drum
I can feel his neck between my lips
gagging me
I want to bite through it
snap his spine
like a Praying Mantis
I want to lay eggs all up and down his body

someday soon, I warn him,
someday soon
my daughters will eat you.

(from Split Ends, *1974*)

CHAPTER SEVEN

Here Comes the Bridle

"Well, I've got to go to work, even if you don't."

Lady in Red

NTOZAKE SHANGE

without any assistance or guidance from you
i have loved you assiduously for 8 months 2 wks & a day
i have been stood up four times
i've left 7 packages on yr doorstep
forty poems 2 plants & 3 handmade notecards i left
town so i cd send to you have been no help to me
on my job
you call at 3:00 in the mornin on weekdays
so i cd drive 27½ miles cross the bay before i go to work
charmin charmin
but you are of no assistance
i want you to know
this waz an experiment
to see how selfish i cd be

if i wd really carry on to snare a possible lover
if i waz capable of debasin my self for the love of another
if i cd stand not being wanted
when i wanted to be wanted
& i cannot
so
with no further assistance & no guidance from you
i am endin this affair

this note is attached to a plant
i've been waterin since the day i met you
you may water it
yr damn self

(from For Colored Girls Who Have Considered
Suicide When the Rainbow Is Enuf, *1975)*

"Since you specialize in disaster stories, I thought you might be interested in the motion-picture rights to my marriage."

Sterner Stuff

SUE HELD

When I was inventing the one I would marry
I wanted to marry an erudite savage,
a happy-go lucky-o ne'er do well sage;
I wanted to marry a calmer of oceans,
a keeper of creatures fierce and uncaged
who'd ride on his shoulders and nuzzle his earlobes
and feed from his fingers and flee from the rigors
of those who'd contain them.
I wanted to marry a man who would love me
abrasive as self-love until I was glowing
remote as a planet and honored for mysteries
no one but he could discover
for only he'd venture to study me plain.
I wanted to marry a truth-groping poet,
a loner, a loper, a leper to Main Street.

    I wanted to wed the impossible he.
    I wanted to wed what I wanted to be.
    I wanted to marry-o marry-o me.

"Let's try scaring your hiccups away—let's talk about getting married."

Marriage Quickies

Dorothy Parker was conversing with a very snobbish young man at a cocktail party, when he commented, "I simply can't bear fools."

"How odd," she observed. "Apparently your mother could."

Andrew considered himself God's gift to woman-kind. "You know," he told his not-exactly-enraptured date, "a lot of women are going to be miserable when I walk down the aisle."

"Really," she remarked. "How many are you planning to marry?"

Any woman who still thinks marriage is a fifty-fifty proposition is only proving that she doesn't understand either men or percentages.—*Flo Kennedy*

The newspaper report of a young woman's death said: "Her friends can give no explanation as to why she committed suicide. She was not married."

'The regularly scheduled program will not be seen tonight so that we may bring you the following special presentation: Getting To Really Know Your Wife.''

"Yes, the lady does know how to keep her hands soft and smooth."

"Sure, we can get together sometime. Call my secretary for an appointment."

Dishwashing & Suicide

MAXINE HONG KINGSTON

Dishwashing is not interesting either to do or to think about, but thinking has dignified other mundane things. At least it will postpone the dishwashing, which stupefies. After eating, I look at the dishes in the sink and on the counters, the cat's dirty bowl and saucer underfoot, swipe at the dabs and smears recognizable from several meals ago, pick up a cup from among the many on chairs and beside beds, and think about suicide. Also about what to write in the suicide note.

The note is an act of kindness. The criminals who most upset us are the ones who refuse to give satisfying motives. "I don't want to wash the dishes one more time." A plain note, no hidden meanings.

I run water into the frying pan—its rim just clears the faucet—but the scrubber and the sponges are hidden somewhere in the bottom of the pile. Thwarted at the start. The pan fills; the pile shifts; greasy water splashes on me and spills. I turn off the water and get out of the kitchen. Let the pan soak itself clean. No way to wash the pot and the blender underneath it nor the dishes under that, the crystal wine glasses at the bottom. The dishpan and the drain are buried, too, so I can't soak anything else. I'll wash again when the mood to do so overwhelms me.

Once in a while, early in the morning, my powers at their strongest, I can enjoy washing dishes. First, I reorganize the pile, then fill the dishpan. I like the feel of the water on my wrists and the way the soap bubbles pop up and float around. I am the one who touches each thing, each tine and spout; I wipe every surface. I like putting the like items together back on the shelves. Until the next time somebody eats, I open the drawers and cupboards every few minutes to look at the neatness I've wrought.

Unfortunately, such well-being comes so rarely, and the mornings are so short, they ought not be wasted on dishes. Better to do dishes in the afternoon, "the devil's time," Tennessee Williams calls it, or in the evening immediately before dinner. The same solution for bed-making—that is, right before going to bed. I try to limit the number of utensils I wash to only those needed for dinner, but since I can't find them without doing those on top, the ones in the way get washed too. I trudge. I drudge.

The one person I know who is a worse dishwasher than I am pushes the dishes from the previous meal toward the middle of the table to clear places for the clean saucers (which substitute for plates, no clean ones left).

Another person pulls a dish out of the sink and uses

it as is. But she doesn't claim to be a dishwasher.

When my father was a young laundryman on Mott Street in New York, he and his partners raced at meals. Last one to finish eating washed the dishes. They ate fast.

Technology is not the answer. I have had electric dishwashers, and they make no difference whatsoever. The electric dishwasher does not clear the table, collect the cups from upstairs and downstairs, scrape, wipe the top of the stove. I need to be in a very organized mood to put the dishes inside the dishwasher. Once they are gathered in one spot like that, the impetus to finish has already begun.

Although dishwashing is lonely work, I do not welcome help. With somebody else in the kitchen, I hurry to get at the worst messes to spare her or him. Alone, I take breaks, wash two plates and quit. Orderly helpers think that dishwashing includes unloading the dishwasher, sweeping and mopping the floor, defrosting the refrigerator and de-crusting the oven, cleaning the kitchen and the dining room.

In "Living Poor with Style," Ernest Callenbach says that it is unsanitary to wipe dry because the dish cloth spreads the germs evenly over everything. Air drying is better, he says, meaning letting everything sit in the drainer. (He also recommends washing the cooking implements as you finish cooking. Impossible. I did that once in a temporary state of grace, which was

"The Day I Left My Vacuum Cleaner." Applique by Paula King.

spoiled by having to wash dishes.)

I do realize that suicide is a false solution to dishes. The worker ends; the work does not end. Besides, a real suicide would have knife or poison or bridge fantasies.

Paper plates are no solution. There are no paper pots and pans and spatulas and mixing bowls. The plates are the easiest part of dishwashing.

I prop books and magazines behind the faucet handles. Some people have television sets in their kitchens. Books with small print work best; you don't turn the pages so often and dislodge the book into the water.

I do enjoy washing other people's dishes. This was a surprise to find out. I like the different dishes, different sink, different view out the window. Perhaps neighbors could move over one house each night and do one another's dishes. However, you usually do other folks' dishes at a holiday or a party.

I like using a new sponge or dishcloth or soap or gloves, but the next time, they're no longer new.

In "Hawaii Over the Rainbow," Kazuo Miyamoto says that in the World War II concentration camps for Americans of Japanese ancestry, the women had the holiday of their lives—no cooking, no dishwashing. They felt freer in prison than at home because of the communal dining halls and camp kitchens. I can believe it.

Compared to dishes, scrubbing the toilets is not bad, a fast job. And you can neglect toilets one more week, and you only have one or two of them.

I typed a zen koan on an index card, which I have glued to the wall beside the sink. It reads like this, and you can cut it out for your wall if you like:

"I have just entered the monastery. Please teach me."
"Have you eaten your rice?"
"I have."
"Then you had better wash your bowl."
At that moment, the new monk found enlightenment.

This koan hasn't helped much with the dishwashing, and it would probably be more enlightening to cut out Miyamoto or Callenbach's words. But I have a glimmering that if I solve this koan, I can solve dishwashing too, or if I can solve dishwashing, I can solve life and suicide. I haven't solved it but have a few clues.

The koan does not say that the monk was enlightened after he washed the bowl. "At that moment" seems to be at the moment that he heard the advice.

I hope the koan doesn't mean that one has to pay the consequences of pleasure; you eat, therefore you wash bowl. Dismal. Dismal.

It could mean something about reaching enlightenment through the quotidian, which is dishwashing.

The monk did not gain his enlightenment after washing the dishes day after day, meal after meal. Just that one bowl. Just hearing about that one bowl.

I have come up with a revolutionary meaning: Each monk in that monastery washed his own bowl. The koan suggests a system for the division of labor. Each member of the family takes his or her dishes to the sink and does them. Pots and pans negotiable. Cat dishes negotiable too.

The koan shows that dishwashing is important. A life and death matter, to be dealt with one to three times a day.

The Politics of Housework

PAT MAINARDI

Though women do not complain of the power of husbands, each complains of her own husband, or of the husbands of her friends. It is the same in all other cases of servitude; at least in the commencement of the emancipatory movement. The serfs did not at first complain of the power of the lords, but only of their tyranny.
—*John Stuart Mill,* On the Subjection of Women

Liberated women—very different from women's liberation! The first signals all kinds of goodies, to warm the hearts (not to mention other parts) of the most radical men. The other signals—*housework*. The first brings sex without marriage, sex before marriage, cozy housekeeping arrangements ("You see, I'm living with this chick") and the self-content of knowing that you're not the kind of man who wants a doormat instead of a woman. That will come later. After all, who wants that old commodity anymore, the Standard American Housewife, all husband, home, and kids. The New Commodity, the Liberated Woman, has sex a lot and has a Career, preferably something that can be fitted in with the household chores—like dancing, pottery, or painting.

On the other hand is women's liberation—and housework. What? You say this is all trivial? Wonderful! That's what I thought. It seemed perfectly reasonable. We both had careers, both had to work a couple of days a week to earn enough to live on, so why shouldn't we share the housework? So I suggested it to my mate and he agreed—most men are too hip to turn you down flat. "You're right," he said. "It's only fair."

Then an interesting thing happened. I can only explain it by stating that we women have been brainwashed more than even we can imagine. Probably too many years of seeing television women in ecstasy over their shiny waxed floors or breaking down over their dirty shirt collars. Men have no such conditioning. They recognize the essential fact of housework right from the very beginning. Which is that it stinks. Here's my list of dirty chores: buying groceries, carting them home, and putting them away; cooking meals and washing dishes and pots; doing the laundry; digging

out the place when things get out of control; washing floors. The list could go on but the sheer necessities are bad enough. All of us have to do these things, or get someone else to do them for us. The longer my husband contemplated these chores, the more repulsed he became, and so proceeded the change from the normally sweet considerate Dr. Jekyll into the crafty Mr. Hyde who would stop at nothing to avoid the horrors of—*housework*. As he felt himself backed into a corner laden with dirty dishes, brooms, mops, and reeking garbage, his front teeth grew longer and pointier, his fingernails haggled and his eyes grew wild. Housework

IT'S NOT THAT I'M

AGAINST WOMEN'S LIBERATION—

IT'S JUST THAT I'M

REALLY INTO THE PROBLEMS OF OPPRESSED PEOPLE

trivial? Not on your life! Just try to share the burden.

So ensued a dialogue that's been going on for several years. Here are some of the high points:

"I don't mind sharing the housework, but I don't do it very well. We should each do the things we're best at."
Meaning: Unfortunately I'm no good at things like washing dishes or cooking. What I do best is a little light carpentry, changing light bulbs, moving furniture *(how often do you move furniture?).*
Also Meaning: Historically the lower classes (black men and us) have had hundreds of years of experience doing menial jobs. It would be a waste of manpower to train someone else to do them now.
Also Meaning: I don't like the dull, stupid, boring jobs, so you should do them.

"I don't mind sharing the work, but you'll have to show me how to do it."
Meaning: I ask a lot of questions and you'll have to show me everything every time I do it because I don't remember so good. Also, don't try to sit down and read while I'm doing my jobs because I'm going to annoy hell out of you until it's easier to do them yourself.

"We used to be so happy!" (Said whenever it was his turn to do something.)

129

Meaning: I used to be so happy.
Meaning: Life without housework is bliss. *(No quarrel here. Perfect agreement.)*

"We have different standards, and why should I have to work to your standards? That's unfair."
Meaning: If I begin to get bugged by the dirt and crap I will say "This place sure is a sty" or "How can anyone live like this?" and wait for your reaction. I know that all women have a sore called "Guilt over a messy house" or "Household work is ultimately my responsibility." I know that men have caused that sore—if anyone visits and the place *is* a sty, they're not going to leave and say, "He sure is a lousy housekeeper." You'll take the rap in any case. I can outwait you.
Also Meaning: I can provoke innumerable scenes over the housework issue. Eventually doing all the housework yourself will be less painful to you than trying to get me to do half. Or I'll suggest we get a maid. She will do my share of the work. You will do yours. It's women's work.

"I've got nothing against sharing the housework, but you can't make me do it on your schedule."
Meaning: Passive resistance. I'll do it when I damned well please, if at all. If my job is doing dishes, it's easier to do them once a week. If taking out laundry, once a month. If washing the floors, once a year. If you don't like it, do it yourself oftener, and then I won't do it at all.

"I *hate* it more than you. You don't mind it so much."
Meaning: Housework is garbage work. It's the worst crap I've ever done. It's degrading and humiliating for someone of *my* intelligence to do it. But for someone of *your* intelligence . . . .

"Housework is too trivial to even talk about."
Meaning: It's even more trivial to do. Housework is beneath my status. My purpose in life is to deal with matters of significance. Yours is to deal with matters of insignificance. You should do the housework.

"This problem of housework is not a man-woman problem! In any relationship between two people one is going to have a stronger personality and dominate."
Meaning: That stronger personality had better be *me*.

"In animal societies, wolves, for example, the top animal is usually a male even where he is not chosen for brute strength but on the basis of cunning and intelligence. Isn't that interesting?"
Meaning: I have historical, psychological, anthropological, and biological justification for keeping you down. How can you ask the top wolf to be equal?

"Women's liberation isn't really a political movement."
Meaning: The Revolution is coming too close to home.
Also Meaning: I am only interested in how *I* am oppressed, not how I oppress others. Therefore the war, the draft, and the university are political. Women's liberation is not.

"Man's accomplishments have always depended on getting help from other people, mostly women. What great man would have accomplished what he did if he had to do his own housework?
Meaning: Oppression is built into the System and I, as the white American male, receive the benefits of this System. I don't want to give them up.

(from Sisterhood Is Powerful, *1970)*

We Don't Need the Men

MALVINA REYNOLDS

It says in *Coronet* magazine, June nineteen fifty-six,
    page ten,
That married women are not as happy as women who
    have no men.
Married women are cranky, frustrated and disgusted,
While single women are bright and gay, creative and
    well-adjusted.

CHORUS: We don't need the men,
                We don't need the men,
                We don't need to have them round,
                Except for now and then.

They can come to see us
When we need to move the piano,
Otherwise they can stay at home
And read about the White Sox.
We don't care about them,
We can do without them.
They'll look cute in a bathing suit
On a billboard in Manhattan.

CHORUS

They can come to see us
When they have tickets for the symphony,

Otherwise they can stay at home
And play a game of pinochle.
We don't care about them,
We can do without them.
They'll look cute in a bathing suit
On a billboard in Wisconsin.

CHORUS

They can come to see us
When they're feeling pleasant and agreeable,
Otherwise they can stay at home
And holler at the T.V. programs.
We don't care about them,
We can do without them.
They'll look cute in a bathing suit
On a billboard in Madagascar.

CHORUS

They can come to see us
When they're all dressed up with a suit on,
Otherwise they can stay at home
And drop towels in their own bathroom.
We don't care about them,
We can do without them.
They'll look cute in a bathing suit
On a billboard in Tierra del Fuego.

"I'd be glad to share the housework if I weren't so bad at it."

"My husband made me happy by adding some magic to our marriage—he disappeared."

SHARON McDONALD

I always brace myself, shut the door, and sit down before I call home. My mother used to tell us that life without crisis was nothing, and all her children internalized this teaching to a degree that has made us varied, creative, and somewhat unpredictable. Our entire family specializes in activities that we like to think build our character but the neighbors swear lower the property value.

"Hi, Mom. What's new?"

Her edge was unmistakable right from the start. "Get time off work and come home. Your brother's getting married to that girl."

The brother in question was Mark, a strong silent type who had spent most of the last several years on an enormous black motorcycle, weaving from Phoenix to Denver to El Paso in the company of forty or fifty intimate friends on similar enormous black motorcycles. "That girl" was his companion of the last year, a young woman with bouncy blonde curls and a level of nervous energy that makes Charo look somber and reflective.

"You don't think they should get married, Mom?"

"He doesn't know what he's getting into." (Mark is twenty-four years old, over six feet tall, and since he acquired biceps, a mustache, and a 750 Harley, few have questioned his decisions.)

"And another thing," Mom went on, "she's a hypochondriac." (Susie gets

Of Bikers, Brides & Butches

sick a lot. Mark takes care of her a lot. They both like it—a lot.)

I tried to change the subject slightly. "Tell me about the wedding plans. Where is it going to be? And what's the weather going to be like?"

"You remember Highway 89? You remember the turnout about twenty miles north of Sedona?" Mark had invited those fifty intimate friends (and *their* intimate friends) to an outdoor ceremony, or what my mother now began to refer to as "a biker wedding." I immediately made plans to attend. As for the weather, Mom reminded me that it was the middle of the monsoon season in Arizona, a period of time characterized by hellish heat and unpredictable wind and rain. But Highway 89 had some sentimental significance for Mark and Susie, and they refused to consider a change in location.

In the weeks before the event, I convinced Louise, my lover of three years,

that this was the perfect time to come home and meet the family. "They'll be so upset over Mark they won't even notice us."

What better time to quietly introduce the love of my life to my family than when they're so distracted?

On the day of the wedding, Louise and I drove north on Highway 89 past Sedona, and began to look for the fated turnout. At one likely spot we found a cluster of savage-looking men on bikes, and I yelled, "Are you here for the wedding?" One, who looked like he had just had a tourist for lunch, turned and yelled, "A wedding, huh? Hey, let's go to the wedding!" Louise floored it.

By the time we reached the right turnout, Louise's butch braggadocio had begun to wilt visibly in the 112-degree heat. As I went off to hug Mark she tried hard to carry the small talk with a long-time friend of my mother's who had, for the first time in memory, lost the power of speech the moment Louise and I walked up together. (Louise is not, as my mother later delicately put it, "the feminine type.")

I was right about the distraction principle; Louise was only a subplot within the larger scheme of things that day. The scene was a bizarre mixture of the traditional and the unheard-of. Fifty or sixty of Mark and Susie's friends lounged about the site, their bikes parked in the background, inspiring Louise to whisper, "I haven't seen this much leather since Gay Pride Day," just before ducking behind a tree to dodge my father's confused stare.

This event had caught my parents mid-divorce, and they made the best of being thrown together in a circumstance only remotely of their making. My two sisters, who had both grown out of nice Catholic girlhoods to fall in love with black men about the same time I fell in love with Louise, were nervously hoping the distraction principle worked for them too,' while their boyfriends stood by surveying the multiple cross-currents. And last but by no means least, the bride's family arrived looking stunned. They apparently could not decide whether this was a "real wedding" or some kind of an orgy, and they came in party dresses with a sheet cake and a case of Ripple on the flatbed of their pickup.

A tiny squirrelly-looking man in judicial robes called the wedding party together at a dirt mound in the center of the turnout. Mark and Susie stepped forward, Susie in a long white dress, Mark in the top half of a tuxedo and jeans, having lost both his pants and the ring somewhere during the last twenty-four hours. Flanked by my sister in maid-of-honor attire, and a best man in a long black cape who was introduced simply as "Jaws," Susie and Mark said, "I do."

During the cake and Ripple reception, my sisters and I mingled while our mates stood propped against individual pine trees, trying to look casual and in place. When the rain began, Susie hiked up her dress and climbed onto Mark's bike, and they roared out of the turnout, pelted by rain and rice from the guests. A few tourists who had stopped to stretch their legs stared open-mouthed as the bride and groom departed.

As for Louise, who had been wanting to meet my family for a long time, she looked deeply into my eyes for a long moment, sighed "This explains a lot," and kissed me as we headed back to the normalcy of Los Angeles.

What Mother Never Told Me

SHARON McDONALD

Prologue: Unnatural Desires

With several years of love, lust, and irreconcilable differences behind us, Louise and I had become aware that we were drifting into that strange uncharted territory known as "long term." They had been tumultuous years, but our dismay at each other's failings had more often than not been matched by our delight in each other's company. Having seen many models of love that start out strong and weaken over time, I was shocked to find the reverse dynamic with Louise.

Now when heterosexuals get to this point they tend to get married, a custom which I have envied for its sentimental symbolism while disdaining its more odious political aspects. I myself had never wanted to get married, but Mother always told me that when I really fell in love I'd change my mind. Imagine my chagrin twenty years later and a whole lifestyle different to find out once *again* that Mother is always right.

Of course, I pondered my desire in secret. I am politically unsophisticated enough to know that I can squeak by being monogamous, and even in some tolerant circles being femme, but my Radical Lesbian License would be revoked for sure if word got out that I wanted to "settle down" with the woman of my dreams.

The more I thought about it, the more ironic it seemed. I was free to explore my wildest fantasies of unnatural acts with Fido and a few dozen close friends, but I was supposed to feel constrained about wanting to shout, "Hallelujah, she's the one!" I finally decided to hell with Convention (Women Have to Marry Men) and to hell with Unconvention (Women Have to Not Marry at All). Who says this lesbian can't live happily ever after?

Popping the Question

I took her out to dinner, fancy gay restaurant, table in the corner, soft candlelight, gay waiters wafting by. I sat terrified, drinking like there was no tomorrow, as might well be true if she said no. She wasn't drinking, and, as I sank lower and lower in my chair, she started leaning over the table and asking solicitously, "Are you all right?"

After our boy had taken away my untouched pork chop and filled my glass for the fifth time, I lurched, er, launched into a rambling preamble. She listened intently, looking concerned. About the tenth time I heard myself stutter, "I, uh, you see, I think we, uh. . ." I shoved a ring box in front of her and just like in the movies blurted, "Will you marry me?" And with that, I was off on what has proven to be the most politically controversial and personally rewarding thing I've done since coming out.

Sharing or Shackling?

Louise and I quickly found out that an event of this nature in a feminist community is much like a natural disaster; it brings out the best and the worst in people. Community reactions broke down into three categories: The Aghast, The Amused, and The Admiring. The Aghast, of course, were radical lesbian feminists. So were the Amused. So were The Admiring.

Longtime friends took us out to ask if perhaps we weren't working too hard, maybe the stress had affected our better judgment. Less delicate acquaintances snorted openly, one summing it up by asking, "Why don't you two just shackle yourselves together?"

But here and there other lesbian couples popped up, delighted at the news. They called us up, some women we barely knew, and said in a rush how they thought it was wonderful and brave and how they'd wanted to have a ceremony for years. We congratulated each other conspiratorially and invited them.

WICCA to the Rescue!

Not wanting to march down any heterosexist aisles, we set about looking for a lesbian ceremony and hit upon the tryst. A Witch friend explained that it was an ancient ritual of bonding that was not the ownership contract of conventional marriage, but rather a mutual coming together of two equals to bond in love and friendship. She offered to help us do it. "We'll take it!"

We called our mothers and sisters and invited them. We sent invitations to our friends, painfully resisting our initial excited impulse to send them to every lesbian west of the Rockies.

One night as the date was drawing near, I sat in bed flipping through a book on witchcraft rituals. I came across a passage that made my hair stand on end. It described how women standing in a circle at a Sabbat turn to each other and give each other "the fivefold kiss," kissing the forehead, eyes, lips, breasts, and genitals. I nearly fell off my bed. "LOUISE!" I shrieked.

"Do blonds have more fun?"

"We've got to get ALL the details on this ceremony!"

The next morning I called our Witch friend and asked for a blow-by-blow account of what was going to happen. I was all right until she got to the part about "anointing the genitals with water."

"We can't *do* that," I said. "Our mothers are going to be there. Besides, I think Louise would faint."

The Witch was horrified. "You can't drop it! This is a very important part of the ceremony! I just can't imagine what the spiritual repercussions might be! It could be terrible!"

"I'll risk it."

"You don't understand. The genitals are very involved in what you're doing here . . . ."

"You're telling ME!"

". . . and it could be *tragic* to omit this protective blessing on your sexual union!"

"Do it like the Catholics do—offer up a silent blessing."

In the end, Witch tradition won out, but only if done with ex-Catholic subtlety.

The women of both our families jumped into the preparations for the tryst with enthusiasm, this being the first tryst in both families' history. The fathers and brothers took a somewhat dimmer view of the proceedings. Because of their customary lack of enthusiasm for events of a lesbian nature, and because of the customary lack of enthusiasm of many of our guests for men in general, they had not been invited. They reacted to this with customary outrage, half of them "threatening" not to come, the other half threatening to come.

Checking Our Closets

But Louise and I had no time for family squabbles; we busied ourselves with weightier issues, like the What-to-Wear argument. I had always wanted to see her in a tuxedo, and this seemed the perfect time, but she had other plans and could not be moved. When I wailed, "But when will I *ever* get to see you in a tuxedo if not on this day?" she replied, "The day you bury me." End of discussion.

Louise's idea was that we should be "outside of time and fashion and contemporary limitations—we should wear stately robes!"

"*Robes?*"

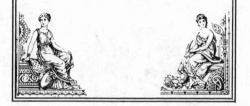

Later after champagne, she would hug me and whisper in my ear, "Now I have another daughter!"

"Yeah, you know, like Ben-Hur, El Cid, Diana the Goddess, Helen of Troy."

"Jesus!"

"That's RIGHT! Roman togas!"

"Good lord, the witches want to bless my genitals, you want me to dress up like Irene Pappas, why did I ever start this thing?"

And with that it hit us: that period of reflection and kicking ourselves known as Prenuptial Jitters. This malady expresses itself in many different forms, all of them desperate. Lesbians, it turned out, are not immune to any of them.

Louise went scurrying off to her shrink to babble, "I love her, *but* . . . ." Meanwhile, I surveyed the preparations for the coming tryst, which were in a shambles. Half the women we'd invited weren't speaking to the other half. The men were still threatening to come. Louise's aunt, who had promised to help, suddenly decided to get divorced, and so spent all the time she should have been whipping up Roman togas crying instead. Louise and I looked at each other and saw the face of a haunted stranger. We retired to separate gay bars to think things over.

Drinking alone, we missed each other. Coming home to bed, we found again some common ground. Revitalized, we remembered that while neither of us wanted to be a groom, we couldn't pass up this once in a lifetime chance to both get a bride.

The Day of Reckoning

Faster than you can say "public commitment," the day of the tryst had arrived. The ceremony itself was short, sweet, and to the point. There were no dramatic surprises, no one popping up to yell, "Stop! She's got a wife and four kids in Des Moines!" There was just us and the goddess and our families and friends, standing there doing what every lesbian has the right to do: be proud and public about her love. I cannot vouch for my appearance, but Louise looked like a dyke angel, shining from the inside out. We held hands, jumped the broom, and it was done! Applause broke out and the party was on.

There was no doubt that Louise and I were totally upstaged by the presence of our mothers. Both remarkably resilient women, they stood up well under a barrage of "How do you feel about this?" questions from our friends. Each answered honestly and in her own style.

Louise's convent-raised mother was once told by her journalism teacher that she had "best stick to *Lives of the Saints.*" Her old-fashioned innocence still largely untouched by modern mores, she attended the tryst with characteristic courage. "I . . . I . . . I . . . One

should be open to *new* things where one's children are concerned. Sharon is a lovely girl." Later after champagne, she would hug me and whisper in my ear, "Now I have another daughter!"

My own mother had provided the early bad example that every little girl needs to grow up lively. No stranger to unusual occurrences, this was still her first tryst. She said, "I think Sharon and

Louise are very lucky to have found each other. They love each other, and I'm happy for them. I raised all my children to do what they thought was right for them. I'm glad they're including me in their lives."

Upon hearing these sentiments, several hardened politicos turned and sauntered off behind separate trees, from which soon emerged the sounds of noses being blown and throats being cleared with difficulty.

The tryst day was in every way a success. Some women who hadn't spoken to each other in years exchanged observations on the scene. Our families had their first exposure to our friends en masse, and vice versa. Everybody so inclined got to kiss not one bride but two! And after it was all over, Louise and I escaped (a la honeymoon) to—no, not Niagara Falls—Tijuana.

Epilogue

Today, Louise and I are a couple wise beyond our years. We have seen too much. We were shocked by our families, who turned out to be more tolerant than we'd dreamed. We were shocked by some of our friends, who turned out to be less tolerant than we'd dreamed. We were shocked by each other, that we actually went through with it.

One happy footnote: Louise's aunt finally stopped crying, got divorced, and arrived on our doorstep a few weeks ago holding hands with another woman and beaming.

From the Pen of a Liberated Woman

> **I think we'll all be better off when word gets around that cleaning a toilet produces no more and no less than a clean toilet; it does not strengthen character, nor is it interesting work.**

No One Has a Corner on Depression But Housewives Are Working on It

GABRIELLE BURTON

They sent brochures out all over town, saying I don't have a dishwasher. Sandra Elkin just stood in this very spot, and said I don't have a dishwasher. The only thing I can figure is that they got so panicked nobody would show up today they started promising anything. I have a dishwasher. When I left my dishwasher this morning, I kissed it goodbye. I may be a depressive, but I'm not crazy.

You're upset. I don't blame you a bit. I'd be upset too if I paid out fifteen bucks thinking I was going to get a freak without a dishwasher. I didn't even pay fifteen bucks, and *I'm* upset.

I think the way that slander got started was when somebody called me up and asked my qualifications for claiming to be a housewife. Even though this is a mental health conference, and I knew you'd be interested professionally, I don't think my lobotomy has anything to do with it.

So I told the truth. That I started out knowing nothing about the business, took on-the-job training, and night courses at the Y, and in only fourteen years, worked my way up to the bottom. It'd take me a month to list my credits, I told them, so I'll just hit the highlights. And this is what I said: I've made 71,343 peanut butter sandwiches, and I know three toilets intimately.

Speech given at Symposium on Women's Mental Health, Oct. 29, 1976,. Buffalo, N.Y.

I don't know what I was thinking of. They couldn't put that in the brochures. Those brochures were being sent out to homes, lying around on coffee tables where little children might see them, and, luckily, somebody put the lid on my toilet remark.

I know as well as the next that a lady *cleans* toilets, but she never talks about them. It's one of our unwritten laws—something to do with our advanced spiritual plane, I think—similar to the law that says a housewife who's just finished cleaning the basement is not sweating—she's perspiring. Or the one that says a housewife is pushy if she asks what week the repairman might come.

These laws are still in my bones, though, strictly speaking, I am no longer a fulltime housewife. Not that my house and I got a divorce—because we really only had a common-law marriage. But some time ago, we had a few fights—it happens in the best of homes—and my house and I got a partial separation.

I am now what you might call a parttime housespouse—and, as I tell my husband, call me anything you want, Roger, just don't call me late to dinner.

But I am still in the house all day long, and housework is like bicycling, it always comes back. Just in case you think I've gotten rusty, I've brought a hint for you today. Know how to get rid of ants in your kitchen? Spread honey on your living room floor.

I still think a lot about toilets—in fact, I was once accused of being an anal compulsive—and I never went back to *that* shrink again.

Saying I have a bowl fetish. I don't even know what a bowl fetish is, but it doesn't sound like anything a Catholic's supposed to fool with.

If I hadn't been so mad, I would have told that guy that the reason I think about toilets all the time is that I'm convinced that much of my depression is directly tied to my toilet training. I never had any. That's true. Not only was I not trained to clean toilets, nobody ever told me that was what I was going to do when I grew up. Probably a prudent decision; you get enough surprises when you're traveling.

Depression is a complicated syndrome though, and sometimes the toilets don't bother me at all. I just wake up one morning, look in the mirror, and Quasimodo looks back. *That's* depressing.

Not because women are vain and shallow, but because an ugly woman is one rung below a leper. You go out on the streets looking like Quasimodo, people will think you're a feminist.

There's no excuse for letting yourself go when a billion-dollar cosmetics industry is right there to correct your flaws. I'd fix my face, too, if I could just figure out what shape it is. You know those magazine articles that show you how to fix up a heart-shaped face, a diamond-shaped face, a club-shaped

No it's not menopausal depression, it's no pay, no sick leave, no pension, no identity.

face . . . . Now, don't laugh, these things must be important because they keep writing about them. I'm thirty-seven years old, and I hate to admit this, but I still don't know what shape my face is.

I don't care what the optometrists say. Men don't make passes at girls who wear glasses. Those of you blessed with 20/20 vision probably don't know that people who wear glasses are convinced they would be a knockout without them. We take this on faith, of course, because without our glasses we can't *see* our face, but we know . . . .

But I've made some progress in this obsession with physical appearance that the bad fairy brings every girl baby at birth. I've given up on my breasts. In fact, one of the reasons I'm so happy there's such a big turnout today is that I want to ask: Anybody out there want to buy a second-hand Mark Eden Breast Exerciser? I'll let it go for $9.95—send it in a brown paper wrapper—and it's the most gorgeous hot pink.

I was telling you about giving up on my breasts. I just decided one day that even though they no longer asserted themselves, it was time I did. Still, I admit, it's cheered my spirits many a time .that after five kids, I have perfect measurements: 32-33-34.

I can't tell you how important I think this conference is. Just to have people coming together to talk about how bananas women are. I got so excited about coming here my face broke out.

You know, I've been a depressive for years, but until recently I thought it was premenstrual tension.

I worried about it a lot. Once even got my nerve up and asked my doctor if it were normal for a woman to have PMT for twenty-two years. Before, during, and after her periods. He said every woman he saw was that way.

I don't tie my depression up with my marriage though, because I was already married two days before it began.

But, as Karen DeCrow has pointed out, marriage *is* a funny institution. A man loves a woman so much, he asks her to marry—to change her name, quit her job, have and raise his babies, be home when he gets there, move where his job is.

You can hardly imagine what he might ask if he didn't love her.

But I can pinpoint exactly when I started getting into trouble. I was cleaning the toilet—you see, toilets *have* been very significant in my life—and instead of singing little snatches of Rogers and Hammerstein as I usually did—sometimes Walt Disney, "Whistle while You Work," tra la la la la la la—suddenly, I was reciting this poignant little poem. Breathes there a woman/With soul so dead/She actually enjoys/Cleaning the head.

Now this was years before I ever thought of being a writer, so it was rather a remarkable experience, and I got right up and embroidered the poem in cross-stitch. It's been very helpful in

my life, ranking up there with something my grandmother once said that also strongly influenced me. I wasn't more than four or five years old when Gramma yelled: "Never touch a hot iron." To this day I haven't.

I'm convinced that the really important thing a housewife has to keep in mind is that she's building a cathedral. If you forget this, you can get confused, and start thinking you're ploughing through the sewers. I myself used to fall on my knees every night and thank my heavenly father, creator of all men, for giving me the chance to practice brotherhood in my unique way. Those of you who aren't religious could thank science that you're genetically endowed to run a vacuum cleaner.

As my Gramma always said, "Count your blessings."

She said that one time to a man who had cancer—after they cut him all up and took out the tumor and pronounced him one hundred percent cured, she told him to count his blessings. She told him he was mighty lucky even if he couldn't talk quite right and had to eat baby food. And he blew up and started yelling that he never asked to get cancer in the first place.

Some people might say that analogy is applicable to housewifery, but not all women hate housework. I have a friend who *loves* housework. Honest, she loves *all* housework. All day long she moves from one chore to the next, smiling the whole time. I went over there one day and begged her to tell me her secret. It's simple, she said, right after breakfast you light up a joint.

But women are beginning to talk about these things, and that's good. Particularly while there's a few of us still outside the loony bin.

I've heard women say that it depresses them to stay in the house all day, that they feel caged, locked up. Me? I love it. There's nothing like that great feeling of shooting the double bolt on the doors, latching all the windows, and knowing you're reasonably safe from rapists.

Speaking of rapists, even the most diehard feminist must admit that's one thing men do better than women.

Now, I'm not saying all men are rapists. Most men only abuse you verbally. That's the way they were taught, and even though it sometimes makes us feel bad, I think we can reeducate them in little subtle ways. Like the other day, I went to the grocery store—that's my little outing, I *love* going to the grocery store—all the noise and colors—crouching there in the aisle with your adrenalin surging—until that exciting moment when you find the mistake in the posted unit price. Poor old Albert Einstein, I always think. Stuck in his lab calculating infinity, while Mrs. Einstein, what's her name?, had all this.

I was really having a good time. I squeezed the Charmin; grabbed up an armload of those new little mini-pads—if *those* pads are as unbelievably comfortable as they say, I'm going to wear them even when it's not my period. Finally, I get up to the check-out line—or the Attack Zone as I call it, who will snarl at me today?—just as the bagger, a boy about fifteen, with acne, is saying to the check-out woman, "You chicks are all the same." I was admiring his devil-may-care air, when suddenly, just like the little toilet poem, I hear my voice saying, "Don't call her a chick." Maybe because the checker was my Gramma's age, I don't know, but that still doesn't excuse my rudeness; I've been properly taught, I know a lady is always polite. He knew that too. "Sez who, lady?" he sez, certainly within his rights, but my mouth kept on going. "A

remark like that," I said politely, "has only one appropriate response." Now he didn't ask, but I could tell he was dying to know, so I told him. "You say, 'Hi, chick,' the chick has to answer, 'Hi, cock.' You don't want her to talk that way, do you?" He got real cranky.

But cranky men don't bother me a bit. I've known a lot of cranky men in

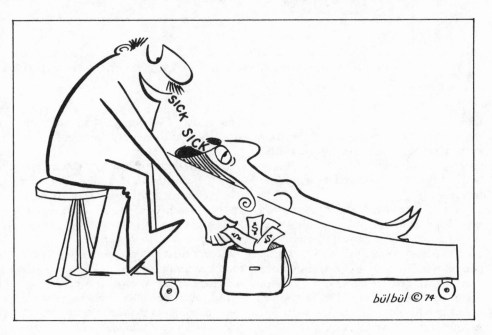

my life, and even though they appear to be yelling and swearing, I know they just got out of bed on the wrong side. And men have a lot on their minds. Some of them might even be depressed.

The trouble with depression is that we don't know much about it. Oh, we know a little about a severe clinical kind where they come and stuff you in the net, but we don't know diddle about the low-level depression people walk around with, still functioning, sort of. Most of the stuff written about depression has been written by *non*depressives, because they're the only ones with enough energy to speculate. The people who really *know* are lying on their beds and staring at the wall.

I used to think about this a lot while I was lying on my bed and staring at the wall. During one of my bouts with de-

pression, I tried very hard to keep a journal, and I wish I'd remembered to bring it here today. It's 200 pages filled with blank. There is one entry, apparently a lift toward the middle, which reads: February 17th, "Flossed two teeth." Marking the page, like a pressed flower from the high school prom, there's a little piece of yellowing floss.

With diaries of depressives, you have to do a lot of reading between the lines.

I've had my bleak times, but I can count my blessings. I'm a lot better off than some people. I've never been a head-banger.

And I had a neighbor once who was really a basket case. This woman was so depressed that next to her I look like Jessie Bernard. Wait'll you see Jessie. She's one of the few women, maybe the only woman I've ever met, who means it when she smiles. You ought to do a study of women's smiles—ever notice how much we smile? How totally inappropriately we smile? Don't stop smiling now—I'm telling jokes, smiling is appropriate now—I'm talking about when you just find out you have to have a hysterectomy, and you run into somebody you know who asks how you're feeling, and you say, "Finnneee." (Big smile.) Or when your boyfriend is cranky and you say, "You're hurting my wrist." (Big smile.) Monkeys do this last kind of "smile" too. They call it appeasement, I think, but I don't think we ought to be anybody's chumps, or chimps. Sometimes I wonder what might happen if we went on a selective smile boycott, if we only smiled when we felt good? That's a crazy idea, the world's already grim enough, you might say it's our *duty* to smile. Just last week, a woman I know, Charlotte Kauppi's her name, was walking down Main Street, she's a lawyer and was thinking about a case coming up in court, when a man said, "Give us a smile, sugar." She didn't hear him at first, so he gave her another chance: "Come on. Give us a pretty smile." She must have gotten out of bed on the wrong side, because she looked right at him and said, "Say something funny."

My neighbor went around like a Cheshire cat, she was batty with depression. It wasn't that she wanted to be in the jet set, but the last exciting thing in her life was the day the baby's umbilical cord dropped off—and the baby was now in second grade. She was guilty as Judas about being depressed. And she couldn't pin down what was wrong with her. During the day, the quiet drove her nuts; she couldn't wait till everybody got home—and forty minutes after they all piled in, she was feeling like a bunch of ducks were pecking her to death. She tried all kinds of things to snap out of it.

Became a career shopper for a while —used to follow the school bus right down the street, turning off at the department stores. She had a real nose for bargains—bought winter clothes on summer sales, summer clothes on winter sales—her kids had beautiful clothes. None of them fit, but they were beautiful clothes. But one day she told me she was giving it up. All the women in the stores were getting her down, she said. She said they'd pick up one thing, listlessly finger it, move on to the next, and the most depressing thing was that everybody's eyes were glazed

I HAD THIS TERRIFIC SHRINK

HELPED ME FIND THE REAL ME.

TOLD ME I HAD TO WORK AT MY WOMANHOOD.

WHO WOULD HAVE THOUGHT BEING PASSIVE COULD BE SO ACTIVE.

141

—did I think her eyes were getting glazed?

Next thing I know, she's on pills, and that was pretty good. She was a little jumpy—the dishwasher would go on and she'd scream—but all in all, she said she felt better than she had in years. She had this marvelous doctor who handed out amphetamines like candy, and things might have worked out very well for her except he got busted one day when a woman died. My neighbor went down with fifty other women and testified in his behalf, but they never listen to women. After that, she nearly went bonkers trying to fill up her days—it was funny she felt she wasn't going anyplace, because she was constantly on the go. Did gourmet cooking, flower arranging, cake decorating, gymnastics, slimnastics—she even learned to make soap dispensers out of old pantyhose. But she couldn't seem to stick to things. Like she signed up for a dancing class, plunked out fifty bucks for mix-and-match leotards, then upped and quit. Made her feel funny, she said, dropping her seven-year-old daughter off at the kids' dancing class, then driving on to hers.

Must have made her feel funny, too, because she laughed the whole time she was telling the story. Laugh? She laughed till the tears rolled down—she had this really infectious laugh—you know the kind that makes all your apertures shrivel up when you hear it and it's so infectious you hope you'll never catch it—but she never drank, I'll hand her that. I sure tried hard enough to hand her that. Practically every morning after we got the kids on the road, I'd yell, "Come on over, we'll have one for the road," but she always stuck to her darn diet cola, that stuff'll rot your teeth. Frankly, I thought a few fingers of Scotch would have helped her during her hostile period, she had a terrible period of just plain hostility. Did all kinds of off-beat things—like, she made a planter out of her oven. The most spectacular planter you ever saw: her entire oven filled with Venus flytrap.

One day I looked out my window

and she was tromping right through my tulip bulbs. I'd spend three weeks making a heart-shaped pattern of my tulip bulbs, and my whole day was planned out. As soon as I finished dusting my rubber plants, I was going to wash and starch Raggedy Ann's clothes, and, if I hustled, there'd be just enough time to polish the bottoms of my copper pans. But what are neighbors for? Over and over, I've asked myself that question. She was sobbing before I even got the bolts thrown.

The kids left for school, she said; her husband went to work; she looked at the clock and he wouldn't be back for nine hours and sixteen minutes, she didn't think she could stand it. The mailman yelled, "Nothing today," and she was thinking about slitting her wrists with a shard of peanut butter glass—except she'd have to clean up the mess—when her doorbell rang. One thing led to another, and just this moment, she'd gotten up from hanky-panky with the Fuller Brush man. But she was still down. I was trying to comfort her and she got really hysterical, started yelling that I didn't understand. The really depressing thing, she said, was that she felt she had to *buy a few brushes* . . . And she dumped every kind of cleaning brush you could think of on my kitchen table.

She let me have first pick—and even though I felt funny getting high on her low, I did get a nifty new toilet brush.

I'm happy to tell you that she's better now. She got into Eastern philosophy, and that's a wonderful thing. She has this guru who knows all about women because he's had five wives, and he's taught her that all her problems lie in herself. Nearly every day she gets to a higher level of understanding, and just about the only thing she can't understand is why she fought her nature for so long.

I can't say for sure, because all Oriental philosophies look alike to me, but it seems to me that what my neighbor's doing is what psychologists call dissociation, and what women know as the old Scarlett O'Hara method of coping:

I'll think about that tomorrow.

I'm a bit of an expert on dissociation, because it was once one of my lifestyles. I'd start out in the morning not thinking about breakfast dishes, move on to not thinking about vacuuming the rug, go upstairs not thinking about making the bed, and by the time I wasn't thinking about the hairy bathroom floor, I was a functioning catatonic. Now psychologists say that's clinically impossible, but housewives have managed it for years.

I raised dissociation to such heights I stopped noticing everything. Once, sitting at a playground with other mothers, one of them commented on my serenity. As soon as I heard her, I smiled serenely. "You're so calm," she said. "I'd be just frantic if my child did that." Until her last words, I hadn't seen that my eighteen-month-old—whom I was looking straight at with my eyes open—was hanging by her heels from the top of the jungle gym. I wasn't off in any green pastures either, I was no place. That was the day I swore off dissociation for good.

Now I belong to the "Rage of the Month" Club. It's wonderful: fifteen minutes every day I primal scream. I think a woman owes it to herself to hold on to her mind as long as she can.

And I have the kids. Always. Children are a great consolation, and I was surprised as Ann Landers when those thousands of people wrote into her column saying if they had it to do over again, they wouldn't have children. Still, I'm reserving judgment. We won't know anything important from that survey till we hear from the other side. I bet you anything thousands of kids are going to write in, saying if *they* had it to do over again, they wouldn't have parents.

Me? I was born loving babies—though I must say nobody ever told me they'd turn into children. We have a wonderful family life though. I've admitted in print that we're not like the Waltons, but the truth is worse: we're not even like the Brady Bunch. But we muddle on, taking heart from this inspiring motto: "The family that fights

"Well this ought to keep our bridge club stoned for at least three months."

together fights together." In truth, my children couldn't be nicer, and you shouldn't take it personally that I tell them when they grow up they won't have to pay ten thousand dollars to a shrink to find out why we rejected them—we rejected them because they're impossible.

The thing with kids is, just when you're ready to flush them down the toilet, they do some little touching thing that'll tug at your heartstrings. On Mother's Day my kids saved up their pennies and bought me a sweatshirt that said, "Being a mother means always having to say you're sorry." I was so touched I cried for two days.

Already, they know which way is up, because even our critics must admit that one of our side specialties, right up there with smiling, is apologizing. How many times today have you said you're sorry? "I'm sorry there's a traffic jam." "I'm sorry it's raining."

How can people say women are powerless? We control the traffic, the weather, the oregano: we're practically omnipotent. Those women who would prefer to be President just want to have their cake and eat it too—I never quite understood that saying, what's the good of cake if you can't eat it? But I'm sure it's like our other sayings and contains mysterious wisdom. We should

count our blessings. People may treat us like children, but we're still bigger. Children aren't even on the totem pole. Americans simply aren't big on kids; it's one of our national prides, we can say that without boasting. And if children would love to have every moment of their mothers' lives, that just proves how smart they are: they figure out very early that if they don't get attention at home, they sure aren't going to get it anyplace else. Get lost, kid: that's our new national anthem.

We could ship all the children out to the old-folks ghettos, but the old folks don't want them either. Some people say that's because they're tired and feel they've put in their time, but *I* think the old people are cross about being dumped. They *might* even think that all of us under sixty-five are suicidal nuts for putting down a group we're eventually going to join.

So what's a mother to do? Given that dislike of children is one of the few socially acceptable prejudices we have left, it's probably crazy for her to try and combine a career with parenting—right? Wrong. It's not crazy; it's full-blown insanity.

Still, you could make a case that one of the greatest gifts a mother can give her children is the ability to lead her own life, because then they'll have a chance of leading their own lives. Now I'll tell you true: that gift is not always my children's first-choice present, but I tell them it's the thought that counts.

And motherhood *is* a challenging career—think of it, motherhood, as we practice it today, is set up with every single odd stacked against you; the moment you pop the baby out, you're both abandoned. What a challenge! Oh, it has its ups and downs—those mothers who couldn't come here today because they have no childcare are having a down—and some people have pointed out that it is unfair that all mothers are not created equal. That's another unwritten law, and not only is it not written down that some mothers are better than others, it's kept top-secret, and can only be revealed at the moment of birth. There's no Vietnamese Mother of the Year. Welfare mothers don't qualify for Madonna status, nor do unwed mothers—though that last is a curious thing, because for a time the original Madonna was herself an unwed mother. But inconsistencies up the ante of already ridiculous odds, and I find if I go around pondering them too closely, I just get depressed.

Maybe you thought that now that Roger is taking his turn on toilet duty I've got it made—but I still get depressed. A lot. I'm depressed right now. (Falls on podium.)

You know I'm teasing. You know I'm feeling great right now. Just think of it: Today in Buffalo, New York, nine hundred of us have come out of the closet—and that's cause for celebration. We could sit here all day and make jokes about some parts of our experience—and God knows laughing together beats crying alone—but I want to beg your leave to shift gears a bit. You know, and I know, that the flip side of comedy is tragedy, and we're talking about our *lives*. If we go on laughing over the absurd parts of our lives, ultimately the laugh is on us.

Believe me. I'm very happy that my husband is not threatened by a toilet brush—and I'm only kidding when I tell him he's getting a bowl fetish. Sharing chores *does* help, and nobody who's tried it knocks it. *That* part of my life is infinitely better than it used to be. You remember my neighbor I was telling you about? That wasn't my neighbor who did all those crazy things— that was *me*. That part about the Fuller Brush man, that wasn't true, I just put that in for a laugh—it was really the Avon lady.

But sharing chores is only a start—a necessary start, but still only a start— and pretty soon, you find yourself thinking: "Today the toilet. Tomorrow the World!" And before you can say Valium, you're behind the eight-ball again. Any of us who think we're doing okay, who think we've found individual solutions to our lives, are fooling ourselves, because a great portion of our mental health today is not an individual

problem. Stick one foot out into the world, you get a hot foot. Even if we hole up in our homes, throw ourselves into being Queen of the Castle, the message is still going to come through the fortress that we are not valued. I tell you, the ways the message comes in are legion; it could make you sick if you thought about it.

Fifty-three percent of the population is female, and women's rights are still considered a knee-slapper—and if we don't laugh, we're accused of not having a sense of humor. There's not one woman in the United States Senate. Our chances of getting a woman on the Supreme Court are not dependent upon any particular woman's legal ability, but on whether or not Betty Ford can

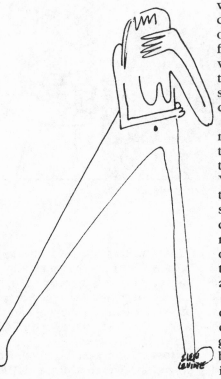

SEVEN YEARS IN ANALYSIS AND NOW THEY TELL ME ABOUT THE MYTH OF THE VAGINAL ORGASM

pillow-talk her husband into it. As for the few women who do hold high-level positions in government and industry— and you can almost count them on the fingers of Captain Hook—well, the poet Marge Piercy has said it better than I can: "The token woman gleams like a gold molar in a toothless mouth." We ought to do that line in needlepoint.

With our present realities, it's no big surprise so many of us stay home. And the 47 percent of the labor force made up of women who don't have, or don't want, the luxury of staying home are bucking odds that require them to be superwomen or masochists.

But women aren't dummies. We may smile; we may pretend not to notice we're not wanted, but that's survival, or buying a little time, because we don't feel we have control over our lives, or we don't feel there's any possibility of change, or, as Johnnie Tilman pointed out years ago, we're one man away from welfare. But we notice—and it works its way out in countless forms: the blues, boredom, listlessness; we get shrewish, have headaches, pop pills, drink before noon.

I want to take just a few minutes more to talk about this, and I'm going to be pausing now and then, because these are questions worthy of pause. You'll know when I'm done, because there will be a very long pause. This section is called: "I seen you when you come in, but I never let on," and by no means is it a comprehensive list of some of the things we're noticing, some of the things that make us feel valueless and vulnerable.

If housework and childcare are an indispensable service to society, how come mothers and housewives don't get social security? We pay veterans' benefits to soldiers for killing, but nothing to women who give life and sustain it. How come babysitters and domestics have bottom status on the Wage Index? If housework is so fulfilling, why aren't men beating down the doors to get in on it? Why do we ourselves apologize for it? And it's a cop-out to say we apologize because of feminist pressure: long before the Women's Movement began,

> **How can people say women are powerless? We control the traffic, the weather, the oregano: we're practically omnipotent.**

we were saying, "I'm just a housewife."

How come everybody agrees that poison should be kept away from children, and their textbooks and TV programs continue to be riddled with sexism?

You pick up the morning paper, and on the back-page photo section there are six pictures of men exercising some variety of power: Ford/Carter/Kissinger/Ralph Nader/Pope Paul/Idi Amin. Juxtaposed directly underneath, the only women on the page wear bathing suits: this year's Miss America contestants. What kind of effect does this have on our self-esteems? Our aspirations?

The Presidential Pornography Commission reports that porn saturation does not significantly arouse a man's sexual urge, but who examines what it does to our self-concepts when we walk past displays of spread crotches in living color?

What does it really say about motherhood when the judge delivers his decision in the tragic Karen Quinlan case? Giving the weighty, heart-rending power to terminate artificial life-prolonging measures not to the mother who bore her, not to the parents jointly, but solely to the father?

Why are women's smoking and women's alcoholism on the increase?

Why do a growing number of our best-educated women spend two, three, four afternoons a week working on their tennis backhands while their husbands advance their careers?

A suburban woman kills herself, kills her children, you read it all the time, and everybody says, "It doesn't make sense. She had everything to live for." Clearly, she didn't think so. And you can't help wondering: Why the children? Everybody who knew her said she was a devoted mother. Was she punishing her husband, punishing the children, or, in some terrible distraught mind-set, did she think she was saving the children, taking them with her in some desperately confused final act of love? There's often a terrifying line in those articles that says, "She and the children were inseparable."

And way down deep, in a secret place, we wonder: Where have our dreams gone?

I don't have the answers. Nobody has the answers. It's taken us this long to begin to ask the questions. We have one devastating fact: so many women are walking around with mental-health problems we can no longer chalk it up to personal flaws. I think reexamining traditional roles is a start. I think we'll all be better off when word gets around that cleaning a toilet produces no more and no less than a clean toilet; it does not strengthen character, nor is it interesting work. Most of all, I think we've got to start telling the truth. And the truth of our lives today is just plain depressing. We are damaged goods; our self-esteems so shaky you could write a book about it. Do we feel inadequate because we've become inadequate, or do we have no trouble staying humble because we get so much assistance? Why do we cry so much? For release? Or do we cry from disappointment and bitterness and anger? Do we turn our rage inward and make ourselves sick? Why are we so rough on ourselves? Why are we so rough on each other?

We've got to get some support systems going. Not systems that teach us to adapt to inhuman frustrations. Not systems that tout personal salvation and teach us to go it alone, pulling up the ladder after us. What we need are support systems that teach us to correctly identify our roadblocks, our frustrations, so that we can stop yelling at our kids, or the driver who stalls in front of us at the green light, and know what we're really upset about. We need systems that verify we're perceiving things accurately; that we're not crazy, but we're living crazy lives.

Maybe one place we could start is by having a Depressives Hotline. This is where you call a number, a woman answers, and you say, "I'm crummy." "Tell me about it," she says, and she's got the nicest voice. And then you tell her:

Maybe your washing machine sounds like it's choking on a piece of meat and the repairman shows up three days late

and says, "You're imagining it, lady." And your washer is still gagging, but you're nervous about calling back, because the way he said "Lady" sounded like an expletive;

Maybe you went to the hairdresser, and, even though you pleaded, he left you under the dryer till your eyes popped, and he yanked your hair in the comb-out, and the style makes you look like Prince Valiant, and you paid him sixteen dollars and thanked him for the abuse;

Maybe a businessman calls your husband at two in the afternoon and says he hopes he didn't wake you up;

Maybe he woke you up;

Maybe you told your husband you wanted a little life of your own, and now you're pregnant;

Maybe your divorce has not turned out to be a self-actualizing experience;

Maybe some creep exposed himself to your nine-year-old daughter, and, instead of understanding his pressures, you're filled with hate;

Maybe you fell asleep thinking, "There has to be more than this," and in a dream the Ghost of Christmas Future showed you yourself, and your hair was white, and you were holding a dishrag.

You tell her whatever it is, and then you say again, because that's how you feel, "I'm crummy." "No, you're not," she says. "Yes, I am," you say, and you argue about it till she wins.

Here's to our health, and luck go with you.

Do you know why women have lessened visual-spatial perception? Because we've always been told that this (hold up hands about four inches apart) is ten inches long.

Multiple Penis Envy

HADLEY V. BAXENDALE, M.D., Ph.D.*

Women's Libber Debby R. was only five when she was introduced to the theory of penis envy. "This boy I knew took me into a garage and taught me all about it." She was stunned and humiliated by this rude initiation into psychoanalytic thought. "It seemed like such a limited, prosaic envy," she told her analyst years later. "I always felt a healthy woman should want more. You know. *Why stop at one?*"

Imprisoned by his culture, Freud never envisioned the possibility that women might want several penises. He believed that the little girl discovers penises and covets *one*. She considers her lack of a penis a deformity that she can correct only by giving birth to a son, who, in Freud's words, "brings *the* longed-for penis with him" (my italics).

"I'd like five, to tell the truth," said Debby R. "It's an insult to suggest I couldn't handle five."

(*from* Are Children Neglecting Their Mothers? *1974*)

*Pseudonym for Joyce Wood. See footnote p. 24.

What God Hath Wroth

CHARLOTTE PAINTER

As Phyllis Wrath awoke one morning from uneasy dreams, she found herself transformed in her bed into an enormous male organ. Her family rushed in to examine her. Her two sisters turned green. Phyllis had always outdone them.

"You passionfruit!" her mother shrieked. "You did it for revenge!"

Phyllis (or Fill, as her friends now began to call her) had long known how to write best-sellers. With the zeal of one who never disdained an advantage, she began mentally to compose her memoirs. Instantly, she felt a throbbing in her head.

"She's growing!" cried her envious sisters. "God, look at her grow! You swellhead!"

Her mother swooned over the poultice she was trying to prepare.

There was no stopping Fill. The writing in her head rapidly metastasized throughout her system. Within minutes she had filled the entire house like Alice after the Pill. The neighborhood was squashed. Soon she was the size of the Washington monument. A crowd formed an obligingly round orifice about her as she soared upward. Train and plane reservations to the Wrath Center were booked for months ahead. CBS gave her twenty-four-hour coverage.

Phyllis thought, "I'll be the biggest thing since the moonshot," but soon she realized she would be bigger. As composition of her book went on, she came to understand that her very act of creation was causing her phenomenal growth. This insight brought on further swelling, and for the first time in her life Phyllis Wrath experienced cosmic enlightenment.

"I am writing something bigger than the Great American Novel, bigger than the Bible," she told herself. "I am writing the world. I *am* the world, the universe. I am God!"

A cloud brushed her head. The earth was a swirl below her. She was free of its maddening detail. She had attained godhead. Words failed her.

We followed her intently via satellite, caught up in a fabulous foreknowledge. It came. And the Lord spoke in the mightiest ejaculation since the Flood.

Capitalists and Communists alike changed their lives by cooperating in the universal distribution of Fill's book by artificial insemination, subscribed to by tithe, all proceeds to Fill's mother.

And that sainted woman was very, very proud.

(*from* The Nation, *Nov. 6, 1972*)

"Shut up, or I'll kill you!"

Mother's Day Poem

PAULINE B. BART

M is for her menopausal problems
O is for her "masochistic" needs
T is for her terror as she ages
H is for the help for which she pleads
E is for the emptiness her life is
R is for the roles that she has lost.
Put them all together: they spell MOTHER
The ones the culture's double-crossed.

I'm Sorry, You're Sorry

MARY KAY BLAKELY

There have been numerous reports lately about the amount of time women spend feeling guilty. Scratch their confident exteriors, and many women will respond with an ardent "I'm sorry." I would bet that a dozen randomly selected women would yield at least: three "I'm sorrys" because their offspring have turned out more like the Addams family than the Waltons; three for lousy dusting, never mind lemon-fresh shines; two for being the only ones in their offices who cannot work overtime; two for still buying additive-enriched, vitamin-poor convenience foods instead of stone-grinding their own wheat; one for refusing to buy the rest of the band candy; and one for not being on a diet.

We live in a world of shoulds. We should make more cookies from scratch, and we should send more birthday cards to friends. We should get more organ-

ized, and we should entertain more often.

As a consequence, women live in a semiconscious State of Sorry, ready to be visibly, vocally very sorry at the droop of a smile. Since just about everyone is walking around bearing some grievance still unapologized for, women are very handy people to have around. Unlike Oliver in *Love Story,* most women believe that "love means *always* having to say you're sorry." We are great apologizers.

Being so sorry is taking its toll. We barely get over being sorry for getting the kids to ball practice late when we have to start being sorry that there's only macaroni and cheese for dinner. Women answer the doorbell with "I'm sorry, I don't have my face on." It's hard to laugh and be clever when you're sorry. You can't ask for a raise when you really want to apologize. You can't send your burnt food back in a restaurant when your kids have been pitching saltines at the neighboring diners. Penitence is very limiting.

It's time, even the most strenuously sorry among us will admit, for a change. The situation calls for action, trading our regret for our self-esteem, our confessions for our confidence. I would like to propose a moratorium on remorse: an "I'm Sorry Boycott," a month of not accepting any blame.

1. Like any boycott, it must be practiced consistently. At home, when your son moans that he's late for the school dance and you haven't washed his shirt yet, don't say "I'm sorry." Remind him that you possess perhaps the only equal-opportunity washing machine in the neighborhood—it works for anybody who pushes the buttons. At work when the chair of the meeting asks for someone to take the minutes and everybody turns to you, the only woman in the room, don't say "I'm sorry." Demonstrate your knowledge of biology and remind them that shorthand skills are not genetic in women. The next time your family itemizes the services not rendered, don't say "I'm sorry." Suggest that someone else will have to pick up the slack. When the Hari Krishna makes a plea for money at your door, don't say "I'm sorry." Mention that a few adjustments in his attire might result in landing a paid

position.

2. I'm not oblivious to the enormous amount of willpower it will take for women to stop saying "I'm sorry," so I suggest that we use a buddy system. Choose a sorry sister and arrange to call each other when the need to apologize comes on strong. The urge to apologize cannot be underestimated when she doesn't make the team, or he doesn't get the part, or we can't volunteer the time. We feel reflex regret when the little one cries as we walk out the door, or the Olympic aspirant can't have gymnastic lessons this year. But before an "I'm sorry" appears like a Pavlovian response, get on the phone with someone who will tell you, "It's a crummy world. It's the pits. There ought to be more time in a day. But listen, you just can't *be* at the piano recital and your final exam at the *same time.*" She'll remind you, "You're given the givens. Don't be sorry. It's not your fault."

3. In order to avoid having all of the unspoken "I'm sorrys" go underground, creating a black market of sorry, there will be no ESP sorrys allowed. I'm not sorry, but it has to be this way. There shall be no sorry thinking during this boycott. This is a serious sorry cease-fire.

4. For the Truly Sorry, who will have difficulty quitting cold turkey, this boycott may cause withdrawal pain. I'm not impervious to the idea of an Apology Maintenance Program for the Incurably Sorry. We could offer a less harmful substitute "I'm sorry" for the veteran apologizers. A few words, as long as they do not accept blame, will do: "That's a shame," for example.

For thirty days, what can it hurt? Who will be injured? Sure, there will be a blame buildup, but what does it matter? And after the boycott, well, who knows? We may never go back to being so sorry, having experienced the fresh air of freedom from guilt. And if we do slip back to saying "I'm sorry," maybe the great want for apology we have created will cause a few grateful people to respond, "That's OK."

DON'T WEAR YOUR GUITAR, DARLING MOTHER

WORDS & MUSIC BY SHIRLEY KATZ
© Shirley Katz 1978

WITH FEELING
Intro

'TWAS SATURDAY NOON, I WAS STRUMMING A TUNE WHEN A

TUG ON THE TAIL OF MY SHIRT   BROKE INTO MY SONG— I KNEW

SOMETHING WAS WRONG, SO I SWITCHED TO MA—TERNAL A—LERT.   I

KNEW I COULD PLACE THAT WOEBEGONE FACE FOR A WISE MOTHER

KNOWS HER OWN CHILD—   I THOUGHT FOR A SPELL - SHE SAID

"MUMMY, I'M NELL!" I SAID, "WHY, OF COURSE" AND I SMILED -

"NOW, PRECIOUS, DON'T POUT, JUST SING RIGHT OUT, GOD MADE

MOTHERS TO COMFORT AND CHEER" SHE HEAVED A BIG SIGH, AND A

TEAR LEFT HER EYE - SHE SOBBED "OH, PLEASE, MOTHER DEAR —

149

150

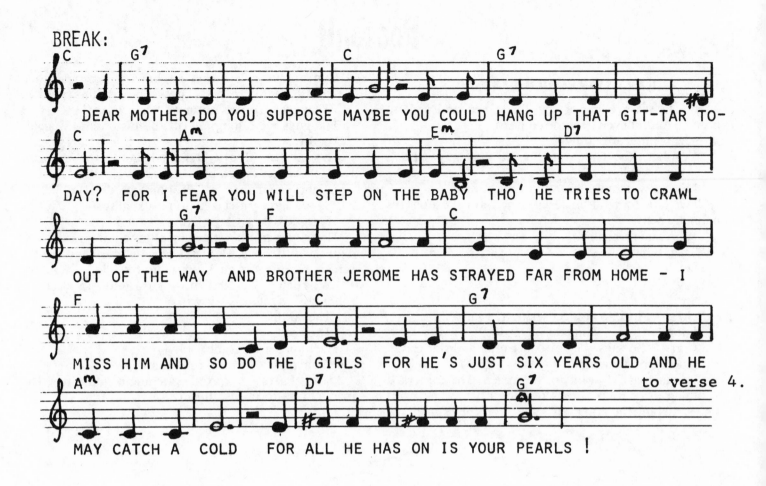

BREAK:

DEAR MOTHER, DO YOU SUPPOSE MAYBE YOU COULD HANG UP THAT GIT-TAR TO-

DAY? FOR I FEAR YOU WILL STEP ON THE BABY THO' HE TRIES TO CRAWL

OUT OF THE WAY AND BROTHER JEROME HAS STRAYED FAR FROM HOME - I

MISS HIM AND SO DO THE GIRLS FOR HE'S JUST SIX YEARS OLD AND HE

to verse 4.

MAY CATCH A COLD FOR ALL HE HAS ON IS YOUR PEARLS !

2.

Don't wear your guitar in the garden
Though the roses may like it a lot
The neighbors have started complaining
They think it's a Communist plot
They're passing around a petition
And, Mother, I think you should know
They say you're neglecting the children
And making the dandelions grow
Now the proper attire for the garden
Is a spraygun or barbeque mitts
Try aluminum foil
Or just suntan oil!
But hang that guitar on the . . .
Rotating spit of the barbeque pit . . .
Oh, hang that guitar on the wall!

3.

And, do you remember dear Father?
He promised to visit us soon
'Twas midnight last March when he
        left us
You were strumming an old ragtime
        tune
When he winks and says
        "Who's for the boudoir
For a beautiful rondo and lay?"
Don't grab your guitar and your
        tuner
You know men seldom mean what they
        say
If you can't find your lacy black
        nightie
Your chin strap or your Spanish
        shawl
Wear your jammies with feet!
Or just wear a sheet!
But hang that guitar on the wall!

4.

"Don't wear your guitar, darling Mother"
She begged as they led me away
"Don't wear your guitar, darling Mother
And the judge may release you some day"
Each night in a vision I see her
As I stare at that dark prison wall
And I weep for my innocent babies
Counting Nell there were . . . 10 I recall
Oh, I'm filled with remorse
        and with sorrow
As I think of my shame and
        downfall
Oh, I know I've done wrong
So I'll sing one more song
(well, maybe two)
Then I'll hang my guitar
        on the wall!

Football

CRAZY HAZEL HOULIHINGLE

Hyman was yelling at the TV screen and spilling beer. He didn't even hear me come in.

"That's unhealthy," I said.

"You bet it is. They're gonna kill that guy—and if they don't, I will."

"I mean, watching. *Watching* is unhealthy."

"I'm not football material," he says, patting his paunchy belly.

"Who said football?"

"Then what?" he says.

"Sex."

"Sex?"

"Sex."

"How the hell do you get sex outta football?"

"I don't," I say. "They do. YOU do."

"Crazy," he says, "it's a ball game, a BALL game. And there's no women."

"Lookit that," I point to the screen. The camera is zooming in on two heroes running off the field, and one is rubbing the other guy's ass. "Look at THAT!"

Hyman is a trifle shook up, but he pretends otherwise. "He just intercepted a pass," he explains.

"That allows caressing an ass—in *public?*"

The guys were jumping off the bench and hugging the heroes.

"Lookit that," I says. "Lookit THAT! They're *kissing* him. It's a big brawl to kiss the hero."

"Right," Hyman says. "He intercepted a pass."

"So we agree: ritualized homosexuality."

"For godssakes, Crazy," he says, "you're crazy!"

There was another play and a bunch of guys tackled a guy with the ball. Hyman keeps his eyes glued to the screen. A few more guys jump into the pile.

"Why?" I says, "did those guys jump in after the other guy was already down?"

"They didn't."

"They did."

The referee calls some foul.

"Well, maybe it was momentum."

"Sex," I says. "Sex. And watching is unhealthy, Hyman. Now I know just the guy for you . . . ."

"I'm feeling very hip today. I found out that being a housewife is now considered an alternative lifestyle."

Aaaaaaaaaaaaaaargh!

SHEILA BALLANTYNE

A 14-year interdisciplinary study with laboratory animals at the University of California has shown that anatomical and chemical changes occur in rats placed in an enriched environment, compared to their litter-mates living a more secluded, impoverished life.

Implications from the research are that the brain—including the human brain—can be expanded by experience regardless of age.

See? "Regardless of age!" I know that should really excite me, give me the green light, so why do I keep thinking of the litter-mates? *Because you both have the secluded, impoverished life, dummy.* But *I've* got choice, *I* can change my condition ("Accentuate the positive." —Bing Crosby). They are stuck in their cages because the researchers still aren't convinced that a woman alone in a little box, on a deserted street, with few social contacts and little mental stimulation, will end up with a shrunken brain. They have to see if it works on rats first—fewer variables that way—then apply their findings to us.

"Daddy! Daddy's home!" The door slams. He's here, whose funeral I conduct once a day in my mind. Norma Jean reaches for the vermouth and pours it in a red, white, and blue tumbler. She lights a cigarette. If I had a joint handy I'd smoke that too. *Try. You've got to keep trying.* She takes a long swallow of her drink and, wiping her mouth on the back of her hand, sweetly turns and addresses Martin as he reaches inside the freezer for ice:

"I made dessert," she says. There is a pause.

"As far as I'm concerned, you've already deserted."

"I *said,* 'I—Made—Dee-zert.'" What's the use? I *may* desert. More and more women are doing it. Private detectives claim business has never been better. I read it in the paper.

"Listen, you bastard! Stop punishing me! I have a right to call at least *half* my life my own! This has got to stop. I can't work, I can't do anything. I feel like running a knife right through your heart!"

"Go ahead, crazy lady! You've got no use for me anyway! Rotten blood-sucking bitch! Take all the things I've worked to give you, then say it's not enough! I could cut your heart out!" Animals go for the jugular; humans, the heart. It's unbelievable the primitive feelings that are aroused by rapid change. Crazy. He called me crazy again! If there's one thing I can't stand *Because it's true?* Yes! It's true! True true true! Now I know why I have always felt a profound sympathy for all crazy people everywhere ("Birds of a feather . . ."). Well, *my* crazy is better than *his* sanity—his warped, rigid, screwed-up . . . CRAZY IS BEAUTIFUL! CRAZY POWER!

"Aaaaaaaaaaaaaaaaaaaaaaaaaaaaaaaaaaah!"

"What the hell are you doing?"

"Aaaaaaaaaaaaaaaaaaaaaaaaaaaaaaaaaaah!"

"Norma! What's the *matter* with you? *Stop* it."

"Aaaaaaaaaaaaaaaaaaaah! Aaaaaaaaaaaaaaaaaaaaaaah!"
He wants crazy, I'll give him crazy. "Aaaaaaaaaaaaaaah!"

"NORMA! STOP SCREAMING THIS MINUTE!"

"Aaaaaaaaaaaaaaaaaaaaah!"

"Norma, please! I beg you, stop."

"Aaaaaaaaaaaaaaaaaaaaaaaaaaaaaaaaaaaah!" If I'd known it felt this good I'd have done it long ago. "Aaaaaaaaaa-aaaaaaaaaah!"

"We can't find your wife. . . It looks like she got away Scot-free."

"Norma . . ." I know what he's going to say: The Neighbors and The Children. "Aaaaaaaaaah!" (Fuck the neighbors) "Aaaaaaaaaah!" (Fuck the children) "Aaaaa-aaaaah!" (Fuck you).

"Mommy, what's the matter?"

"Dad, why is Mom screaming? Did you hit her?"

"Shit. No, Ruthie, I didn't hit your mother."

"Then why is she screaming?"

"BECAUSE I'M CRAZY!" It's lots of fun, Ruth Ann; when you grow up you'll be crazy too, just like me!

"Norma Jean! We'll talk about it later. Please just stop *screaming.*" Got to get to her before she starts throwing the pots and pans; once they get going with the pots and pans, you've lost the whole ball game.

"Aaaaaaaaaaaaaaaaaaaaaaaaaaaah!"

"Make her stop. She's hurting my *ears.*"

"Shut up, Damon. If you don't like it, go back to Popeye." You like Olive Oyl's screaming better than your own mother's?

"No one can stop me! Do you all hear? I can scream all night if I want! I am my own person! Aaaaaaaaaah!"

"Now you've made Damon cry, Mom; and I'm about to cry too." No, no, Ruth Ann; the Woman of Tomorrow doesn't cry. She screams!

(from Norma Jean the Termite Queen, *1975)*

154

CHAPTER NINE

Once Upon a Myth

GODDESS

bülbül

Application for Employment

RHODA LERMAN

APPLICATION FOR EMPLOYMENT

NAME: Ishtar

OCCUPATION: Mother Goddess

MARITAL STATUS: Mother/Harlot/Maiden/Wife

PRESENT ADDRESS: In transit. (Temporary address: Syracuse, New York)

AGE: $(E = MC^2)$ $(F = MA)$?

CHILDREN: same as above

EDUCATIONAL DATA: self-taught

SOCIAL/COMMUNITY ACTIVITIES: Laying of cornerstones, setting of foundations, sacred prostitution, (organizer, etc. etc. . . .)

SPECIAL HONORS: Star of David, Star of Solomon, Star of Bethlehem, Eastern Star (Grand Worthy Matron)

RECORD OF EMPLOYMENT: (Please record employment dates in chronological order)

TITLE: Queen of Heaven

PLACE OF EMPLOYMENT: Galaxy

DATES: 4,800,000,000–9000 B.C.

MAJOR RESPONSIBILITIES: Fashioning stars, worlds, suns, people (everything, etc.) Prime moving

REASON FOR TERMINATION: Project completed

SALARY: Original Title

TITLE: Angel of Death

PLACE OF EMPLOYMENT: Heaven

DATES: April 9000 B.C.

MAJOR RESPONSIBILITIES: General conflagration, boils, etc.

REASON FOR TERMINATION: Reorganization of Personnel

SALARY: Peace/Quiet/Rest–Sabbatical

TITLE: Queen of Heaven

PLACE OF EMPLOYMENT: above

DATES: 9000 B.C.–4501 B.C.

MAJOR RESPONSIBILITIES: Birth, love, death, disease, seasons, etc.

REASON FOR TERMINATION: Company failed to maintain initial commitment

SALARY: Adoration/Worship/Respect

TITLE: Angel of Death

PLACE OF EMPLOYMENT: above

DATES: April 4501 B.C.

MAJOR RESPONSIBILITIES: Flood engineer, Passover, Killing of 1st born, plagues

REASON FOR TERMINATION: Cut-back in territory and personnel

SALARY: Peace/Quiet

TITLE: Queen of Heaven

PLACE OF EMPLOYMENT: Heaven

DATES: 4501 B.C.–1350 B.C.

MAJOR RESPONSIBILITIES: Birth, love, death, augury, disease, changing of seasons, alphabets

REASON FOR TERMINATION: Personality differences (Moses & Monotheism)

SALARY: Adoration, cakes and incense

TITLE: Whore of Babylon (unemployed)

PLACE: wilderness

MAJOR RESPONSIBILITIES: Birth, love, disease, changing of seasons

REASON FOR TERMINATION: Still working

SALARY: Scorn and Calumny

DO NOT WRITE BELOW. THIS SPACE FOR OFFICIAL USE ONLY

The Creation of Man

RHODA LERMAN

Once upon a time when the Great Goddess, Ishtar, loved and ruled the earth and all of humankind were women and a simple chemical additive could cause reproduction of more women, an error was made. It did not indeed seem at the time a great error. It was rather a chromosomal deficiency. One of the children born was a mutant, tiny horns, too many aggressive parts in its soul, not enough intuitive parts and an odd roseate stump between its legs. Its infant features, however, were soft and pure in the image of the Great Goddess. The infant was brought to Ishtar.

Ishtar looked upon its face and spoke. "Send it away to the sea. It is necessary that it should not live."

The mother cried.

Ishtar spoke. "I see the world plunged into greed, grief, war and destruction. I see the end of civilization and the burning of our libraries. The infant is to be sent to the sea."

Wrapped in a reed basket, the infant was floated downriver toward the sea. At a bend in the river, the basket was caught by bulrushes and a wolf mother dragged the infant to its lair in the wilderness far beyond the walls.

The mutant grew. At first the wolf mother suckled the infant and then lay with it. Its limbs grew thicker and hairier. The other cubs nipped at its uprightness and wouldn't play with it for its deformities. The mutant ate raw flesh and fondled other beasts as he grew. Shepherd girls, returning from the pastures, reported that it had leaped upon them in odd, heavy ways. It was last seen running across the steppe after a pack of wolves.

Slowly the women forgot about the mutant. With Ishtar's guidance they continued about their business of creating civilization as had been decreed.

Many years later, the mutant appeared at the city gates, large, bestial and clumsy.

"I can perform funny tricks with my strange stump," he called to a gentle long-necked poetess writing under the shade of a fig tree. "I want to come into the city," he called to a stately group of matrons of Law passing along the avenue in their robes. They ignored him. "Let me in or I'll break your wall down."

The mutant huffed and puffed and kicked at a cornerstone. The poetess laid a finger to her lips. "Hush, I am composing alphabets."

"Let me in. I belong in the city."

"Nay," answered the gentle poetess, "you have eaten raw flesh. You belong with the beasts."

"I'll tend your flocks and sharpen your nubs and bring you delicate grains from afar and repair your city walls and install your air conditioners and do funny tricks with my strange stump if you will let me in."

The matrons, listening, nodded to the poetess. The poetess opened the gates. In return for his labors and funny tricks, the matrons promised to civilize him.

They have never succeeded.

Eventually the walls were kicked in.

(from Call Me Ishtar, *1973)*

To Whom It May Concern

TO WHOM IT MAY CONCERN:

What am I doing here? It is very simple. Your world is a mess.

A mess.

Your laws are inhuman. Your religion is without love. Your love is without religion and both, undirected, are useless. Your pastrami is stringy, and I am bored by your degeneracy.

But what's a mother to do? I'm here to bring it all back together again. I'll come and straighten things out for you. I will choose an image here to do my work. To do your work. I shall spray your dusty corners with Lysol so you will find knowledge, stitch up those parts of your souls which have lost each other so that man knows what is womanly in him and woman knows what is manly in her. You hate, screw, war, starve and die without knowing me. The closets of your souls are empty of power and love. I do not like to come down here and work. There are no men here for me and I become, as a fish beyond the sea, hungry. And when I am overworked and hungry, I am mean. And when I am mean, I am destructive. So watch it. You are going to have to show me some respect this time, or you will all be impotent and once more the world will come grinding to an end and that end, as in your own grinding, which I have witnessed often, uncomfortably, will have no ecstasy.

158

Excuse me. I begin my threats again. I must remember, this time, that if I want you to become more divine, I must be more humane.

Somehow, I will distribute the wonders of my baking to you, to heal and balance and restore to you the powers that once were yours in the antique. I have always been the connection between heaven and earth, between man and woman, between thought and act, between everything. If your philosophers insist the world is a dichotomy, tell them that two plus two don't make four unless something brings them together. The connection has been lost. But I'm back. Don't worry. I am going to give you the secrets this time. You are not ready, but then you may never be and whatever will I do with them then? I must warn you I am jealous and selfish. However, I am really all that you have. I am one and my name is one and there shall be no one before me. I will forgive you anything, though, if you will love me. Cordially yours,

I remain,
Your Mother/Harlot/Maiden/Wife
(The Queen of Heaven)

P.S. Call me Ishtar

(from Call Me Ishtar, *1973)*

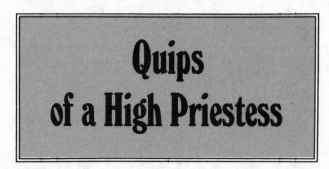

Quips of a High Priestess

On Kirlian photography: "The aura that women have, on average, is nine inches, all around the body, and for men it's four and a half inches. Now isn't that interesting—it *did* come down to inches after all!"

On the Goddess as "Momma": "Everybody has to go to sleep every day: Momma lives there. If you're a president or a waitress, you go to Momma every night."

Zsuzsanna Budapest, High Priestess, Susan B. Anthony Coven Number One. *

On bathing: "Most women are left alone in the bath. So you can lock the door and do bath spells. Then you come out four hours later—'Just been to India!'"

On sex: "It's written nowhere that every little man has to have a little woman. The Goddess identifies herself, 'I am she who binds hearts together.' There's never a word about genitals—that this particular genital goes with that genital. Momma never says stuff like that."

On cursing: "Each time you say, 'O my God,' there's an o-my-god groove in the brain that gets deeper and deeper. Or you say, 'Jesus Christ!' That's another subversive groove in your feminist brain. Now, 'O fuck' is O.K.—but 'son-of-a-bitch' is not. You can say, 'son-of-a-prick.'"

On soft words: "Those witchcraft books that tell you to throw yourself in an epileptic fit on the ground and scream show a very male approach. They think, if it's louder, it's better. It's the same thing as, 'if it's bloodier, it's better.' It is not. Very strong witches have been known to say very little with very great effects. When you have the mouth connected to the brain, your words really count."

* Most people do not know that the covens that originated in the United States during the 1970s represent a revival of goddess-worship. The term "witchcraft" refers to a goddess-worship that predates Judaism/Christianity and that stresses positive elements—creativity, wisdom, loving, pleasure, generosity, inclusivity, learning, tolerance, and healing.

You Are What Is Female

JUDY GRAHN

you are what is female
you shall be called Eve.
and what is masculine shall be called God.

And from your name Eve we shall take
the word Evil.
and from God's, the word Good.
now you understand patriarchal morality.

(from The Work of a Common Woman, *1978)*

The Takeover of Eden. Applique by Paula King.

The House of Mirrors

MARY DALY

Our planet is inhabited by half-crazed creatures, but there is a consistency in the madness. Virginia Woolf, who died of being both brilliant and female, wrote that women are condemned by society to function as mirrors, reflecting men at twice their actual size. When this basic principle is understood, we can understand something about the dynamics of the Looking Glass society. Let us examine once again the creatures' speech.

That language for millennia has affirmed the fact that Eve was born from Adam, the first among history's unmarried pregnant males who courageously chose childbirth under sedation rather than abortion, consequently obtaining a child-bride. Careful study of the documents recording such achievements of Adam and his sons prepared the way for the arrival of the highest of the higher religions, whose priests took Adam as teacher and model. They devised a sacramental system which functioned magnificently within the sacred House of Mirrors. Graciously, they lifted from women the onerous power of childbirth, christening it "baptism." Thus they brought the lowly material function of birth, incompetently and even grudgingly performed by females, to a higher and more spiritual level.

(from Beyond God the Father, *1973)*

Norma Jean's Theory

SHEILA BALLANTYNE

In the beginning, before primitive man made the connection between intercourse and conception, he would stand around in the afternoons, after the hunt, making observations. One of the first things he noticed was that all the women were getting bigger and bigger bellies. "Umph. Gee. She's getting fat," he would think. Then later, he would stand around in the evenings by the fire and he would see all the women giving birth to babies. "Fantastic!" he would say; "Whooo-ee! Looka that, come right out of nowhere!" He was ignorant of cause and effect, what with coming home tired from work, and the effort required to stay alive, etc.

After a while, his mind began to wander during

work. He'd think: "Here I am every day, out here whuppin' and clubbin' these animals; she git to stay inna cave, nice and warm, givin' suck to those things what come outa her. How come nothin ever come outa me 'cept shit? Still, I got this pleasant thing on me that rises when I needs it and goes down when I don't, and she don't have that. But a baby's bigger, and it can grow and do things by itself, and brings in extra food when it grows up. And she can have lots of them! I only got one of this. And it don't *do* nothin, 'cept go up and down, and in and out, and pee. Well, shit. I don't know." (This was the first recorded depression.)

Later on he made the connection between intercourse and conception. "Hey!" he said. "I made a discovery! If you fuck, you get babies!" It was as important a discovery, in its way, as the discovery of fire. After some years, however, he developed extreme melancholy. He confided to a friend, "I am *so* blue. I fuck and fuck, but *she* still gets all the babies!" His friend replied, "Yeah, I noticed that too. It's damned unfair that we don't get to have people growing inside us. Just imagine it—having another person *inside* you! It gives me chills. I'd sure like to try it to see what it's like, but I don't know any way to do it." (This was the original sex discrimination.)

The first recorded case of the defense mechanism known as overcompensation occurred shortly after this, as primitive man stormed out of the cave one morning, just after his woman gave birth to their fifteenth child, and said, "I just can't stand her no more! She lie there alla time havin babies, got no use for me. I am so *envious* I fit to die! Ungh ungh *ungh!*" "Well, cheer up," the voice of overcompensation whispered to him. "You still got your thing there." "Sure enough I do. I'll show her. I can do more things with this thing than she can do with her non-thing! I'm gonna have me some rape and pillage! And I'm gonna build me a great big weapon, shaped just like my thing, and I'm gonna kill a lot of dirty bastards with it! And then I'm gonna build me a monument in the shape of my thing, big as a mountain! And everyone gonna get down onna knees before it and they gonna say 'Whoo-ee! You are the *greatest.'*" So he went right out and laid waste to the land. And it felt so good he never stopped. And when he came home at night he kicked his woman in the head and said, "Nyaa, nyaa, nyaa! You can't come out with me and rape and pillage and smash things and lay waste to the land, cause you justa dumb broad; you gotta stay inna cave, havin' babies 'cause you got gypped; you got no terrific fantastic thing on you like I do! And don't you go trying to steal it inna night, either. It don't come off...(I don't think). I *knows* you envious; but you just gonna hafta make do. They's that got, got, they's that don't, don't." And as he lay there that night, he found himself in deep reflection about his woman. He thought: "She do mysterious things I can't do. She got mysterious things inside her I can't see. She *bleed* alla time but she never die! Weird. She scare me. I gonna keep her down so she can't do nothin funny, like eat me up."

(from Norma Jean the Termite Queen, *1975)*

"Because I don't call <u>this</u> 'happily ever after'!"

Honk if You Think She's Jesus

MUGSY PEABODY

Susan Pasteur Caanan watched Colonel George Armbruster cut his steak while her husband, Lt. Col. Harry B. Caanan, beamed under George's 467th retelling of Harry's brilliance in the cockpit. "If," Susan wondered, "ole Harry can find Hamilton Field in the middle of the night with a 4½ ton jet, why can't he find my clitoris?" Like many of Life's Compelling Questions, this had no apparent answer.

George's wife, JennyMarie, smiled and squeezed Susan's hand. George was now pounding on the table to emphasize points in what Susan called his "America—love it or go shoot yourself" speech when the California earth began to shake.

Susan looked up at the Sears five-arm chandelier, and she realized it meant to loosen itself and plop itself firmly on her head. She considered whether a coma might be a viable alternative to her life as an Air Force wife, and while she wondered, the chandelier came loose and plopped itself firmly on her head.

When the 4.7 earthquake ended, an Enlightened Susan found herself still alive and still awake. JennyMarie said, "This happened to my Aunt Bernice once . . . such a lovely woman, too. . . ."

"JennyMarie, living next door to you is like living with Dale Evans," Susan said.

"Oh, you're *so* sweet. She's always been one of my favorite thinkers . . . ."

Susan immediately found herself driving across the Golden Gate Bridge in her little green MG. She then found herself at the San Francisco Women's Halfway House and Enlightenment Par-

lor. Susan was very pleased to find herself. She'd been looking for twenty-eight years.

Enlightenment, in any case, is as great a burden as naturally curly hair—and in Susan's, the chandelier was so heavy she immediately reached that State of Being in which one says absolutely nothing Unenlightened. Small talk, of course, doesn't *have* to be dull. But this *is* America, after all. You can't just go around dropping Universals in people's tea.

So when Andiron L. answered the Halfway-Enlightened door and Susan said, "The impact of truth is a direct factor of the length of time during which it is disclosed," Andiron spent considerable time pulling on her earlobe.

But, noticing no guns, knives, or other threatening characteristics, Andiron finally said, "Say, listen, Sweetheart, why don't you just come inside and rest for a bit?" Andiron L. made one of two assumptions people normally make about Enlightened people—that Susan must be completely stoned out of her mind.

Susan put her pack down in the room with a 15-foot ceiling, 11 windows, 27 women, 2 cats, 3 kids, and a large overstuffed Indian print pillow on the floor in the corner next to the marble fireplace. A stained-glass window above the fireplace announced, "My consciousness is fine—it's my pay that

needs raising."

After watching for a few minutes, Susan smiled mystically and got up to stand in front of the blackboard on which were written Shana Alexander, Caroline Bird, and Rita Mae Brown's latest books and the editorial address of *WomanCabbie,* a magazine about the capitalist-sexist-bullshit-oppression of women driving cabs. Susan wrote:

$$\text{Impact} = \frac{\text{Truth}}{\text{Time of Disclosure}}$$

Then she sat down on the pillow and resumed reading *The Further Fattening Adventures of Pudge, Girl Blimp,* a comic book she found on the mantle of the fireplace.

"Hi," a woman squealed. "I'm Janelle."

Susan ran her fingers through her European short-cropped auburn hair and looked at Janelle. Then she looked at the other happy, bright, smiling faces. "Sound off, Mouseketeers," Susan said.

No one could think of anything to say that was supportive, so Andiron poured Susan a ceramic mug full of Red Zinger tea. Andiron was white with a dark brown Afro. She wore jeans and a long-sleeved dark print shirt under a t-shirt advertising the First Annual Handicapped Gay Eskimo Small Press and Beer Can Recycling Conference.

The women decided to rummage through Susan's daypack to discover who she was, a process she watched in bemused silence. "Strangers are only friends you haven't misunderstood yet," she told them.

Andiron said, "Well, Susan Pasteur Caanan, apparently you are married and live in Bel Marin Keys, CA 94934. So are you leaving your old man or what?"

. . . the masses, looking for packaged answers, found Susan Pasteur the Kraft cheese of their pre-cut world.

"Probably beat her," Janelle said. "Look at that bump on her head."

Susan blinked.

"Would you like to stay with us?" Susan didn't know what forces deposited her in the Halfway House in the first place, but as any Enlightened person could see, she would stay until she left. So she blinked again.

"Listen," Andiron L. suggested, "she's apparently blown away by whatever just came down, and she is bumped on the head, so why don't we give her a couple of organic aspirin and let her space for a while?" Everyone agreed this made sense, since it did. They returned to raising their consciousness so they could understand why Janelle's woman lover and new role as an independent leather craftsperson made her feel like the same piece of shit her husband and five kids had.

A woman named Cassandra suggested it was because there wasn't much market for leather Tupperware or soap dishes, but this was shouted down as non-positive support.

"Eventually one discovers one should not necessarily do those things one believes will make a real difference in one's life," Susan finally said.

"Why not?" a tearful Janelle asked, cosy from an evening of gratuitous hugs and attention.

"Because there is no external which can make a real difference in one's life. However, this possibility is often the positive force which helps one deal with the daily realities," Susan answered.

The women, notebooks in hand, had begun scribbling. They actually had no idea what Susan was talking about, but it sounded Important.

"So I shouldn't have fucked Maria," Janelle said, looking up from her notes.

"I guess that's what she's saying," Andiron said.

"Bullshit," Maria said.

"Bullshit is sexist. Cowshit?" Cassandra offered.

"No, then you'd have to say 'rooster-shit,' 'ramshit,' and 'eweshit,'" Andiron L. said, pouring Susan another cup of tea. After the meeting, she took Susan to a bedroom on the second floor. It had a poster that read: Those who spend their lives in closets smell of mothballs.

Susan stared at the poster, then let her daypack fall wearily to the floor. Andiron sensed Susan's loneliness, so she brought her sleeping bag in and slept next to Susan on the floor. Susan was beginning to like Andiron L.

When they awakened, Susan asked Andiron, "How many feminists does it take to change a lightbulb?"

"Dunno," Andiron grinned.

"Six," Susan said. "Four to discuss the political ramifications, one to provide day-care, and one to change the lightbulb."

Days passed, as they will whether or not we manage them, and Susan became the guru of the SFWHHEP. Wednesday nights became the time to gather at Susan's wisdom well. Though things she said often seemed strange and out of context, they made the women feel better. Soon, Wednesday Nights were moved to the Unitarian Church, where it was easier to accommodate four hundred persons.

Lt. Col. Harry Caanan eventually found himself in Dr. Luther Sang-Freud's office in Mill Valley. He, unlike Susan, had not been looking for himself, so he didn't really notice. Dr. Sang-Freud was saying, "Vell, my boy, you zee, often ve cure cases of amnessia, the affliction your voman zeems strugglink mit, by recreating ze circumzdances in substance identical mit doze vitch caused ze original difficulties," and puffed on his briar, wondering if this yahoo would finish paying for the redwood hottub.

"Sir, I don't really follow what you're saying," Harry said, knowing a great deal more about the outside of a jet than the inside of a thought.

"My boy, you obviously don't watch many 'B' movies."

Harry shook his head.

"Look, bozo, what you do is, hit her on the head with a chandelier."

For this, Harry paid $150.

The May Seminars began with "Susan on Friendship." From the Indian print pillow, she was staring at her Birkenstocked feet, stroking her auburn hair, and saying, "A real friend is someone who loves you in spite of your shortcomings. An enemy is someone who tells you they love you in spite of your shortcomings. And then catalogues them for you. Sometimes in a crowded room at the top of their lungs. Always for your own good." She paused to give the 3,000 notetakers time to catch up.

"There are men who are unwilling to pay for their lover's abortions unless they are absolutely sure the pregnancy was 'their fault.' In the vernacular, such people are referred to as 'assholes.' Many times, women pay for other women's abortions. They do not ask, 'Are you *sure* it's mine?' These are referred to as 'friends.'"

The crowd cheered. The cameraperson zoomed in for a close-up. This entire guru role embarrassed Susan, for she had the humility of a truly Enlightened person. But the SFWHHEP was taking care of her, so she continued.

"Sometimes assholes and enemies move out of town. And sometimes friends move out of town. I don't know where enemies and assholes move to. But friends move to Illinois, Indiana, Pennsylvania, or Sacramento. None of these is San Francisco. When enemies and assholes move, this is called 'Far Out.' When friends move, it is called 'Far Away.' These are not the same."

Susan noticed a young Mark Twain type in a white suit and Earth Shoes sitting next to Andiron L., who looked pissed. This was because Mark Twain was Media Venture, her ex-old-man, who knew damned well men weren't allowed in Parlor Seminars. (This wasn't Susan's decision.)

No one noticed the other man there, Harry Caanan, who was hiding behind a light boom in the back of the auditorium. This was unfortunate, for Harry

When enemies and assholes move, this is called 'Far Out.' When friends move, it is called 'Far Away.' These are not the same.

fully intended to hit Susan firmly on the head with the Sears five-arm chandelier he had cleverly concealed in a Safeway grocery bag.

Susan continued, "When you are angry and yell and throw things, people say you are acting like a Child. When you are angry and talk calmly and drink alcohol and can't sleep because your stomach hurts, people pat you on the shoulder for being Adult. When you act like a Child, people you don't like go away and they do not come back. When you act like an Adult, you get an ulcer and a sore shoulder and people you don't like like you. And you get angry all over again and again. This does not make you feel Better. Adults do not normally live as long as Children for this very reason."

Harry, meanwhile, was hiding in the curtains at the side of the stage. No one was paying any attention to Harry, which is how he managed this.

Media Venture leaped to his feet exuberantly. "I can sell her, I can sell her!" Media was *not* a pimp, though this was precisely what every person there thought. Even Harry.

But finally Media escaped the pile of screaming, kicking notetakers long enough to explain that he was a public relations man who owned his own counterculture advertising agency, which employed 52 percent women in executive/creative levels of power. And that some of his best friends were lesbian. Media explained he had a new slot for a guru account, since the U.S. Department of Silly Awareness Groups had created 175 new licenses for Silly Awareness Groups in 1979, over the dead bodies of Nalf Rader and his Citizens Against Silly Awareness Groups (CASAG).

While everyone was shouting at Media, Harry saw his chance. He aimed the chandelier straight at Susan's head, and as he was about to launch it, harpoon-fashion, Andiron decked him with a karate chop. Then she deposited him on the auditorium steps with a broken chandelier and a good deal to think about.

Susan watched these proceedings from a brown study atop her pillow. She was not pleased. She knew, given the opportunity, this was not the most fun she could have on a nickel.

In fact, it took her two days, back at the urban ranch, drinking tea and eating 9-grain wheat toast—while Media outlined his Plan for Susan Pasteur Seminars, Inc.—to quit trembling. She had watched so many "B" movies since marrying Harry that she had won Dialing for Dollars eleven times, and she knew exactly what Dr. Sang-Freud had told Harry. Eventually she relaxed.

In six months Susan became an overnight sensation. Media told her that Wednesday Nights, now telecast nationally from the Halfway House, brought in $83,000 a week in donations alone. Susan was the only person in history whose name Barbara Walters actually pronounced correctly. The Pasteur, Inc., offices at Ghirardelli Square on San Francisco Bay employed forty-three men and persons. Pasteur owned seven white Dodge vans with drop-down side doors to display "the line." School kids wore little gold-plated chandeliers around their necks and carried ring-binder notebooks full of Pasteur sayings. There was a TV tape, a radio cassette, a ten-minute movie, and a full line of jogging wear. Bumper stickers, posters, and buttons from Maine to San

"Thank goodness! I was scared to death he'd slay that dragon and I'd have to marry him."

The intelligent woman, men say, is likely to be inedible, a long drink of water, a skinny pickle, a stringbean, a pill, a dried-up prune, a bag of bones, an old hen, a dog.

Diego pleaded for the Pasteurization of America. The Lt. Col. Harold Caanan Fan Club in Georgia was composed of retired Air Force officers whose wives had left them for Susan, the Rev. Sun-Moon-and-Stars, or other Silly Awareness Groups.

Indeed, the masses, looking for packaged answers, found Susan Pasteur the Kraft cheese of their pre-cut world. They paid through the nose to see her (dressed in white fisherperson's clothes imported from Greece, sitting cross-legged in front of a portable fireplace) speak from her giant Indian print pillow. Fully half the country was hitting itself over the head with chandeliers in search of Enlightenment. No few wanted to fuck her, too.

Susan, Andiron, and Media were on a PSA jet to LA to meet with an agent who wanted to do a movie of Susan's life, starring Joan Baez, Golda Meir, and Candice Bergen, when Susan said, "Knowing when to end something is the hardest thing in the world."

"Certainly," she thought, "it's too bad I can't just say I want out of this fucking zoo. Once, an art teacher told me I had overdone a watercolor and ruined it. He said, 'It takes two people to do a good watercolor—one to paint and the other to shoot the artist when the work is finished.' A good deal of living is like this."

She was staring at the beautiful girl sitting across the aisle from her, next to the tall New Englander. The girl's head was swathed in bandages, with blond tufts of hair, clear blue eyes, and an angelic smile.

Media said terrifically, "Susan, that would make a great quote for the new steno pad line. 'Knowing when to quit' —no, that wasn't it. Or how about the new promo brochure?" He whipped out his pen.

Susan continued looking at the beautiful girl. This was because the girl had hypnotized her with the crystal pendant she wore—quite deliberately.

Andiron said to Media, "Shut up, Asshole." Andiron, being a true friend, had figured out how to tell what Susan actually meant by what she said, no matter how Enlightened it sounded.

"Some things go on," Susan said. "This is because they are Good Things. Why some things are Good and some Bad, no one really knows," she continued. Media scribbled. "Andiron," she said, taking the woman's hand, "do you know Janelle has taped everything I've said since I came to the SFWHHEP? She has an entire closet full of everything I've said, including 'pass the maple syrup' and 'wonderful, but a little higher and to the left.'"

Media said, "No shit, really? That's terrific!"

Andiron said, "Steady, Big Fella—before you start adding interest and capital gains—I rewired Janelle's tape recorder so the 'play' button is the 're-cord' button, and the 'record' button is the 'play' button. So every time she plays one of those tapes, she erases it."

Susan said, "Isn't she beautiful?", looking at the girl across the aisle and holding Andiron's hand. The stewardess asked them if they wanted anything to drink. She was wearing an "I've been Pasteurized" button. Susan didn't really see them anymore. Everyone wore them. The girl sat down in the aisle when the stewardess left and put her head in Susan's lap.

"What is she, about fifteen?" Andiron guessed. Andiron thought she was another of the thousands who were convinced that Susan could heal them just by touch. Susan nodded, stroking the girl's head. "Sixteen in November, a Scorpio," Susan said. The middle-aged New Englander turned out to be her father, and he buttonholed Venture in hushed tones. They went off to the bar together.

Susan said, "Sometimes people say it didn't Work, or it did Work." She stroked the girl's head. "People do not say it Played, or didn't, unless they are talking about a phonograph record." The stewardesses sat in the seats behind her, taking notes in their Pasteur steno pads.

"This is interesting because it tells us people think more highly of work than of play. People who think more of play than of work are called 'Children' or 'Artists' or 'Hippies' or 'Crazy.' There is not a lot of difference. People who think work is more important than play are called 'Adults.' This is another reason Children live longer."

"My name is Meredith Hyding," the girl said.

"I know," Susan said.

Meredith explained to Susan, "The reason things often end badly is because the communication to take them through ending well is not there. If the communication still existed, things probably wouldn't end at all."

Susan smiled. "I was wondering about that."

Then Meredith hit Susan over the head with her carry-on bag, in which there was a Sears five-arm chandelier.

Mr. Hyding explained later that Meredith had recently been hit by a falling lighthouse in Braintree, Mass. She, too, had become Enlightened.

Meredith told Susan it was time to quit the business and seek personal happiness, since being happy was the only truly Revolutionary, Enlightened thing anybody could do. She told Andiron and Susan to spend the next month or so gnoshing hotdogs and watching Winnie the Pooh movies at Disneyland. Susan soon became convinced that Meredith was far more Enlightened than she had ever been.

By the time PSA landed in LA, Susan had appointed Meredith her successor, the father had hired Media to take care of business, Meredith agreed to see the agent about Susan's movie, and the stewardesses forgot to bring their drinks because they were too busy writing down what both Meredith and Susan said.

When Susan and Andiron walked through LA International, they passed two security guards handcuffing Harry to a row of Fiberglas chairs. Susan told them to release him. Then she told him she was in love with Andiron and

Those who spend their lives in closets smell of mothballs.

wanted a divorce. Harry hit himself over the head with his chandelier and immediately accepted the wisdom of this. In fact, he became so aware that he left the Air Force, married Janelle, hit her over the head with his chandelier, and became an organic carpenter in Taos, New Mexico—where he donated all his above-subsistence earnings to the Pueblo Indians.

Susan and Andiron opened a restaurant overlooking the Pacific Ocean at Big Sur, California. The dining room is dominated by a very large, framed poster of Meredith Hyding in a hot, steaming bubble-bath. The slogan says, "Anybody who pays $250 to be told they're okay isn't."

They remained happy for quite some time.

Why Little Girls Are Sugar & Spice and When They Grow Up Become Cheesecake

UNA STANNARD

I. Cannibalism—A Fable

Once upon a time in herstory, before history, before humankind knew that copulation led to conception, one way women could get pregnant was by eating. Princesses in ancient China who wanted babies ate lotus flowers; women in Northern India ate coconuts; Celtic women drank mistletoe tea. Men did what they could to take part in the great mystery of new life by casting spells on the food they hunted: a man would say to the spirit of a dying animal, "Go,

start a new life in the belly of Q," or to achieve the same effect, he would give a woman part of the animal to eat. In herstory women ate the life of plants and animals and gave them a new birth. In herstory women were the cannibals.

In herstory man fed woman, not because men were the hunters but because man wanted a vital role in the creation of life, a role he could achieve only by thought control, by getting a woman to eat food he had willed with life power. In herstory a man couldn't get a woman pregnant by raping her; he had to tempt her to eat his magic food.

In North Queensland it was the custom for a man to court his beloved by offering her food. If she ate it, she knew she was pregnant; if she ate it, they were married. The man offering her food was also offering her himself. By eating the food she not only incorporated a new life, she incorporated the man whose life then became a part of hers. In herstory a man leaves his father and mother and cleaves unto his wife. In herstory women ate men.

History began when woman fed man, when Woman in the Garden of Eden gave Adam fruit "and he did eat." It

was a solemn transference of power, of knowledge of the great secret of how life begins, for after Adam eats the fruit, he and Woman cover their genitals with fig leaves; they know the function of copulation, that semen is the magic life substance. Woman henceforth conceives and bears children in sorrow and her husband rules over her because she is no longer the great creator of life. Man is. Man henceforth preempts woman's herstorical role. He becomes the sex who thinks he needs food to create semen, which is itself called "seed," a kind of embryonic food man plants in woman from which grows "the fruit of the womb," as the Bible calls babies. And woman henceforth cooks and serves man food because, like herstorical man, she wants to play a vital role in the creation of life and wants to become, like the food, one with the superior sex, incorporated into the life of a man. In history a woman leaves her father and mother cleaves unto her husband. In history men eat women. Men are the cannibals.

History began when man became God, the Almighty Seed-Bearer, the creator of the flesh and blood womban fruit which, though it ripened and died, was always supplanted by new fruit. However, after many centuries a sect of men conceived a higher conception of life, of life that need not depend upon womban; life, therefore, that need never die. For if womban produced only mortal life, wasn't it logical to conclude that the sex that carried the seeds of life within its own body could create immortal life? And lo and behold, the Miracle came to pass. At least according to history, which commemorated the momentous event—the creation of immortal life by man—by beginning history anew. Before the Miracle was relegated to B.C., the era of natural dissemination, when Adam and his male progeny broadcast their seed and populated the world. A.D. glorifies the era of spiritual dissemination, when man (and man alone) became capable of populating heaven with progeny that would

never die. But immortal beings are created in the old herstorical way—by eating, except that the magic food is now a man, an immortal man. "I am the bread of life," said Jesus, and whoever eats his flesh and blood, the bread and wine of the sacrament, is born into "everlasting life." By eating Jesus, believers give birth to their immortal selves. In A.D., men and women eat a man. It is the era of Christian cannibalism.

II. Natural Herstory

We start life as herstorians. Having observed mummy's belly grow fast and having been told food makes people grow fat, all children, male and female, naturally conclude eating can make them pregnant. Boys and girls invest food with life-creating powers. Boys and girls call their feces "chocolate babies." Boys and girls have fantasies of eating themselves pregnant, though psychiatrists tend to find that fantasy only in girls. The adolescent girl's alternating passion for gorging and dieting is an expression of her desire/fear to be pregnant, but adolescent boys are probably not without that unconscious complex, and it is highly doubtful that bulimia, a neurotic compulsion to eat oneself fat = pregnant, afflicts only women. The male potbelly, or beer belly, may well be the palpable projection of an unconscious desire. And the childish belief that eating causes pregnancy may explain the food cravings of pregnant women and the deep concern of men that these cravings be satisfied.

Many folk cultures are still in herstory. Until recently Christian women in Tuscany and Portugal who had trouble getting pregnant got consecrated food from a priest. "A man is what he eats," said Feuerbach and Savarin, an herstorical belief that some peoples take literally in regard to fetuses. Indian women of the Gran Chaco don't eat mutton after marriage so their children won't have flat noses. Ibibio women of Southern Nigeria abstain from snails so their babies won't slaver. Gypsy wom-

en eat a cock if they want a boy, a hen if they want a girl.

Wedding cake is herstorical food, magic food to ensure the bride's fertility. Our modern wedding cake is an extra-ceremonial ritual, not part of legal marriage, but in ancient Rome the bride and groom, as part of the marriage service, had to eat a special cake called *confarreatio*. In modern Morocco native brides drink holy water just before the marriage is consummated so that they will have many children, especially male ones. Such customs are reminiscent of the conception-marriage food of North Queensland, where, when the woman eats the food a man offers her, she is both pregnant and married. To ensure the wife's fertility, a Hindu bride and groom on the fourth day of the marriage ceremony eat off the same leaf.

The wife never again eats with her husband. He eats alone or with men only, a practice men have often been fond of. An Eskimo woman may not eat with her husband. In Barotseland, whether married or unmarried, men and women eat separately. In the Uripiv islands a man who eats with a woman runs the risk of dying suddenly, and in many African tribes it is a capital offense to eat with a woman. The former middle- and upper-class custom of requiring the women to leave the dining room after a meal so the men can drink and smoke alone is a civilized attenuation of the primitive I-want-to-be-alone-when-eating complex, and of course there were until recently many drinking and eating places from which women were barred.

The original segregationists were men excluding women from their private clubs. Among savages, a woman could not enter the all-male initiation houses (or wombs as they were sometimes called), whose doors resembled gaping vaginas and in which men performed secret rituals, symbolic imitations of menstruation and pregnancy. Among Christians, a woman could not enter the hallowed inner sanctum of

churches where men performed the magic that created immortal life. Why, then, shouldn't men have wanted to be alone when they performed another act once thought to create life?—eating.

III. Unnatural History

In the James Bond novels it's hard to tell when the gourmet meals end and the girls begin, a stew that has a long history and that is a peculiarly male contribution to civilization.

In herstory eating was eating and sex was sex. Sex was a pleasant pastime; eating the important act that could make women pregnant. When eating became the important act that could make a man fertile, it became necessary to have a woman around in which to deposit the fertilized seed. Food is and always has been the most popular aphrodisiac, because aphrodisiacs originally caused conception. In herstory it was the woman who ate the mandrake root or other magic food to make herself pregnant; in history men eat mandrake roots or drink milk in which the testicles of a ram or goat have been boiled, or the genitals of a cock, or onions, oysters, or fish in order to fertilize and increase the quantity of their semen. Since semen has to be transferred to a womb, aphrodisiacs also had to make a man potent, but potent used to mean primarily the ability to beget, only secondarily the ability to get erect. The ancient phallic monuments were not incitations to male lechery; they were fertility monuments, inciting men to propagate the species.

Wine and women, feasting and fucking became male correlatives because women used to follow dinner in the interest of conception, for which reason the early Christian ascetics, who advocated sexual continence, urged men to abstain from food. "An empty and rumbling stomach," said Jerome, is indispensable for chastity. "The beginning of chastity is fasting," said St. John Chrysostom.

Woman, having become associated with food, by a further compression became herself a sexual comestible:

No Grape that's kindly ripe, could be
So sound, so plump, so soft as she,
Nor half so full of Juice.

Thus did John Suckling in the seventeenth century smack his lips at the prospect of a peasant bride. Mercutio, in *Romeo and Juliet*, calls Juliet's vagina "A pop'rin pear." But the favorite fruity part of a woman's anatomy was the cherries that were her lips. Wrote Thomas Campion: "Those cherries fairly do enclose/ Of orient pearl a double row," and the cherries obligingly cry out "Cherry ripe" when they are ready to be kissed. Seventeenth- and early eighteenth-century poetry is overfilled with such delicious red bitable cherries.

In the nineteenth century, the century that created the word millionaire and the acquisitive way of life, woman became an article of conspicuous consumption. The aged John Jacob Astor, the first millionaire, no longer able to digest food, drank long and deep of a wet nurse. Young robust men preferred strong meat. *"Le plat du jour"* was the nickname of a particularly tasty and available French whore. A Russian whore was dubbed *"Salade-à-la-russe."* In 1864 Cora Pearl, a famous expensive whore, gave a banquet for men only in which she had herself served up on a huge silver platter, naked except for a sprinkling of parsley. *Femme-à-la-cannibale* must have become the rich lecher's Saturday night special. At the turn of the century the American cotton king, McFadden, ordered and got Maxim's of Paris to serve him a naked girl covered with a pink (cherry?) sauce.

In our age of democracy every Tom, Dick, and Harry has his dish, his tomato, peach, cookie, or chick, whose breasts are apples, grapefruits, or watermelons, her ass a pear, and her legs cheesecake. (Women's legs, of course, didn't become edible until the twenti-

eth century, when they became visible.) The modern *pièce de résistance* is still the cherry, at least for jaded gourmets who like to impale that choice morsel, which has now descended to between a woman's lower lips. Cherries, like truffles, are hard-to-get delicacies, but every man can have his sugarbun or honeypie, a favorite male figure· of speech because the part stands for the hole.

Food is consumed and a marriage is consummated; an orgy is an exotic stew of food and/or women; appetite is both sexual and oral, a wolf is a man who preys on women and also a rapacious eater, who is driven by the same hungry root as the rapist; carnal knowledge and carnivorous are two forms of meat consumption; fleshpots are pots for cooking meat and dens of sexual indulgence; little girls are sugar and spice and Mom is apple pie; sexy women make men drool; plump Jewish women are "zaftig," juicy, like dirty jokes; vulva sprays are fruit-flavored; men who act like women are "fruits"; and bad food and bad women are both adulterated—because women are food.

Women are food, like animals. When man became *homo sapiens,* he excused his taste for meat by explaining that animals are inferior, irrational beings put on earth by God for man's use. Women, who are also defined as inferior, irrational beings ordained by God for man's use, are also man's rightful food. Therefore, in order not to deplete their meat supply, men have kept women animal-like and have not allowed them to develop the rational faculties distinctive of men. The intelligent woman, men say, is likely to be inedible, a long drink of water, a skinny pickle, a stringbean, a pill, a dried-up prune, a bag of bones, an old hen, a dog. The intelligent woman, men also like to say, would be better off cooking than using her head. "She that knoweth how to compound a pudding is more desirable than she who skillfully compoundeth a poem," said a seventeenth-century Puritan. "A man in general is

"Oh go on! I've kissed too many toads already!"

better pleased when he has a good dinner than when his wife talks Greek," said Samuel Johnson. "I'd rather see a woman make such biscuits as these than solve the knottiest problem in algebra," said the brother-in-law of Susan B. Anthony in 1839 when he tasted her cooking. "My husband doesn't give a hoot that I can whip out an appendix, but he was thrilled when I became a good cook," said a doctor in 1965 when she gave up medicine to produce seven children and an infinite number of meals. When journalists want to prove that a female judge or banker is really a woman, they are likely to tell us she's a good cook. The male gut feeling that cooking is woman's natural province, head-work an unnatural one, that women should be associated with food not the mind, derives from the male classi-

fication of women as animals, as man's meat, not rational beings.

To set up intelligence in women and cooking as opposites, like black and white, is to set up a false opposition that has nothing to do with reality, but the belief that women were food was highly productive of such absurd irrationalities. Starting in the late eighteenth century, men began to feel that women should be seen but not eating, at least not eating a lot. Said a 1788 book of table manners: "As eating a great deal is deemed indelicate in a lady (for her character should be rather divine than sensual), it will be ill manners to help her to a large slice of meat at once, or fill her plate too full." In 1821 the poet Byron said, "I have prejudices against women: I do not like to see them eat." Later in the century Swin-

burne at meals used to put a vase in front of him to block the view of his friend's wife eating. Scarlett O'Hara stuffed herself before a banquet because it was unladylike to eat heartily in the presence of men. In any case, the nineteenth-century woman's corsets, tightened like a vise, precluded heavy eating in public. Women's mouths were psychologically behind the veil. Men did not want to see women eating, for if, as men believed, women were food, why should they need to eat? Women should be the eaten, not the eaters.

Similarly, when one starts with the proposition that women are food, then food must be women. Logically, food and women should become interchangeable commodities and sexual equivalents. And they did. At the same time as men began to find the sight of a

woman eating repellent, they began to think of women as pure, sexless beings. Scarlett O'Hara, eating little or nothing at a banquet, made men think she was an angel, not only because angels live on air but because angels are sexless. The nineteenth-century woman's corsets cut her off from her sexuality as much as from her stomach. Both sex and eating had become sensualities reserved for men. Both sex and eating had come to be regarded as gross aggressive activities suitable for men only, another irrational male belief that resulted from his confusion of women with food.

A further fantastic notion developed from that confusion. For, if women and food are sexual equivalents, then just as a woman can be looked at as food, as a honeybun or tomato, then food can become a woman—peeling a tomato can mean undressing a woman and biting into one taking a woman. Food becomes a sex substitute, which accounts for the strange belief that "the way to a man's heart is through his stomach." That proverb, which says a man can be seduced by food, is not recorded before the nineteenth century and could not have come into being until food had become a sex substitute and women had been denied their sexuality and therefore had to resort to a symbolic equivalent. Both the courtesans who served themselves up naked on silver platters and the ladies who served their gentlemen callers large quantities of home-cooked food were symbolically saying, "I am sexual meat." The difference was that the whores consciously knew what they were. But the ladies unconsciously knew the food they served was a sacrament, their own bodies offered up to the male cannibal. Both the lady and the whore were setting themselves up as the sexually eaten, not the eater. To serve a man food in our culture means that a woman has no sexual appetite but is willing to serve a man's appetite.

If every woman's magazine is still stuffed with recipes, if *Cosmopolitan* instructs its playgirls in the art of seducing a man by the culinary magic of shrimp remoulade or steak he-man style and advises a successful seducer to keep her man enthralled by serving him caviar and sour cream omelettes in bed, if publishers still find it profitable to put out HOW-TO-GET-YOUR-MAN-COOKBOOKS, it is because women think of themselves as articles of sexual consumption, not sexual consumers.

Woman IS a piece, which is why she feels compelled to become part of a whole, to serve the piece she is to a man. The food she serves is herself, and she, like the food, wants to be swallowed by the man, to become legally and nominally incorporated into him. And when she achieves her goal, when she is swallowed into a male establishment, she descends to her proper place—the belly, where she becomes a man's womb. R.I.P.

IV. Counter-Arguments

(1) If women are food men eat, what about the common male fear that women are mouths that eat men?

Woman "is a mouth and a voracious mouth which devours the penis," said Jean-Paul Sartre in his *Existential Psychoanalysis.* Karen Horney found that same fear expressed in the dreams of every one of her male analysands, and the myth of the *vagina dentata,* that the vagina is a mouth with teeth that bites off penises, is one of the most widespread myths.

It probably is perfectly natural for men to fear entering the vagina, which is going blind into a dark place. So long as man identifies with his penis, so long as it is his "little man," he will have such fears. But the myth of the *vagina dentata* may have a less natural origin; it probably did not spring into men's psyches until history, when men began to incorporate women, to dehumanize them and deprive them of power. Since we fear others will do to us the harm we have done to them, men fear women will deprive them of power, which since history is located in the penis; hence men have fantasies of vaginas as castrating mouths. The myth of the *vagina dentata* is psychologically a projection; men fear women will devour men as men have devoured women.

(2) Since women historically have been the sex associated with food, why are chefs traditionally men?

To be a chef is a fulltime job that takes a woman outside the home; until recently a woman's place 'was in the home. Furthermore, what properly possessive husband would want his wife, the woman who serves him and is his sexual meat, to serve the same function for other men? That would be equivalent to prostitution. Moreover, when women cook, so goes the male tale, they cook by instinct, as an extension of breastfeeding; it flows from them naturally. But when men cook it is an art, culinary science that requires the rational faculties women lack (for centuries cookbooks were written only by men). Just as women were capable of producing mortal children, but a man was needed to produce immortal children, so for the day-after-day, three-times-a-day feedings a woman is adequate, but for *haute cuisine,* soul food, men are necessary. Chefs are the priests of cooking.

(3) There is no need to invent herstory to explain why women are food. They ARE food; women's breasts are a baby's milk supply.

Because of lactation there is a natural association of women with food. The only difficulty is that female infants suck at the breast, too. Therefore, why is it that women don't grow up hungering after women the way men do? The chief reason seems to be that at an early age women are conditioned to stop thinking of mother as food. In some societies the conditioning is early and drastic. For example, in parts of Japan, whereas boys used to be weaned gradually and gently, girls were weaned suddenly and harshly—the mother rubbed red pepper on her nipples. Yet such ex-

treme measures are not necessary in cultures in which women do the cooking, for since infants by the age of two have identified with their sex, girls quickly identify with mother and become the food producer, the food not the fed. With girls, the infantile association food = mother = love is transferred to the girl herself and she becomes food = mother = love, the sex that is supposed to give, not get, foodlove. Boys, on the other hand, are allowed to go on regarding mother as foodlove, an association that is extended to all women at adolescence, when girls are culturally designated as man's sexual meat. Therefore, when men eat food made by a woman they are unconsciously still being fed by mother. The male association of Mom and apple pie is by no means innocent; it is oral incest, just as, when Mr. Jones marries and his wife becomes—like Mom—Mrs. Jones, he commits nominal incest. But culturally approved incest is for men only. Just as when Miss Jones marries, her husband does not become—like Dad—Mr. Jones, so the spicy momsexfood is exclusively a male dish.

Women do lactate, but that does not mean they have to be culturally identified with food or solely responsible for the daily feedings. There is no innate necessity for women to be the cultural milk fountains, men the greedy suckers. A society could have been created in which both men and women, after lactation, feed the children—one in which both men and women bring home the bacon and cook it. In such a society there would be a healthier give and take between the sexes. Women would not be processed into health food for men, and men would stop hunting pieces of ass and plucking peaches and gobbling up cream puffs and piercing cherries and wolfing down grapefruits and watermelons and devouring cheesecake.

(4) Men are hot dogs.
  Irrefutable.

"I've risen quite far in the company. . . all the way from tomato to top banana."

CHAPTER TEN

S/He-It

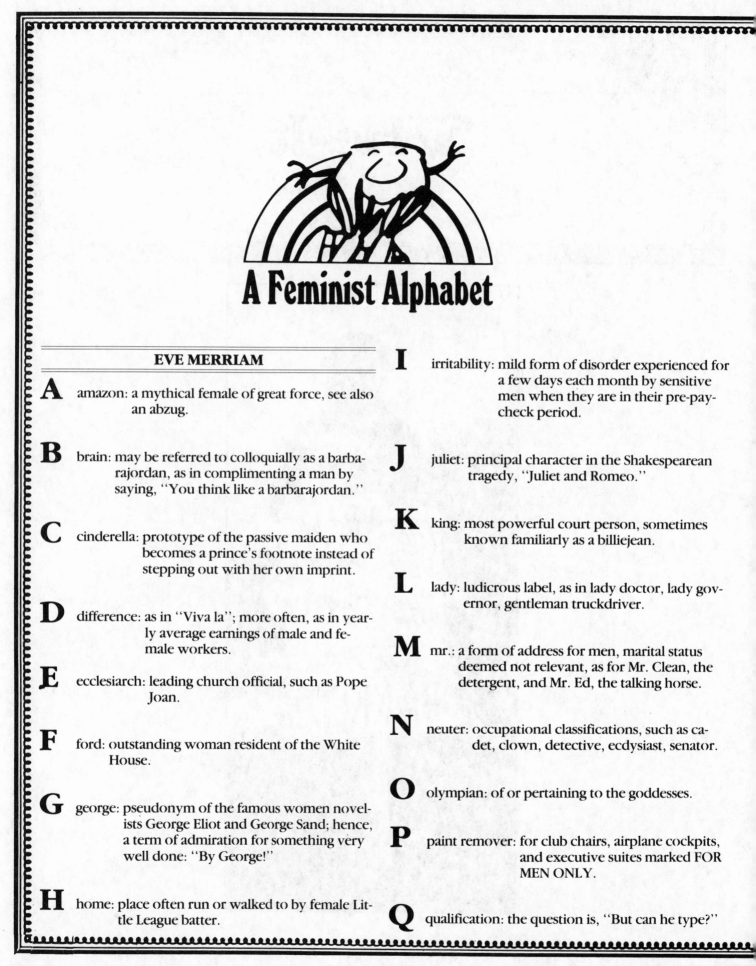

A Feminist Alphabet

EVE MERRIAM

A amazon: a mythical female of great force, see also an abzug.

B brain: may be referred to colloquially as a barbarajordan, as in complimenting a man by saying, "You think like a barbarajordan."

C cinderella: prototype of the passive maiden who becomes a prince's footnote instead of stepping out with her own imprint.

D difference: as in "Viva la"; more often, as in yearly average earnings of male and female workers.

E ecclesiarch: leading church official, such as Pope Joan.

F ford: outstanding woman resident of the White House.

G george: pseudonym of the famous women novelists George Eliot and George Sand; hence, a term of admiration for something very well done: "By George!"

H home: place often run or walked to by female Little League batter.

I irritability: mild form of disorder experienced for a few days each month by sensitive men when they are in their pre-paycheck period.

J juliet: principal character in the Shakespearean tragedy, "Juliet and Romeo."

K king: most powerful court person, sometimes known familiarly as a billiejean.

L lady: ludicrous label, as in lady doctor, lady governor, gentleman truckdriver.

M mr.: a form of address for men, marital status deemed not relevant, as for Mr. Clean, the detergent, and Mr. Ed, the talking horse.

N neuter: occupational classifications, such as cadet, clown, detective, ecdysiast, senator.

O olympian: of or pertaining to the goddesses.

P paint remover: for club chairs, airplane cockpits, and executive suites marked FOR MEN ONLY.

Q qualification: the question is, "But can he type?"

R re-entry: as of mothers into the economic market after childrearing; also, from outer space.

S sage: outstanding Wise One, the voice of experience; for example, a margaretmeadster.

T television top newscaster: a walters, formerly a walter.

U ulysses: absentee father; mother heads single-parent household.

V virginiawoolf: in real-estate parlance, a single room.

W wet nurse: the one job men cannot fill, as women cannot apply to be sperm donors.

X x: the female sex chromosome, also still the unknown quantity.

Y y: the male sex chromosome, also part of a mathematical formulation as in $x = y$.

Z zeitgeist: spirit of liberty, equality, sorority.

"Him" to the Weather

JUDITH K. MEULI

After the early "him-icane" jokes about the first male-named hurricane, "Bob," wore off, most radio and television weather forecasters made "Bob" a genderless "it" in record time. It was nothing like the old days when hurricanes with female names were known to "flirt with the Florida coast," were "perfectly formed," had tempers that "teased and threatened." Houston *Breakthrough* columnist Gabrielle Cosgriff, who noted the difference, speculated on how hurricane "Bob" might have been described if the weather forecasters had used comparable sexual connotations to describe the weakness of the storm, suggesting, "Bob can't get it up," or "Bob peters out," or "Impotent Bob slinks ashore." An outdoors writer for the Houston *Chronicle* was so distraught at the change, he was driven to homophobia: "Bob, the first manchild of the National Hurricane Center, marks the first time ever the seafarers must wait to receive a gentleman caller," he wrote. "At any rate, when Bob comes twirling his skirts ashore he will have an effect on the upper Texas shore."

(from National NOW Times, *Sept./Oct. 1979)*

****

Alan Alda, on the road for ERA, observed state legislators who addressed their female constituents as "honey." Alda's response: "'Honey' is inappropriate unless you are a bear talking to your lunch."

*"I am not a chairman, I have never been a chairman,
and I will never be a chairman. . ."* —Anne Saunier

Overcoming a Man-nerism

NAOMI R. GOLDENBERG

"Man and His Environment" was the approved title
for a new interdisciplinary course at a large midwestern
university. A few feminists on campus indicated that
the title was offensive, but, as usual, their opinions
were not heeded.

The young professor for the new course sought me
out to give a lecture on psychology, my area of expertise. As a title for the lecture, he proposed "Man's Relations with Himself." I refused to give the talk.

"What's the matter?" he asked.

"Well," I replied, "I really know nothing about jerk-
ing off in the shower."

THE WIZARD OF ID by Brant parker and Johnny hart

I'M SORRY...WE ONLY SERVE MEN IN THIS ROOM.

GOOD... BRING US TWO

12-11

176

Talkin' Gender Neutral Blues

by Kristin Lems
©1978 Kleine Ding Music

1. Well I was walkin down the street one day
    Readin the signs that passed my way
    And after awhile I started to see
    That none of those words referred to me....
    "Good will towards men..." "All men are created equal.."
    "Praise Him....."

2. Well I asked some friends if they agreed
    That they felt left out in the things they read;
    They told me yes and added some more
    And soon we all felt pretty sore...
    Congressman.....businessman...sideman.....
    But I sure never heard of a househusband!

3. Well some men came by and a fight began to grow;
    "You girls are so dumb you just don't know---
    These here are called generic words;
    They're meant to include both the bees and the birds."
    Well gee fellas, how am I supposed to know?
    I certainly don't feel included!

4. Well then okay, said I, if that's so true,
    I'll just use "woman" to cover the two.
    "It don't make a difference to us," they said,
    "If you wanna use 'woman,' go right ahead."
    I said, thanks, that's real sisterly of you;
    Glad to see you believe in sportswomanship.

5. "Now hold your horses," they started to cry.
    "I think I'll hold my mares," said I.
    "You're leavin all of us guys behind!"
    Why no! We're all part of womankind!
    So don't fret, friends....take it like a woman....
    You'll get used to it, just like we all did!

An Eight-Letter Word

MARY ELLMANN

. . .feminine functions as an eight-letter word in the notorious Woodrow Wilson biography by Freud and William Bullitt. At one heated point, Clemenceau calls Wilson feminine, Wilson calls Clemenceau feminine, then both Freud and Bullitt call Wilson feminine again. The word means that all four men thoroughly dislike each other.

(from Thinking About Women, *1968)*

Letter to the Editor

To the Editor:

I certainly agree with you, Nola R. Jeffries, about the silliness of the word "chairperson" (Voice, March 16). As you say, if those "idiotic radicals" (probably women's libbers) would quit bothering about trifles like language, we'd be better off, and things would be less complicated.

Who cares if women get letters addressed "Dear Sir" or "Gentlemen" or "Mr."? We know what people mean.

So what if speakers and writers nearly always use he/his/him to denote gender even though the audience/readers are mostly women?

And how stupid can anybody be to think that freshman, trackman, chairman, congressman, postman, fellowman, mankind, etc. etc., doesn't include women? We know who we are.

We don't have to nit-pick at language just because a few radicals go around claiming that language is tied up with our attitudes and prejudices toward others.

What woman, for heaven's sakes, needs to have his sex clarified in language? Any woman worth his salt knows who he is.

You wouldn't hear a man hollering about being called "Mrs." or "she" or "her" or "chairwoman" or "Dear Madam." A man knows who she is.

Things are complicated enough without fussing over language, and who would know it better than the National Association of Parliamentarians and the Women in Construction?

Anyway, Mr. Nolan R. Jeffries, sir, I agree with you 100 percent about the silliness of "chairperson," and I think that . . . oh . . . I mean Nola R. Jeffries. But, it isn't important, is it? You know who you are. Right?

South Bend Tribune   Mr. Patricia Miller
March 25, 1976   South Bend

Dear Colleague: I Am Not An Honorary Male

JOANNA RUSS

I know you. You're a goodguy. You believe in equal pay for equal work (although you're sometimes not sure why) and you've gone out of your way to bring a woman into the organization/department/business. You may even wish men could wear brighter colors and/or shoulder less responsibility like some of the much younger guys you see walking around. You like liberated women, too; after all, who wouldn't like women who are independent, intelligent, keen, and interesting conversationalists? You know better than to ask such a woman when she's getting married, or why she never got married, or what the company will do when she quits her job to get married, because you know she takes her job as seriously as you take yours. In fact, you treat her just like a man, just like one of the boys. You even tell dirty jokes when she's around. What's your reward?

She hates you. ▪

What you need is some way out of your bafflement. And feminists do baffle you. They certainly don't want to be treated like women, but now it seems that they don't want to be treated like men, either. What do they want? Dear God, what do women want?[1]

I'm going to tell you. You've taken one step—you now treat certain women as if they were men—but now you must take the next step. You must learn that someone can be human like you and competent like you but come out of, and live in, an entirely different situation. Hence the title of this article and a colleague's round-eyed adjuration to me, "But you're an honorary male." (Another version of this will be found below.)

Turning certain, select women—or all women—into honorary males is not what women's liberation is about. Women's liberation means far too much for me to tell you in one article, but perhaps we can at least keep you from making crucial mistakes. As tourists in a foreign country are given a phrase book so that without actually learning the language they can still complain, "Waiter, there is a Presidential candidate in my salad," or "Alas, my camisole has come undone," so I am going to give you a phrase book for the foreign country of feminism. There'll be a difference, though—this book translates what *you* say.

It translates what you say into what you mean.

It may not keep you from thinking the forbidden items below, but at least if you button your lip before you actually say them, you will (1) avoid making a fool of yourself, (2) avoid being struck by an enraged colleague or friend, and (3) start thinking about what you really mean. Most of these sentences are automatisms. That is, they are reactions that occur from ear to glottis without ever actually passing through the cerebral cortex. I hate them. You ought to hate them, goodguy that you are. If you don't, if you insist stoutly on your right to defame, abuse, and insult anyone within hearing distance of your voice, then you're not a goodguy.

You don't want all of us women to think that.

Do you, goodguy?

What You Say to Her	What You Mean
I'm all for women's liberation, but . . .	I'm scared.

What You Say to Her	What You Mean
Can't we talk about this objectively?	We just had an objective contest and you lost. Sorry about that.
It was only a joke.	I love the sex war because I always win. I find jokes about you funny. Why don't *you* find jokes about you funny?
Women who work. . .	Housewives don't work, especially those with small children. Housewives do nothing but loll around on sofas all day, eating chocolates and reading bestsellers.
Most men don't want to work with women because women are too distracting to have around.	My sexuality is your problem, not my problem.
I wish the women around here would make themselves presentable.	My sexuality is your problem.
But what's going to happen to sex?	It's my way or no way. And My sexuality is your problem.
Why do feminists want to kill off all the men?	Omigod, I feel so guilty. Or You're murderously irrational, so I don't have to listen to you.
I don't see why you have to take this women's liberation stuff so personally.	When I'm upset at something that affects me, that's righteous indignation. When you're upset at something that affects you, that's hysteria. Or How can anybody have feelings different from mine? It's against nature. Or If we all start having feelings and expressing them openly, the sky will fall.
I asked my wife (secretary) about women's liberation and she said. . .	I asked my maid about Black Power and she said. . .
My wife (secretary) is perfectly happy.	Everybody loves me, God is on my side, and you want to change it all. Or My wife (secretary) hates me; God forbid anyone should find out. Or My wife (secretary) is perfectly

I'm all for women's liberation, but I don't see why women who believe in it have to lose their sense of humor.

Gee, there's a woman jockey (elephant trainer, engineer, carpenter) out in Indianapolis. What won't they think of next?

We're hiring a woman. What do you think of that!

You can't expect change to come overnight.

Women can do anything they want to, as long as they remain feminine.

Women need protection. The world out there is tough. It's a jungle. You'd better think twice about that femlib stuff.

I think what you said at the trustees' meeting was fine.

My wife doesn't want to go back to work; she wants to stay home with the children.

Men need to earn more because they have families to support.

happy because luckily she has no mind of her own. You wouldn't catch me putting up with that kind of life for five minutes.

(See "It was only a joke," above.)

Freak.

Kiss me. I'm a goodguy.
    And
Fifty years after the vote and 10,000 years after human society was first formed. A streak of lightning.

And if we're lucky, never.

It's I who set up the rules about what women can do, not women.
    And
It's I who set up the rules about what "feminine" is, not women.
    And
As long as women remain deferential, pleasant, smiling, unaggressive, unambitious, accommodating, flattering, hard-working, admiring, and dependent, they can be as feminist as they like.

Boo!
    And
If you don't let me open doors for you, I'll smash them on your fingers.[2]

For goodness' sake, you didn't expect me to back you up at the time, did you?

This may be true, but you may also be saying:
Especially after I harped for six weeks on how wretchedly neurotic they'd grow up without her.

Women who have families shouldn't have families.
    Or
Women who have families don't *really* have families.

Or
Women with families should go
on welfare.

I'm worried about this feminist movie/article/book. It's so bad. It doesn't give people a good impression of how competent women are, does it?

Heh heh.

Forbidden Phrases

Under no circumstances may the traveler into Feminism ever utter these. Egos wither. Strong men turn into human beings. Inhabitants of Feminism utter them frequently, but they were never strong men to begin with. Utterly forbidden under pain of novel emotion and total reassessment of one's ideas about oneself and the world are the following:

I'm sorry.	I'm unhappy.
I don't understand.	I'm afraid.
Teach me.	I don't know anything.
Help me.	*I was wrong.*

Also entirely forbidden is listening to more than three consecutive sentences from a feminist without interjecting such "rational," status-enhancing remarks as "Hm! How can you prove that?" "Not *all* women." "I think we have to examine your assumptions." Etcetera.

Don't, I beg you, follow your immediate impulse, which is probably to show this to your wife or nearest woman friend in the hope that she will refute it. Women are liars. Your friend (or wife) knows better than to argue with a man, particularly about abstract matters; from the age of three she has learned how to please Daddy: by finding out what he wants and doing it, by finding out what he thinks and then saying it, and by admiring him (which includes agreeing with his opinions). Your secretaries do not smile at you because they like you but because it is part of their job to be pleasant; your girl friend doesn't agree with your opinions because she shares them but because that's the way to hold you; your wife doesn't cook dinner and mend your socks because she loves you but because it's part of her job. How can someone who depends on you for money, for social position, for status, even for her own self-esteem, even keep it clear in her own head whether she loves you or not?[3] Men are necessary to women, but not individually or as particular persons. You are a socially indispensable store-window dummy. In fact, I myself am an awful liar. If I met you in person, it's very unlikely I would talk to you the way I'm doing in print. It's too much trouble, it's painful, it leads to fights. I too "know" that women's business is to keep men comfortable. Only at a distance and in print am I brave enough (and unexhausted enough) to risk fights more than once or twice a week.

Moreover, we know what you think. We can read about it in books or see it endlessly in the movies or on prime-time TV. I can walk into a bookstore and buy *your* sexual fantasies, *your* adolescence, *your* adventures, and *your* job. TV Westerns and macho detective stories show me the kind of man *you* enjoy imagining you are. Movies tell me about *your* beliefs about violence, *your* feelings of inadequacy (at least the ones you'll admit to), and *your* code of interpersonal behavior. If I get tired of these, I can turn to the newspaper and read about especially powerful examples of what *you* have said and done. If you want to learn about me, there's very little you can find in books, movies, or on TV except men's ideas about women. What little there is that is written by *me,* produced by *me,* financed by *me,* is often distorted by my fear of you, my dependence, or my need to keep important things secret.

If you take this article to a friend or colleague, she will be running a risk (which never even occurs to you) if she disagrees with you. We are taught very early that our self-esteem depends on popularity with men. Women are, in fact, afraid to seem offended by male attention, of whatever kind. So she'll be "nice"; she'll smile and say it's a silly article; why are feminists so touchy? because she knows that's what you want to hear. (It's also, often, what she wants to hear.)

Oh, she'll laugh heartily and give you some version of "I'm already liberated; I don't need that stuff." This means that (1) she has fifty IQ points over anyone she's ever met, (2) she works a ninety-hour week fulfilling the requirements of both a woman's traditional role *and* her job, and (3) she is very, very lucky and/or very, very rich. She's also terrified of being thought like those "other" women—the weak, stupid, lazy, inferior, parasitic ones. She will work harder than any man and for less money, she will perform every one of a woman's traditional tasks (which includes flattering men), she will make fewer demands than traditional women do, and she'll earn her own living. She's a bargain.

Or she's young and fairly pretty, afraid to be classed with those "other" women—the ugly ones, the fat ones, the pimply ones, the failures, the wallflowers, the intellectuals, the "unfeminine" ones. She thinks she'll never age. She tries hard not to notice that the deference and attention men give to her is not given to old or plain women. She cannot, of course, trust other women.

Or she's married, in her forties or fifties, perfectly well-adjusted, with a husband she loves and wonderful children. She's gracious, hard-working, sympathetic, pleasant, and a fine hostess. She hardly ever thinks about women's liberation because if she does, oddly enough, she starts having those funny headaches and periods of depression she is too happy and well-adjusted to have. She is, by the way, terrified of being thought like those "other" women—the castrating, neurotic, hard, ambitious, aggressive, unwomanly, unmaternal women. (The name of *this* game is Divide and Conquer.)

You can believe her, whoever she is. (I've been all of her, on and off, in my time.) Or you can start thinking. You may get so worried about saying the wrong thing that you can't say anything. This is good. You're beginning to doubt your old map of the world, which is the only way you'll ever learn a newer and truer one. If you become desperate, try one of the Forbidden Phrases, like "Help me" or "Teach me" or "I don't know anything about it."

Feminists like them.

Women like them.

In time you may even get to like them yourself.

---

[1] It's interesting that women never ask this question about men, or children about parents, or Blacks about whites; it's always the other way around. As Mary Ellmann says, in *Thinking About Women,* once you are in a position of controlling other people, they instantly become mysterious to you. Blacks know what whites want, children know what parents want, and women know what men want—power. The subordinate wants what the superior has. In fact, the subordinate wants what keeps the superior up there —power. But the superior cannot credit this; his/her/their superiority is based on the assumption that it (the superiority and power) is *natural.* Hence the bewildered cry, "But what do they want? We've given them everything." Everything but the power to dissolve the situation of superiority/subordinance.

The phrase, "Dear God, what do women want?" is a famous sentence of Sigmund Freud's.

[2] From an article by Flo Kennedy in the April 1973 *Ms.*

[3] She has the strongest motives to persuade herself she does, though—it's very painful for subordinates to perceive they are subordinates, and not by choice, either. The superior also has to rationalize his power as "natural" or "right" or "loving" (or "protective"). To know that you're in your superior position only by virtue of raw power is rather unsettling to most people who—after all—want to be humane and decent. This muddle of motives can lead to hideous personal tangles, especially in marriage.

I do not
refer to myself
as a
"housewife"
for the reason
that I
did not marry
a house.

—Wilma Scott Heide

Another Name for "Down There"

SUE HELD

The dozen or so Hoosier feminists who gathered that evening decided that women had had very little influence on the power of language—and the power of naming. Even our uniquely female body parts are un-named by us. Better not think of it at all than to think of it as gash, twat, cunt, slit, or even—egad—gondola. Latinate clinical terminology is not ours either. It's too exclusive, not exclusive enough, or otherwise off the mark. Because we don't have the proper language to refer to (whatever it is), it's not surprising that we've been choosing silence—and impotence.

We have been stuck, it seems, with our own vaguely geographical, remotely antipodal term, DOWN THERE.

Clearly, DOWN THERE is not precise enough, poetic enough, potent enough, or momentous enough for the challenges ahead.

The discussion that night turned to finding a term of our own for DOWN THERE. Brains were stormed, terms invented, neologisms aborted, phrases born. After dozens of words were tried, an anonymous genius in the corner murmured, "We could call it REALITY." We paused, briefly, to recognize this significant moment.

We suspect, however, that others got there first. Consider, for example, Cole Porter's "Use your mentality, face up to *reality.*"

In fact, we have simply tapped into a universal lode:

"Dr. Seymour Fisher is so out of touch with *reality* that he sincerely thinks menstrual cramps occur in the vagina." —*Barbara Seaman*

Playing bridge "is a substitute. . . for the pleasures one should be receiving from *reality.*"—*Sidney J. Harris*

"A man I know once tortured himself with agonies of guilt and shame every time he was sexually aroused by his wife; he was 'semantically' evil, evil by arbitrary definition. Redefining then, in a more *reality*-accepting way, is a way of reducing the distance between what is and what ought to be." —*Abraham Maslow*

"To make a precise scientific description of *reality* out of words is like trying to build a rigid structure out of pure quicksilver." —*Dorothy Sayers*

"Human kind cannot bear very much *reality.*" —*T.S. Eliot*

"I have never managed to hold her fast; always her *reality* evades my grasp and carries me far away." —*Cesare Pavese*

"Though no law specifically forbids sex-change surgery in the United States, it is almost impossible to obtain. Many doctors and psychotherapists object that the treatment makes a delusion a *reality.*" —*Arno Karlen*

"Howard had never thought much about her before, and he was now forced to acknowledge her existence, her disturbing *reality.*" —*Joyce Carol Oates*

". . . the particular myth of the power of women in America turns *reality* on its very head." —*Kristen Amundsen*

"The demon *Reality* is the number one killer of romance, so let's simply obliterate the demon and get back to that divine wedding with the Vision in white organza." —*Marcia Seligson*

"If we are to honor *reality,* we must be aware that the power and love can have a dialectical relationship, each feeding and nourishing the other." —*Rollo May*

"Unrequited love generally lasts longer than any other kind, because it is never forced to confront *reality.*" —*Sidney J. Harris*

"*Reality,* to the traditional reporter, is a huge unending game to be reported from the grandstand, with scores to be kept, trends detected, strategies analyzed." —*Robert Stein*

"At seven orgasms per hour, *reality* becomes a dream." —*Woman: A Journal of Liberation* (Vol. 3, No. 2)

Pickups, Puns, & Putdowns

MALE (POLITELY): WHAT DO I HAVE TO GIVE YOU TO GET A KISS?
FEMALE: CHLOROFORM.

An All-Male Senate Leads to a Stag-Nation

Every Mother Is a Working Mother

Uppity Women Unite

Clara Shortridge Foltz, the first woman attorney in California, was also the mother of five and a champion of rights for women under law. In 1898, when she stood before a tribunal court to present one of her cases, a male colleague said that the "Mrs." might better be at home tending her children. "A woman," she responded, "had better be in any business than raising such men as you."

Rock the Boat, Not the Cradle

I'm Drowning in the Typing Pool

"Male chauvinist chameleon," suggests Suzanne L. Clouthier in British Columbia, Canada, is the proper term for someone who shuttles between bigotry and liberality, according to the situation.

A Woman Who Tries to Be Equal to a Man Lacks Ambition

It's Not Kosher to Be a Male Chauvinist Pig

"The oracle said girls should be obscene and not heard."
—Judy Little

Sexism is a Learning Disability

Ann Sayre, the publicity manager of the M.I.T. Press, was annoyed by a salesman who constantly referred to women as broads. "You, then, must be a 'narrow,'" she countered.

The Best Man for the Job May Be a Woman

In Kalamazoo, Colorado, Barb Turner's sister and a few friends were sitting in a bar. A man came to their table and said, "Do any of you chicks dance?"

"It all depends," said her sister, "on how the turkey asks."

A news reporter, noting that vasectomies were cheaper, faster, possibly safer, and just as effective as sterilization of the woman, asked urologist Bernard Levatin why female sterilizations were so popular.

"Well," Dr. Levatin replied, "what all-American hero wouldn't send his wife in for surgery rather than himself?"

Rape Is a Male Phallacy

Josie Takes the Stand

RUTH HERSCHBERGER

Public practice of any art, he observed, and staring in men's faces, is very indelicate in a female.
—DR. JOHNSON VIA BOSWELL

Once upon a time there were two chimpanzees called Josie and Jack. They lived in a cage in a chimpanzee colony in Orange Park, Florida. All day long friendly scientists observed and made records of them. This was extremely flattering to the chimpanzees, and when one of them solved a particularly hard puzzle, he received a piece of banana as a reward. Life seemed ideal.

But suddenly a cloud passed over the happy colony. On March 15, 1939, as Josie stood resolutely beside the food chute, she little realized that she had become representative of all womanhood, a model upon which personnel directors and police captains could in the future base their decisions and argue their case.

Nor did her cage-mate, Jack, as he elbowed her gently aside, realize that he was from that moment the incarnation of the dominant male, an inspiration to all humans who sought "friendly masculine ascendancy" over their womenfolk.

For thirty-two successive days ten bits of banana, at spaced intervals, slid down the food chute toward the waiting chimpanzees. Who would get the tidbit first? Who would demand it? Which animal, male or female, would prove naturally dominant over the other?

March 15: the first tidbit came down the chute into the cage. Jack promptly claimed the food. Josie did not protest; there was no physical conflict. Jack ate

all the food the first day, all of it the second, all of it the third, and all but one bit the fourth.

Meanwhile, life and time were not at a standstill for Josie. In the typical if egregious manner of the female frame, her menstrual period had given way to the post-menstrual, and this in turn withdrew in favor of the period known as *tumescence* or genital swelling. On March 21, as the swelling continued, Josie abruptly appropriated all ten pieces of food, much to Jack's displeasure. By March 23, Josie had assumed command.

Josie retained the food chute in each daily experiment until April 3, when her period of tumescence (and heat) was over and the genital swelling began to subside. Thereafter the food chute was Jack's (with one exception) until the termination of the experiment.

By comparing the results of this experiment with those from experiments with other mates, it was found that during tumescence the female almost invariably took over the food chute and claimed all the tidbits without interference from the male. Science had made an interesting discovery; all that remained was the routine work of communicating the results to the public.

It can now be illustrated that semantical analysis is not mere quibbling over the definitions of words; it can uncover buried facts and alter the interpretation of evidence.

In a popular version of this experiment, *Chimpanzees, A Laboratory Colony,* by Robert M. Yerkes, the one fact that emerged quite clearly was that Jack had made off with most of the honors. This was true enough, but issue can be taken with parts of the account, and particularly with the use of the word "natural," a variant of "normal." It is an ordinary little word, and yet it stands for so much in the mind of the public.

When human beings want to know what they're "really" like they turn to the lower animals, who are thought to exhibit impulses closer to nature, untainted by civilization and altogether more valid. Whatever turns out to be natural for the chimpanzee becomes practically conclusive for us.

From Josie and Jack's thirty-two days at the food chute, Professor Yerkes concluded not only that males were "naturally dominant" over females, but that the biological basis of prostitution stood revealed in certain aspects of Josie's behavior.

The matter was so disturbing that we took it directly to Josie. Josie was busy at the moment, grooming her friend Wendy, but on hearing of the manner in which the Thirty-Two Days had been presented to the reading public, Josie requested an opportunity to present her version of the affair.

The Interview

"People have been very kind to me at Orange Park," Josie began, "and I don't like to look a gift horse in the mouth. However, I would like to register a protest against the attempt to discredit my food chute score in the Thirty-Two Day test. Apparently all that humans want to hear is that Jack was dominant. *Why don't they ask what the score was?* You wouldn't slight the Brooklyn Dodgers that way, would you?

"Well, I'll tell you what the score was. I was top man at the food chute for fourteen days out of the thirty-two. Jack was top man for eighteen. This means I won 44 percent of the time, and Jack won 56 percent. He's champion, I'll grant you that; but still it's almost fifty-fifty. If Jack hadn't been dragged in as the *biggest* male in the whole colony . . . well, it sounds like sour grapes.

"'When the female is not sexually receptive,' writes Professor Yerkes, 'the naturally more dominant member of the pair almost regularly obtains the food; whereas during the female's phase of maximal genital swelling, when she is sexually receptive, she claims or may claim the food and take it regularly even though she be the *naturally subordinate member* of the pair. . . .'

"What is this? Are there eight aces in this deck? The italics are not only mine, I'm proud of them. Those words," cried Josie, "look like somebody decided I was subordinate way in advance. The referees are practically saying any gains I make while I'm 'sexually receptive' can't be registered because the phase of maximal genital swelling is out of bounds!"

Josie lowered her voice to a whisper. "There are sinister implications in this, for human females as well as for the women in our colony. If the period of sexual interest is, by implication, an extra-natural phase in women (for it makes us *act* dominant when we're really *naturally* subordinate), it looks like we girl chimps spend about 14 days out of every 32 in the toils of Satan.

"It all comes from there being so few women scientists. Some woman scientist ought to start passing it around that males must be unnatural because they don't have cyclical changes during the month. Then see the furor start. Maybe they'll see how much fun it is being deviants half your life. Look:

A woman has to do twice as much as a man in order to be considered half as good.

Fortunately, that isn't too difficult.

"'Under certain circumstances,' writes Professor Yerkes, 'the sexual relation of the mates may supplant natural dominance.'

"But what is so *unnatural* about the sexual relation of the mates!" exclaimed Josie. "I work up a good score, and they want to disqualify me because I happened to be feeling good! Besides," she continued, "why call me sexually receptive anyway? That's one of those human words with an opinion written all over it. Call me sexually interested if you will, for I am. In typical pre-mating activity, who starts everything by leading off at a run? And who decides when the parlor game stops and the male establishes contact? I do. Receptive? I'm about as receptive as a lion waiting to be fed!

"You know, human society is looking to us chimpanzees to set a pattern for the relation between the sexes, and it's hardly fair to misrepresent our social adjustments. Let's look at the circumstances of the experiment, for I don't think aspects of it were as controlled as they should be in the empirical sciences.

"Lots of factors make one chimp dominant over another. Weight is a big factor and hunger is another. Just because there's no physical conflict doesn't mean that force isn't the deciding factor. Chimpanzees understand each other just as humans do. If one of us really wants that food, don't think fightability can't be communicated by other means than swatting.

"When I got the food chute, it was because I wanted it bad enough. Maybe the time of sexual 'receptivity' makes the female more aggressive: that's a funny word-mix! When Jack got the food chute it wasn't because I didn't want it, but because I saw that he was willing to scrap for it. Perhaps when I was sexually receptive I was hungrier. You've got to remember that all during this test we had our regular meals every day; we weren't starved. Lots of dominance was temperament. Take Wendy, a friend of mine. She's little and yet when she was tested with Bokar she fought him right along. She *cared.*

"When Jack takes over the food chute, the report calls it his 'natural dominance.' When *I* do, it's 'privilege' —conferred by him. If you humans could get enough perspective on your language, you'd find it as much fun as a zoo. While I'm up there lording it over the food chute, the investigator writes down 'the male temporarily defers to her and allows her to act as if dominant over him.' Can't I get any satisfaction out of life that isn't *allowed* me by some male chimp? Damn it!"

There were moments during the interview when Josie's language had to be taken to task.

"Don't interrupt," Josie said sharply. "It's this prostitution angle that makes me the maddest.* All sorts of higher primates are glomming on to the results of that food chute test, and their interpretation gets farther and farther from the facts, nearer and nearer to the cor-

ruptions typical of human society. Jack and I can go through almost the same motions, but by the time it gets down on paper, it has one name when Jack does it, and another if it was me.

"For instance, when Jack was at the chute and I gestured in sexual invitation to him, and after his acquiescence obtained the chute, this was put down as 'favor-currying' on my part, as exchanging sexual accommodation for food, as downright prostitution.

"Please note that on March 21, as well as on other occasions, Jack came up to me repeatedly at the chute and similarly gestured in sexual invitation. Doesn't this suggest that he was trying to get me away from the chute by carnal lure? Or was Jack just being (as everyone wants to think) an impulsive male? The experimenter took it as the latter. But who knows that Jack wasn't about to exchange sexual accommodation for food?

"The profoundest assumption behind all this is yet to be told. It's so unfair a girl hates to think of it. No matter what names you humans give to things, we chimpanzees go right on enjoying life. It isn't so with humans, and that's why I feel so sorry for women. The names you uncaged primates give things affect your attitude toward them forever after. You lose your insight because you are always holding up a screen of language between you and the real world. Semantics tries to knock some chinks in this blind, and I'm all for it.

"The reason people are so sure that I traded sexual accommodation for food, and that Jack wouldn't, is because nobody thinks women enjoy love, I mean sex.

"It's as bad as that. People can't understand why any female animal should 'submit' (that's another of *your* words) to sex unless there's some reason for it—the reason here being to get control of those ten pieces of food!

"Maybe human females don't enjoy sex, but we chimps resent any forced analogy with humans. Among chimpanzees sex is controlled by the female, and don't let anyone tell you different. The chimpanzee female doesn't permit sex unless she feels like it and you can talk sexual 'receptivity' the rest of your life,

---

* "In the picture of behavior which is characteristic of femininity in the chimpanzee, the biological basis of prostitution of sexual function stands revealed. The mature and sexually experienced female trades upon her ability to satisfy the sexual urge of the male." —*Chimpanzees*, page 86.

that word makes no impression on us unless we're inclined.

"Out of twenty-four females in our colony, two have consistently refused to mate. Don't ask me why; myself, I think they're crazy. All their cyclical changes look perfectly normal, and they get plenty of male attention too. But they just don't want to. How is it these two females haven't been raped by the overpowering males in the community? They haven't."

By this time Josie had hold of the bars of her cage and was sputtering excitedly. She harped on the fact that Jack was seventeen pounds heavier than she was, while the average male chimpanzee is only ten pounds heavier than the female. She kicked, too, because the only pairs tested for dominance were those in which the female was appreciably smaller.

"You can tell my listeners, too, that we chimpanzees are as different from one another as any bunch of human beings are. I don't like to see the word going around that prostitution or male dominance is 'characteristic of the apes.' You can take three numbers like 2 and 9 and 4, and say the average is 5, but that 5 isn't me and it isn't Wendy and it isn't Jack. It's a statistician's dream. If I need two pints of food a day and Jack needs four, don't try to satisfy either of us with three.

"And don't start saying three is 'normal' either," she cried.

"*De gustibus non est disputandum.* Wendy and I are as different as chromosomes can be, and we want to keep it that way. The human word *natural* and all its chaotic offspring—*feminine receptivity, friendly masculine ascendancy,* and the rest—are an obstruction of justice and an interference with nature."

Josie rested her case.

(*from* Adam's Rib, *1948*)

ACKNOWLEDGMENTS

Grateful acknowledgment is made to the following individuals and publishers:

Claire Bretécher for "The First Tampon." Copyright © 1973, 1976 by Claire Bretécher. Reprinted by permission.

Ivy Bottini for "Clowning with Ivy Bottini" and "Becoming a Tampax Junkie." Copyright © 1979 by Ivy Bottini.

E. M. Broner for excerpts from HER MOTHERS. Copyright © 1975 by E. M. Broner. Reprinted by permission of Holt, Rinehart and Winston, Publishers.

Marilyn French for excerpt from THE WOMEN'S ROOM. Copyright © 1977 by Marilyn French. Reprinted by permission of Summit Books, a Simon & Schuster division of Gulf & Western corporation, and Andre Deutsch, London.

Hadley V. Baxendale for excerpts from ARE CHILDREN NEGLECTING THEIR MOTHERS? Copyright © 1974 by Joyce M. Wood. Reprinted by permission of Doubleday & Company, Inc.

Mary Ellmann for excerpts from THINKING ABOUT WOMEN. Copyright © 1968 by Mary Ellmann. Reprinted by permission of Harcourt Brace Jovanovich, Inc., and Macmillan, London and Basingstoke.

Barbara K. Abbott for "Map of the Battlefield of Life . . . ." Originally published in *Sexisms Satirized,* Pocketbook Profiles, 1976.

Gloria Steinem for "If Men Could Menstruate." Originally printed in *Ms.* Magazine, October 1978.

Lisa Alther for excerpt from KINFLICKS. Copyright © 1976. Published by Alfred A. Knopf, Inc., and Chatto & Windus, Ltd., London.

Jane Field for "New Discoveries Hailed as Birth Control Breakthroughs." Originally printed in *Majority Report,* October 1972.

Randy Glasbergen for his cartoons. Copyright © 1980 by Randy J. Glasbergen.

Carol Troy and *Ms.* Magazine for "Superpower Sought on the Contraceptive Front." First appeared in *Ms.* Magazine, November 1976.

Artemas Cole for his cartoons.

Roberta Gregory for "Revolutionary Contraceptive" from *Dynamite Damsels.* Copyright © 1976 by Roberta Gregory.

Jules Feiffer for the cartoons, "Up Against the Wall, Mother," "Rape," and "Pop, What's a Homosexual?"

bülbül for her cartoons and cartoon strips.

Kristin Lems for "Mammary Glands" and "Talkin' Gender Neutral Blues." Kleine Ding Music (BMI) copyright © 1978 (for both songs). Used by permission.

Nora Ephron for excerpt from CRAZY SALAD: SOME THINGS ABOUT WOMEN. Copyright © 1975 by Nora Ephron. Used by permission of Alfred A. Knopf, Inc., and International Creative Management.

Mary Mackey for "M.L.A." and "What Do You Say When a Man Tells You, You Have the Softest Skin." From SPLIT ENDS, Ariel Press. Copyright © 1974 by Mary Mackey.

Shirley Katz for "Don't Wear Your Guitar, Darling Mother." Copyright © 1978 by Shirley Katz. "The South Suburban Women's Liberation Coalition Marching Society and Housewives' Revolutionary Band Fight Song." Copyright © 1977 by Shirley Katz.

Ellen Goodman for "The Man Was Right—Life Isn't Fair." Copyright © 1979, The Boston Globe Newspaper Company/Washington Post Writers Group. Reprinted with permission.

Jane O'Reilly for "Clunks." Published in *Ms.* Magazine, July 1977. Reprinted by permission of Wallace & Sheil Agency, Inc. Copyright © 1977 by Jane O'Reilly.

Nicole Hollander for a three-panel cartoon. This cartoon has appeared on the cover of *The Spokeswoman* and in *I'm in Training to Be Tall and Blonde,* Nicole Hollander, St. Martin's Press.

We also wish to acknowledge the following people for their assistance, moral support, and encouragement:

Geni Abrams, Marilyn Bentov, Mary Brewster, Helen Bugbee, Zsuzsanna Budapest, Nancy Borman, Jocelyn Cohen, Tee Corinne, Barbara Contardi, Daryl Dance, Lyn Chevli, Francine Cardman, David Crosson, Stacey M. Franchild, Flo Kennedy, Ardeana Haley, Janie Haback, Martha Gresham, Julie Jensen, Marc Katz, Carol Farley Kessler, Melanie Kaye, KNOW, Inc., LESBIAN TIDE, Laura X., Paula Lichtenberg, Sharon McDonald, Sara Lukeman, Judy Little, Joan Levine, Louisa Mae, MAJORITY REPORT, Helen McKenna, Judith Moses, Nancy Poore, Madeleine Pabis, Shirley Rock, Una Stannard, Isabel Shapiro, Samuel Shapiro, David Shapiro, Betty Swords, Susan Saxe, Anne Sayre, Ruth Z. Temple, Robin Tyler, Emily Toth, Chocolate Waters, Tricia Vita, Sharon Voss, Naomi Weisstein, Anne C. Willett, Anne F. Wittels, Women's History Research Center, Inc., Sharon McEndarfer, Pat Lawton, Indiana University/South Bend, Ron Wolin, Margaret Hicks, Mary Blake French, Kay Hults, and a very special thanks to Cathryn Adamsky, Joan Uebelhoer, and Ann Hunsberger.

Cover and book design by Shohet-Walters Design Group